DOCTOR WHO
THE HANDBOOK
The Fifth Doctor

DOCTOR WHO
THE HANDBOOK
The Fifth Doctor

David J. Howe
Stephen James Walker

First published in Great Britain in 1995 by
Doctor Who Books
an imprint of Virgin Publishing Ltd
332 Ladbroke Grove
London W10 5AH

ISBN 0 426 20458 1

Cover illustration by Alister Pearson

Typeset by Mark Stammers Design, London

Printed and bound in Great Britain by
Mackays of Chatham PLC, Chatham, Kent

Acknowledgements

For help in delving into the era of the fifth Doctor we are grateful to, as always, Andrew Pixley, and also to Martin Wiggins, David Gibbes-Auger, Jon Preddle, the *Skaro* Team, Jan Vincent-Rudzki, Peter Moffatt, John Brace, Mark Stammers, Patricia Holmes, Richard Hollis, Johnny Byrne, Richard Bignell, Anthony Brown and *In-Vision*, Gary Russell, Simeon Hearn and all *Doctor Who* fanzine editors everywhere.

CONTENTS

To Mark Stammers

Foreword

The Doctor's view of the sky was partially obscured by the vast dish of the radio telescope, but he looked up at the small patch of blue that he could see.

There was no pain, and he supposed that his back must have been broken. He had, after all, fallen at least 100 feet from the steel girder upon which he had been so precariously perched. It had been the tilting of the dish that had caused him to overbalance and hang, suspended from some wiring, before his grip had finally given out and he had plummeted to the ground.

Now he looked up at the blue sky, his face devoid of expression.

He was aware of movement and colour all around him. Flashes of mustard and green, purple and white and a rich burgundy flickered in the periphery of his vision. His friends, Adric, Tegan and Nyssa, came to kneel by his battered and injured body.

'Doctor?' Nyssa leant over him. The young Trakenite's brow was furrowed in concern. The Doctor had helped her a lot over the last few days, and his support when she realised that the evil creature called the Master had actually taken her father's body had been vital.

The Doctor's face registered no emotion or change.

'Doctor?' The pronounced accent told the Doctor that this was Tegan, the newest member of his current travelling entourage. She too had needed careful support when the Master had killed her

1

aunt, although she had known him for what seemed like only hours.

There was still no change in the Doctor's expression.

'Doctor?' Adric was more urgent, more demanding than the others. The Alzarian youth had known the Doctor for longer than the other two, and had seen him get out of apparently worse scrapes than this. Surely a mere fall would not stop the Time Lord?

The Doctor's large eyes slowly moved to focus on Adric's face, and his slack mouth gently pulled up into a familiar and very welcome smile of recognition. The three friends smiled back. The Doctor was alive.

'It's the end,' whispered the Doctor, holding Adric with his eyes. 'But the moment has been prepared for.'

He flicked his gaze past Adric and up, towards a spot somewhere above his own head. Adric looked and saw nothing, but the next second there was a hazy, misty figure standing there. The Doctor gently lifted his arm from the ground and gestured at the ethereal figure, which slowly began to walk towards the Time Lord's prone body.

'The Watcher!' Adric recognised this mysterious being who had been following them about and, well, watching – that was the only word for it. When he had asked the Doctor who this creature was, and what it was doing, the Doctor had abruptly changed the subject. Now, here it was again.

As the creature stepped forward, it seemed to pour itself into the Doctor's body. To funnel in through the Doctor's features.

Realisation hit Nyssa hard. 'So he was the Doctor all the time.' This white, ghost-like apparition was some sort of projection of the Doctor, someone who was always there, watching, biding his time and waiting for the right moment.

Now, it appeared, that moment had arrived.

The strange merging of the Doctor and the Watcher completed itself, and the three travellers looked on as the Doctor's face was rapidly encased in the same white fibrous substance that had marked the Watcher's visage. This coating slowly faded to reveal a pair of piercing blue eyes. Fine blond hair replaced the familiar brown tangle. The final traces of the Watcher vanished and, miraculously, a younger man lay on the ground before them.

Adric, Nyssa and Tegan could not believe their eyes. The Doctor had changed. Changed his appearance. And they had seen it happen.

Adapted from *Castrovalva* part one by
Christopher H. Bidmead

Television is a medium that seemingly delights in giving people their fifteen minutes of fame. Its very nature is rooted in change, and as the months pass so new programmes are made and presented, and new stars are born. Some of these shows and individuals go on to win enduring popularity, but far more are never heard of nor seen again.

Since the end of 1974, there had been a single constant for *Doctor Who* viewers across the country: Tom Baker was the Doctor.

It had been a period during which the BBC had arguably enjoyed more success with *Doctor Who* than ever before.

The ratings had soared to an all-time high – higher even than in the heyday of the Daleks in the mid-sixties. The distinctive image of the Doctor – incredibly long multicoloured scarf, floppy felt hat, bulging eyes, tangled curly brown hair and an engaging and disarming smile – was firmly entrenched in the public's consciousness.

Now, however, after some seven long years in the series, Baker was moving on and a new actor had been chosen to take on the lead role. All those who had watched, enjoyed and indeed grown up with Baker as the Doctor must surely have experienced more than a twinge of sadness at the closing moments of *Logopolis*, the fourth Doctor's final regular story. This truly was the end of an era.

The man chosen to succeed Baker was Peter Davison – an actor totally dissimilar in appearance and temperament.

This was nothing new for the series, as each of the previous three Doctors had presented a marked contrast to his own predecessor: Baker's image had been very different from Jon Pertwee's;

Pertwee's had been very different from Patrick Troughton's; and Troughton's had been very different from William Hartnell's. There was however a major distinction on this occasion in that Davison, unlike the others, was already very well known to television viewers when he joined *Doctor Who*, principally from his role as Tristan Farnon in the BBC's veterinary series *All Creatures Great and Small*.

This was by no means the only innovation to occur at this time. Davison's era as the Doctor in fact coincided with a significant change of direction for *Doctor Who* as new producer John Nathan-Turner proceeded to stamp his mark on it. The 20th anniversary was also looming, and the series was taking off in a big way in America. Fandom, too, was becoming increasingly well organised and sophisticated, and the *Doctor Who* Appreciation Society was losing its virtual monopoly on major conventions and other activities.

Elsewhere in the news, Freddie Laker's airline business fell into a state of collapse; Argentina attempted to reclaim the Falkland Islands, provoking a brief war between that country and Britain; Michael Fagan popped into the Queen's bedroom for a chat with the monarch; the *Mary Rose* was raised from the sea bed; long-time Soviet leader Leonid Brezhnev died and was succeeded by Yuri Andropov, who also died just 15 months later to be replaced by Mikhail Gorbachev; and Steven Spielberg unveiled his new blockbuster film *ET*.

It was against this backdrop, and the increasing freedom that technological advances like digital processing, fibre optics and microchips brought to television production, that *Doctor Who* marched boldly into the eighties.

In this book we explain the thinking underlying Davison's casting as the Doctor and the development of his character; recall the stories of the fifth Doctor's era and the contribution that they made to the series' evolving mythology; describe the script editor's function; discuss the production development that occurred during this period; chronicle in depth the making of one particular story, *The Five Doctors*; and detail the marketing and promotion of the series.

Peter Davison brought a fresh charm to *Doctor Who*. His Doctor was an innocent lost in space and time; an elder brother figure intent on righting wrongs and, if at all possible, getting in a good game of cricket too. His era saw him coming up against a wide variety of foes, both new and old, and travelling with a succession of companions – namely Adric, Nyssa, Tegan, Turlough, Kamelion and Peri. It also saw the series making a successful start to the 1980s, despite a number of factors that were not in its favour, and introducing a new generation to the wonders of the *Doctor Who* universe.

Join us as we revisit the era of the fifth Doctor.

PART ONE – THE DOCTOR

1: Peter Davison – In His Own Words

ON HIS EARLY ACTING CAREER:

'I became involved in acting at school in nothing more than school plays. Then I joined an amateur dramatic society and from there took a chance of applying to a drama school simply because I didn't do very well with exams – I like to think that was because I didn't try, but I don't know… At any rate, because I got the equivalent of only one pass, I was able to do what I wanted to do rather than be directed towards a certain profession. So I applied to drama school and, very fortunately, got into the Central School of Speech and Drama, where I was for three years. After that I worked for three years in different repertory companies around the country, and then I had a year and a half out of work. Every actor has to have a year and a half out of work. It teaches him humility – I think. After that I was very, very lucky in that I got two very big television parts following each other. The first was in a thing called *Love for Lydia*. The second was the part of Tristan Farnon in *All Creatures Great and Small*.'

Interviewed by Stephen Collins in April 1983 for *Zerinza* Issue 30/31, published in August 1983.

ON HIS ROLE AS TRISTAN FARNON IN *ALL CREATURES GREAT AND SMALL*:

'Playing Tristan was a very interesting time for me. I know it's been said to me, so it's obviously in print somewhere, that I think

Tristan was the nearest I've ever played to myself, but when I first got the part I thought I was totally unsuitable for it. But there again I can't think of a part that I've ever been offered or accepted that I haven't thought I've been really totally unsuitable for – including *Doctor Who*! It's just that I was really very shy and I couldn't string two words together in a social situation. So, in a way, I grew like Tristan, I suppose. Not that I went around playing practical jokes on everyone like he did. I just think that it brought me out of myself a bit.

'It sounds a terrible thing to say, but it also helped my role that Christopher Timothy walked in front of a car one Christmas and broke his leg. There were whole scenes after that where he did nothing other than stand, and then limp out of shot while someone else spoke. He couldn't move anywhere for about three months, and that meant that a lot of scenes which should have been Robert Hardy and Christopher Timothy became Robert Hardy and me. So that built the character of Tristan up and did me a lot of good. Poor old Chris.'

Interviewed by Stephen Collins in April 1983 for *Zerinza* Issue 30/31, published in August 1983.

ON BEING CAST AS THE DOCTOR:

'John Nathan-Turner had been what was called a PUM – a production unit manager – on *All Creatures Great and Small*. That basically meant that he held the purse strings; he told people what they could and couldn't do with the money available. Then he left to do a PUM on *Doctor Who*, so he wasn't on the last season of *All Creatures*, and he became producer of *Doctor Who* some months later. I would say I hadn't really spoken to him for about a year when he rang me up one Saturday night and told me that Tom Baker was leaving *Doctor Who*, which I didn't know, and I didn't know why he was telling me that. And then he went on to say, "How would you feel about being the next Doctor?" Well, there was a sort of stunned silence. I didn't know what to say. So I told him to ring me back the next night. I spent 24 hours thinking about it; and also asking close friends, or people whose opinion I respected, what I should do. Then he rang me back, and I still really hadn't made any sort of decision, so he asked me to lunch the following week to discuss it.

'So we had lunch the next week, and he got me drunk, and I think about a week after that lunch I said yes. The reason I delayed was not that it wasn't a great chance, but I did feel that it was a fairly extraordinary thing to be offered to me. I felt, as I'm sure a lot of other people felt initially and may still be thinking, that I was fairly young for the part.

'The first Doctor was, sort of… old. He was a grandfather figure, let me put it like that. Subsequent Doctors got younger, and it just took me about two weeks to come to terms with it. I did come to terms with it, and I could then imagine myself doing it, and that was the turning point.

'It also frightened me a bit, I'll admit, because *Doctor Who* is a very big institution. I decided finally when I sat down and I thought "Well, if I say no to this one then it's a great opportunity missed". Also no one knew that I'd been offered it, so I knew that if the BBC got someone else to do it I'd have to keep silent for the rest of my life that I'd been offered *Doctor Who* and turned it down. I couldn't bear the thought of someone else doing it, so I said yes. And I'm very glad that I did.'

Interviewed by Stephen Collins in April 1983 for *Zerinza* Issue 30/31, published in August 1983.

ON FOLLOWING TOM BAKER AS THE DOCTOR:

'Of course I was daunted to be following Tom Baker. It didn't hit me until I sat down and tried to rationalise it. Tom had played the part for seven years and that, I figured, meant that no child under the age of 10 in Britain would ever have known a Doctor other than his. That was one factor. And because he was so identified with the role, one tended to forget – even though I had watched *Doctor Who* from the age of 12 – one sort of forgot about the other ones. It wasn't until I sat down and thought that William Hartnell had played it for three years, Patrick Troughton for three years and Jon Pertwee for five, that I saw myself in that context and was able to rationalise it. But it certainly did worry me, yes.

'I'll tell you about the two times I've met Tom. The first was just after I'd started filming. It was in the bar at the BBC and he'd either just got married or just got engaged to Lalla Ward, I'm not sure which. I went into the bar and there he was with Lalla. Lalla was also at drama school with me – she was in the year above – and I was really amazed to see her. She gave me a little kiss on the cheek, and it was through a combination of that and the fact that the BBC bar is awfully noisy that I couldn't hear the one piece of advice that Tom gave me about *Doctor Who*! It was one of those situations where someone says something to you and you say "Oh, right" and nod. Just by reading lips, I think he said "Enjoy yourself," but I didn't hear it. The other time I met him was at a Douglas Adams party in Islington, and he served the drinks all night. He just stayed behind the bar and served champagne. It's his new-found role!'

Interviewed by Stephen Collins in April 1983 for *Zerinza* Issue 30/31, published in August 1983.

ON RECORDING THE REGENERATION SCENE FOR *LOGOPOLIS*:

'It took about four and a half minutes! It was meant to take much longer than that, but we ran out of time. I had to lie in shot with white goo in my hair. Then I was thrown into the Make-Up Department, my hair washed, and given make-up. Then I was put onto the set and told to sit up and smile!'

Interviewed by Ian Atkins for *Wholook* Issue 2, published in April 1986.

ON HIS ACCEPTANCE BY THE SERIES' OTHER REGULARS:

'There was fairly instant acceptance by the companions, really. Except for Matthew Waterhouse, who is a very nice chap, but who does say some of the most... not tactless things, but he kept saying things like "Oh, Tom used to do this," and "Tom used to do that," until I felt like boxing him around the ears! Of course he didn't mean it the way it came out. When we had Richard Todd playing Sanders in *Kinda* – and Richard is a very well-known British film star of the fifties and early sixties – Matthew apparently took him aside one time and tried to explain to him how to act on television, and where the cameras would be, that sort of thing! You have a slight – I'll rephrase that – an *enormous* inferiority complex when you follow somebody who has done *Doctor Who* for seven years, but apart from that I had no real problems.'

**Interviewed by Stephen Collins in April 1983 for *Zerinza*
Issue 30/31, published in August 1983.**

ON HIS DOCTOR'S COSTUME:

'There was endless talk about the costume, absolutely endless. At one point they wanted me to walk around in a polo outfit: boots, jodhpurs, striped shirt, a riding crop and all sorts of hats... Although the cricket context was my suggestion, the eventual costume isn't what I would have chosen. I would have preferred a slightly more off-the-peg kind of look, but John Nathan-Turner wanted a designed look. I would've preferred the Doctor to go into the TARDIS wardrobe and pick out an ordinary black frock coat and a cricket jumper. I wanted a frock coat as it seemed to me that was a *Doctor Who* "thing". I know Jon, and sometimes Tom, had a short jacket, but I felt the image of the Doctor was slightly more "frock-coatish". So I would have preferred a black frock coat, white cricket jumper, cream cricket trousers and my usual shoes. Tom had the question marks on his lapels, and that's apparently the reason I was given them. And please don't ask me what the significance of the celery is, because I don't know! John decided that the costume needed something on the lapel, and he came to me one morning, a couple of days before we started filming, and said that he had a great idea for what it should be. I said "Yes?" and he said "A stick of celery". I said "Oh".

'He's promised to explain it at some point. I'm looking forward to it as eagerly as I am sure you are!'

**Interviewed by Stephen Collins in April 1983 for *Zerinza*
Issue 30/31, published in August 1983.**

ON HIS CHARACTERISATION OF THE DOCTOR:

'I wouldn't say so much that I'd tried to change the role, but maybe I am now getting closer to what I had originally intended. It's always a dichotomy between what you set out to do and what actually comes over, until you find ways in which to play it to your satisfaction. So I don't think my idea of the character has materially changed but the way in which it is coming over may certainly have done. Because as you gain confidence and knowledge about the part, you get closer to your ambitions.

'I haven't really explored the character to any great extent at the moment. One season, although it seems long when you set out on it, actually is fairly short as far as making the part your own is concerned. So I feel I'm still only on the surface of it to a large extent. I haven't quite decided in my own head yet how the Doctor's mind works. At certain times I can see the line straight through him and know what I'm doing, but at certain other times you rather have to bluff your way through because you haven't quite got his thinking worked out. After all, it is such a complex character in relation to any other character you might be asked to play, you do have to start from scratch. So I just find things in different stories and I say to myself, "I could have done that in the last story, and maybe I'll bring it out a bit more from now on."

'It depends on how much you believe the actor knows best… Tom Baker did the Doctor for seven years and by that time he really did know the character inside out. However, when you've been doing it for only eight months or so you still rely very heavily on the back-up from those more involved with the paraphernalia of *Doctor Who*, who were there before me.'

Interviewed by Jeremy Bentham for *Doctor Who Monthly Summer Special*, published in June 1982.

'Any similarities between my characterisation and Patrick Troughton's have never been deliberate. I would say it has more to do with the fact that I am younger than any of the others. I felt, in a way, I had to be more fallible, because I didn't want to play him as a hero as such – like, dare I say it, a *Buck Rogers* type figure. I was never pushed towards this, but the implication always is that if you get someone younger to play a lead part like that, you tend to try to make him dashing. I felt he should be a sort of anti-hero – not evil so much, but someone who doesn't go about things in the way a normal hero would.'

Interviewed by Jeremy Bentham for *Doctor Who Monthly*
Summer Special, published in June 1982.

'I think the scripts for the whole of my first season had already been commissioned and were already in draft form before I was cast. I'm absolutely certain that the first three stories were written for Tom. But that didn't matter materially, and in fact I quite liked that as I didn't want the scriptwriters to make any prejudgements about the way I played the role. I evolved the character as I went along. I asked John Nathan-Turner if I could have some tapes of the old Doctors, so he got them, and I sat down and I watched. I wanted to take elements from their characterisations, especially the first two as they were the ones I'd watched the most when they were originally shown. Also, I felt I would be on dangerous ground if I tried to take anything from Tom's Doctor. So I really concentrated on the first two.

'The gruffness and slight bad-temperedness that I wanted to get from William Hartnell fitted in very well with the character of Tegan. I was able to give her a hard time! And Patrick Troughton had a certain vulnerability, a certain quizzical attitude that I liked. I wanted to give the impression that you could never be quite certain whether or not the Doctor was doing the right thing. And there was the compassionate side.'

Interviewed by Stephen Collins in April 1983 for *Zerinza*
Issue 30/31, published in August 1983.

'My Doctor does lose his temper sometimes, but so did the early ones. William Hartnell's certainly did. That's really where I picked it up from. Also, I suppose it was initially a thing to counteract the fact that I was much younger. I think I might have dived in a bit with the losing the temper in the first few stories, simply because I did not want to come over as the sort of jolly ex-public schoolboy – which I'm not, as it happens. When I was looking at how to play the character, I wanted to pick up pointers from the other Doctors. Also the companions I was with were rather frustrating, in terms of the story, so it was nice to bring that element into it. Probably, looking back on it, I slightly overdid that bit of it, but when you start off you're not sure how you're going to do it, so you gradually have to work through it.'

Interviewed by Andrew M. Smith on 30 August 1983 for *The Cloister Chamber*, published in October 1983.

'Performance-wise, I was never very happy with the second season. I think it got just a bit dull, and the stories a bit over-complex. I didn't feel that I had a lot of room to embellish the character and I think this is definitely one of the inherent dangers of doing *Doctor Who* – the writers tend to latch onto your first portrayal of the part and stick with that. For me, that presented too limited a challenge. On the other hand, I think there was a conscious effort made during the third season to do something about that, which is why I felt happy about going out on top – or at least at a peak.'

Interviewed by Richard Marson for *Doctor Who Magazine* Issue 106, published in November 1985.

ON THE DOCTOR'S COMPANIONS:

'I would say neither Matthew Waterhouse nor Sarah Sutton left willingly, but neither of them went screaming or shouting either. I don't know whether the problem with Matthew was that he didn't want to leave or that he didn't want to get killed off. I said to him, and I think it's right, that if he was going to leave, then being killed was quite a good way to go. I know it precludes him from coming back, but I do think it was quite a good thing to blow a companion up. It's something that will not be forgotten. Also, it actually makes the companions more important, adds a bit of depth to them, because it means they are vulnerable. The thing with *Doctor Who* and continuing characters like the Doctor and his companions is that although you have cliffhangers, and their lives are always in danger, if you know that nothing will happen to them then something is lost. I know that you know nothing will ever happen to the Doctor, apart from the odd regeneration or four, but the fact that it's a possibility a companion could die, I think that adds to it. And what a way to go, as well, saving the Earth like that. Or trying to, anyway. It was an heroic effort.'

Interviewed by Stephen Collins in April 1983 for *Zerinza* Issue 30/31, published in August 1983.

'The idea was not to keep Sarah Sutton's part on beyond about the first story of my first season. Sarah's was meant to be the first character to go, and she was meant to go fairly early. This is the influence that I've had on *Doctor Who*: I managed to keep her on for as long as possible. That's the one thing I can claim. John Nathan-Turner thought that Janet Fielding was meant to be *the* companion. However, I did feel, and I still do, that a companion has to be sympathetic, and I thought that Sarah's character was the most sympathetic that there was in the TARDIS at that time. So I said that I didn't mind who he got rid of, as long as it wasn't Sarah. Oh dear, I'm really putting my foot in it here!

'The character of Nyssa has been my favourite *Doctor Who* companion, and I feel that it was a character not so much underplayed as eclipsed a bit by Tegan's character, and to a certain extent by Adric's character. I would say this, too: it's a popular misconception that having an Australian companion makes the series more popular in Australia. I think that is why there is an Australian in the series. I would ask you, and anyone else who agrees, to write to John Nathan- Turner and tell him that Nyssa was the most popular companion. Not because of Janet – there's nothing wrong with Janet's character – but I just wish you would tell him that Sarah was the most popular. Would you?'

Interviewed by Stephen Collins in April 1983 for *Zerinza* Issue 30/31, published in August 1983.

'The character relationships were worked out in rehearsal. The Tegan character was meant to be abrasive and a little pissed off at things, not to put too fine a point on it. I think actually the best companions are the ones who scream and say, "Help me! Help me!" There is a danger that if you give the companions too many personal problems, it becomes a bit like soap opera.

'Turlough started off well. John Nathan-Turner is a very good ideas man, and promised Mark Strickson a part with a little more meat to it. Mark was very intrigued with Turlough, but, as it turned out, they kept locking him up so he could do no wrong. Mark would often speak to me about this – he was very worried. That's why he wanted to leave.

'With Kamelion, we had a situation where Gerald Flood would record his dialogue prior to the studio recording of a story, and they'd go away and write a computer program to make the robot's mouth move around the words. We'd have to fit our lines exactly into the pauses, otherwise he would start talking over us.

'He was terrible. He couldn't move, couldn't do anything. When I first saw him, at the beginning of my second year, or maybe at the end of my first, he was just a head and shoulders mock-up, and his mouth and eyes moved and he looked quite impressive. But when we got the real thing…'

Interviewed by Terry and Andy Kerr for *Skonnos* Issue 10, published in March 1985.

'I didn't think Janet Fielding's character worked, which is nothing against Janet, who thought maybe I did have something against her! We actually got on very well, but I don't think that kind of aggressive person, who's always getting at the Doctor, works. I think there's got to be a feeling that they're on the same side. OK, the companion gets fed up with the Doctor when he doesn't do something right, but they're basically on the same side. With Janet's character and with Turlough, I think you came very close to having two companions who very definitely weren't. I think that was a frustration for Mark Strickson too; he couldn't do anything.'

Interviewed by Richard Marson for *Doctor Who Magazine* Issue 134, published in March 1988.

'Nicola Bryant was pretending to be American with everybody. I think it was under instructions from John Nathan-Turner – although

I haven't got quite close to the truth as to whether it was her idea or his idea actually to pretend to *everybody*. The trouble was that we had two reporters with us the entire week we were in Lanzarote for *Planet of Fire*, and I think she had to pretend to be American for them, so they didn't let the cat out of the bag.

'I knew that she didn't have a very strong American accent, but I didn't find out for ages she wasn't even American. What she was telling us was that her father was American, or that she'd been brought up in America. It was all lies...under instruction, but nevertheless, complete fabrication!'

Interviewed by Nicholas Briggs for *Doctor Who Magazine* Issue 215, published in August 1995.

ON THE LACK OF 'HANKY-PANKY' IN THE TARDIS:

'When I joined, because I was younger than Tom Baker, it was felt that there was a danger that people would think there was hanky-panky going on in the TARDIS. So you'll notice that to start with both Nyssa and Tegan were fairly well covered up from head to foot in their differing outfits. The idea was that it would simply stop everyone from thinking about it – you know, what the eye can't see, et cetera, et cetera... But it was pointed out in one or two letters to the *Radio Times* that a lot of the male population quite liked looking at the companions from time to time, and a bit more of the companions than they were seeing! So it was decided to give them both new costumes. I think the girls were in two minds about it. It can sometimes be very cold recording *Doctor Who*, and I don't think they appreciated the fact that they were walking around in slightly skimpier outfits – in one case, a very much skimpier outfit! At the same time, I guess they weren't entirely happy with the costumes of the first season. I think Janet was quite pleased to be rid of the air hostess outfit, but I don't know how pleased she was to get into the costume she ended up with.'

Interviewed by Stephen Collins in April 1983 for *Zerinza* Issue 30/31, published in August 1983.

ON *CASTROVALVA*:

'The thing about *Castrovalva* was that it was really the second part of *Logopolis*, and it was quite confusing. It was in fact the fourth story I recorded. The first three were *Four to Doomsday*, *The Visitation* and *Kinda*. That was so I could find my way around the part a bit more before doing my introductory story, and also, I think, because the scripts for *Castrovalva* weren't quite finished when recording was scheduled to begin. What can I say about it? I don't know. I tried to do little things in it, like the little impersonations of the other Doctors. I don't know that I like the sorts of times when the Doctor is confused, and I seem to have done a lot of scenes like that now, where the Doctor is being diminished, or parts of him are being taken over or he's falling over! Maybe they think I'm awfully good at falling over, or perhaps they think I'm best out of the way. I don't know. But, anyway, there was a fair amount of that in the first two episodes of *Castrovalva*.'

Interviewed by Stephen Collins in April 1983 for *Zerinza* Issue 30/31, published in August 1983.

ON *FOUR TO DOOMSDAY*:

'It was really difficult to establish the character of the Doctor! I was just thrown in at the deep end really, and I was just finding my way around the part. And in instances like this, where you don't know how you're going to finish up, you start off with a sort of non-committal attitude. I didn't want to make any kind of decisions about what exactly I was going to do, so I sort of blandly wandered about for a while. I don't think it was by any means the best story of the season, and that didn't help either.'

Interviewed by Stephen Collins in April 1983 for *Zerinza* Issue 30/31, published in August 1983.

ON *KINDA*:

'I think the good thing about the writer Christopher Bailey is that he creates in his own mind a whole world. The mythology of Deva

Loka was very firm in his mind, and I liked that an awful lot. It was confusing, but it was precise.

'In many ways the fault with some *Doctor Who* stories is that they aren't well enough thought out. *Kinda* was well thought out. Now there may have been a difficulty with everyone else actually following it, and that's the problem that comes from that thinking-it-out process, but I was very impressed with the actual writing and the thought that he had put into it.'

**Interviewed by Stephen Collins in April 1983 for *Zerinza*
Issue 30/31, published in August 1983.**

ON *THE VISITATION*:

'In a way it's easier to do a historical story, as you are dealing with history and therefore facts that can be twisted to a certain extent – as, obviously, in *The Visitation*, where we ended up starting the Great Fire of London. The trouble with the futuristic ones – and I think *Four to Doomsday* suffered from this to a certain extent – is that there is a danger that you view the future only in terms of today's technology. *Four to Doomsday* was about something that was meant to be happening way away into the future with an advanced technology that was capable of crossing the vastness of space, and yet they were still dealing with silicon chips – and, who knows, silicon chips may well be obsolete two years from now. They may be obsolete now, for all I know! So that's the difficulty with doing futuristic ones, whereas you can play around a bit more with historical ones. I liked the Terileptils, too. Very good costume that.

'You know, Eric Saward is one of my favourite writers. It's just a personal opinion, but I like the twists he does at the end of them. I liked *The Visitation*.'

**Interviewed by Stephen Collins in April 1983 for *Zerinza*
Issue 30/31, published in August 1983.**

ON *BLACK ORCHID*:

'I had a rough time with the cricket scenes. They were done in one afternoon, and it was pouring with rain; it was absolutely pouring! The thing about film is that you can't see rain unless it's very, very heavy. So there was the problem of saying to the director, "Shall we assume it's raining in the story, or shall we pretend it's not?" Well, it wasn't really raining heavily enough to say it was raining, and the characters would not have been playing cricket in the pouring rain anyway. So we had to film it in the pouring rain – and that's my excuse for my bad play! I know I look very good – well, I look all right – but that was only after they cut out all the times the ball fell out of my hand when I was running up to bowl! If ever you get to see the out-takes! At one point I swung at the cricket ball that was being bowled at me, missed the ball entirely, and the cricket bat flew out of my hand and ended up at mid-wicket!'

Interviewed by Stephen Collins in April 1983 for *Zerinza* Issue 30/31, published in August 1983.

'I did actually bowl someone out on camera, genuinely! What happened was that the cameraman had got absolutely no idea about cricket, and the director said, "Just take a shot of Peter coming in to bowl." The idea was that he would take a shot of me coming in to bowl, and the extra who was playing the batsman would not be in it at all. He set up the camera and I ran in to bowl, thinking it was just on me. The batsman played the stroke, missed, and the ball hit the wicket. He was out! So I said to the director that it was a terrible shame that this was not in shot, and the cameraman said, "Oh, it was in shot – I didn't know it wasn't meant to be!" So it was actually there, and I bowled this guy out.'

Interviewed by Ian Atkins for *Wholook* Issue 2, published in April 1986.

'I never particularly liked *Black Orchid*, to tell you the truth, mainly because I seemed to spend a lot of the time dressed up like an idiot... a clown, which I never liked. I don't know what it was that

I didn't like about that story… Maybe it just smacked too much of Noël Coward or something.

'I don't like two-parters, really. I just think they're too short. The story's all wrapped up a bit too quickly.'

**Interviewed by Nicholas Briggs for *Doctor Who Magazine*
Issue 214, published in July 1994.**

ON *EARTHSHOCK*:

'The thing I liked about the new Cybermen was the idea that, rather than a totally inanimate face, you could see the hint of something moving underneath. Because there is meant to be something inside the suit; Cybermen are not actually robots. I liked this new side of them. Actually, one of the old stories I had been given to look at right at the very beginning, when I was looking at how to approach the role, was *The Tenth Planet*. The Cybermen had a sort of stocking mask over the face of the actor… and the voice of the actual actor wasn't used. Obviously the man playing the part would open his mouth, but the sound would come from somewhere else; the mask mouth wouldn't move.

'The voices were wonderful as well; not at all like the latest Cyberman voices, which I feel are a bit too Dalek-like. In their first story, the accent was always on the wrong words, and it was really quite jolly!

'Anyway, the Cybermen had to be redesigned for *Earthshock*, and I thought that they looked really very good. There was the perspex chin, of course, but what was underneath it was quite complicated. Maybe you didn't see enough of it? I thought it gave the impression of this shrivelled thing under there speaking. I told David Banks, who played the Cyber Leader, about the early voice, and I thought he was very good, because he incorporated that approach with the modern treatment. I thought he came up with a very good cross between the slightly strange jolliness and the later Dalek-like voice.'

**Interviewed by Stephen Collins in April 1983 for *Zerinza*
Issue 30/31, published in August 1983.**

'*Earthshock* is one of my three favourite *Doctor Who* stories, because I had always liked the Cybermen and it was very dynamic. We had a tremendous time with that one, because although the pressure was on, it had a wonderful guest cast, and yet still managed to give us a lot to do. It had a cut and thrust that was missing from some of the other stories. My other favourites were *Frontios* and my last one, *The Caves of Androzani*.'

**Interviewed by Richard Marson for *Doctor Who Magazine*
Issue 106, published in November 1985.**

ON *TIME-FLIGHT*:

'The problem with *Time-Flight* was simply that they tried to do the exterior scenes interior, and there was this very unsatisfactory thing of cutting from an exterior of Heathrow Airport to the interior of Studio 8, Television Centre – and it was meant to be the same place, billions of years earlier. I think that makes a tremendous difference to a programme. It's really very hard to get a believable story in those circumstances. You're all meant to be in this vast area, and the point of horizon is ten yards away! It was a shame the story was written on too grand a scale for the money we had available. Potentially, it was a well designed set, done to scale so that it was meant to look as if it was fading away into the distance, but it just wasn't possible to do it.'

**Interviewed by Stephen Collins in April 1983 for *Zerinza*
Issue 30/31, published in August 1983.**

'Some of the scripts we had were extremely duff. I found that a big pain. If we ran out of money at the end of a season as well, the whole programme looked duff. *Time-Flight* exemplified that. No money! What do you do? You're stuck there, in Studio 8, with tiny models of Concorde and ridiculous polystyrene granite rocks. It was just absurd.'

**Interviewed by Richard Marson for *Doctor Who Magazine*
Issue 134, published in March 1988.**

ON *ARC OF INFINITY*:

'Funny things happen all the time when we are making *Doctor Who*. For instance, I remember an incident when we were filming *Arc of Infinity* in Amsterdam. I was playing two parts, if you recall – the other being Omega, who was trying to turn himself into the Doctor. Once he turned into me, he started to decay.

'In one of the scenes I had to cross Dam Square, which is in the middle of Amsterdam, wearing horrific make-up – a mixture of Rice Krispies and glue and all sorts of things fixed down one side of my face.

'Anyhow, I had to run through the square – which is rather like our Trafalgar Square, full of people and pigeons. It must have been quite terrifying to these people – who, of course, had no idea we were making a film. They just couldn't believe their eyes as I ran by! It wasn't easy for me, either, having to dodge the trams and cars as well.

'Getting that scene done was really hard work. We had to do it four times, and after all that it was decided it was too horrific and cut from the story.'

Quoted by Peter Haining in *Doctor Who – A Celebration*, published in 1983.

'I had to rescue Janet Fielding from the red-light district. A whole group of us were walking around in the red-light district, and I turned around at one point and Janet was being chatted up by these men. She thought they were just being friendly. I had to explain to her that they thought she was… you know… available!'

Interviewed by Nicholas Briggs for *Doctor Who Magazine* Issue 214, published in July 1994.

ON *SNAKEDANCE*:

'This was probably my favourite story of my second season. I don't really know why; I just liked it as a story. Colette O'Neil was a wonderful guest star; she's terrific. As a sequel, it was almost part two of *Kinda*. It was commissioned almost as an explanation, as the feeling was that there had been a lot of potential in *Kinda* that wasn't well explained, not as amplified as it should and could have been.'

Interviewed by Stephen Collins in April 1983 for *Zerinza* Issue 30/31, published in August 1983.

'This was another chance for Janet Fielding to do heavy, evil acting. I think I saw *Snakedance* as a kind of rest for me. Janet did quite a lot in that, and I would kind of wander in from time to time.'

Interviewed by Nicholas Briggs for *Doctor Who Magazine* Issue 215, published in August 1994.

ON *MAWDRYN UNDEAD*:

'There were an awful lot of holes in the story, I seem to remember. I recall thinking "There's no way this is going to work", because if you sit down and read the script, the plot is like a sieve. But in fact, it's one of those things that you notice when you're doing it, but when you actually watch it back you don't notice any of the holes. That taught me a lesson about plots in general. There can be enormous holes in a plot, but the audience will just never notice. You can do the most extraordinary things and get away with it, as long as the story moves, as long as the audience isn't given time to think about it.'

Interviewed by Nicholas Briggs for *Doctor Who Magazine* Issue 215, published in August 1995.

ON *TERMINUS*:

'We used the sets from *Alien*, which really excited me. The story had interesting ideas but, again, plot holes which caused real problems. For the final scene we had three minutes' recording time left and hadn't even blocked it out. We never had the time to do things properly.'

Interviewed by Graeme Wood, Mark Wyman and Gary Russell for *TV Zone* Issue 16, published in March 1991.

ON *ENLIGHTENMENT*:

'Bizarre story. A very bizarre story that. Never quite got a grip of it.'
**Interviewed by Nicholas Briggs for *Doctor Who Magazine*
Issue 215, published in August 1995.**

ON *THE KING'S DEMONS*:

'*The King's Demons* was a riot from beginning to end. It was just
a riot! We did it at the same time as I was rehearsing pantomime at
Tunbridge Wells. It was mainly a *Doctor Who* panto: Anthony
Ainley was in it, and various other *Doctor Who* people. I was so
tired. We would do half a day rehearsing *The King's Demons*, then
we would go down to Tunbridge Wells and rehearse the pantomime until about nine o'clock in the evening. God, it was murder!
I just remember laughing from start to finish. There was an actor
called Michael J. Jackson in it, whose character died in mortal
combat. His body was brought in and Isla Blair was meant to sob
over it. The sobs were not sobs at all – they were hysterical laugh-
ter! Then the body started to laugh. You can see it if you look
carefully; the dead body is sniggering!

'Of course, the real demon of the piece was the new compan-
ion – Kamelion! It never worked!'
**Interviewed by Nicholas Briggs for *Doctor Who Magazine*
Issue 215, published in August 1995.**

ON *THE FIVE DOCTORS*:

'I have very good memories of doing the special, because we all
got on so well. I think the Doctors were originally kept apart in
the script because John Nathan-Turner worried that we might not
get on, or that one or other would start demanding a better share
of the action, but as it was we all got on terrifically well. It was all
a bit silly in rehearsal, of course, but luckily the director, Peter
Moffatt, knew when to tell us off, and when to let us have a good
laugh. I particularly enjoyed working with Patrick Troughton, and
of course he had a tremendous sense of humour, so we had a whale

of a time. It was also nice to have the Brigadier back again. Nicholas Courtney had made *Mawdryn Undead*, which was a great show to do, and I'd already worked with him in *Sink or Swim* and *All Creatures Great and Small*, so we got on straight away. About the only bad thing about it was the freezing weather on location in Wales, and a sequence where special effects were a little enthusiastic with an explosion, nearly finishing Anthony Ainley off for good!'

Interviewed by Richard Marson for *Doctor Who Magazine* Issue 106, published in November 1985.

ON *WARRIORS OF THE DEEP*:

'That's where we had one of those really absurd things we always used to get: a monster, in this case the Myrka, who couldn't move faster than half a mile an hour and yet caught up with perfectly healthy soldiers and killed them!'

Interviewed by Nicholas Briggs for *Doctor Who Magazine* Issue 215, published in August 1995.

ON *THE AWAKENING*:

'This is the story that famous out-take comes from, with the horse and cart demolishing the gate. I just don't remember much else about it, really. I think I quite liked it. I know we had a kind of re-enactment of a battle on the village green down in Hampshire, which caused some consternation with the villagers.'

Interviewed by Nicholas Briggs for *Doctor Who Magazine* Issue 215, published in August 1995.

ON *FRONTIOS*:

'*Frontios* was excellent, an extremely well-rounded script that got hold of the way I saw the part of the Doctor and made his dialogue and actions fit in with this. I enjoyed it because there was really something there to latch onto in rehearsal and make your own. If you like, it had enough there without the actors having to try to embellish a weak storyline.'

**Interviewed by Richard Marson for *Doctor Who Magazine*
Issue 106, published in November 1985.**

ON *RESURRECTION OF THE DALEKS*:

'OK, so there was lot of mass murder in it, but the Daleks were
quite effective. You always think of the Daleks as being profoundly
ineffective, not able to do anything, but they move around the
studio like greased lightning! I can tell you, they are far more
effective than some of the monsters we had, especially in terms of
moving around. We had one ridiculous creature in the last story I
did – *The Caves of Androzani*, a very good story. It was meant to
devour soldiers and various people, but the thing could only move
at about half a mile an hour. Being chased and caught was a sort of
ridiculous process of "Oh, no, aargh!" type of crawling away, when
you could just have walked away and it would never have been
able to catch you. But the Daleks, no, they were great. Mind you,
we had terrific operators.'

**Interviewed by Ian Atkins for *Wholook* Issue 2,
published in April 1986.**

'I had to have a Dalek story before I left. I'd have been very disappointed if one hadn't been done. The Daleks are so much a part
of everybody's memories of *Doctor Who* that it would have been
terribly sad if I'd not met them.

'*Resurrection of the Daleks* had a good, exciting script with
lots of action and tremendous direction from Matthew Robinson.
It was also the beginning of the end for my team, with Janet Fielding leaving, which was a sad moment.'

**Interviewed by Richard Marson for *Doctor Who Magazine*
Issue 106, published in November 1985.**

ON *PLANET OF FIRE*:

'This was Nicola Bryant's first story. A good reason to be in
Lanzarote. Peter Wyngarde was in it. Great volcanic scenery. I
quite liked the story. Actually, the last two stories I did had a lot of

"acting" to do in them. Much more than was required in the other ones.'

Interviewed by Nicholas Briggs for *Doctor Who Magazine* Issue 215, published in August 1995.

ON *THE CAVES OF ANDROZANI*:

'*The Caves of Androzani* is my favourite of all the stories. It was a terrific story in which to leave. Indeed, I couldn't have got a better exit.'

Interviewed by Richard Marson for *Doctor Who Magazine* Issue 106, published in November 1985.

'Graeme Harper was a very good director, but the most unlikely good director you'll ever meet, actually. For the first three days, I thought, "What is this guy doing?" If you've ever met Graeme Harper, you'll know he's like some kind of human dynamo. He was darting all over the set saying, "I can do this from here, I can do this from here," and I thought, "Oh my God, this is going to be just terrible", but of course it was great.'

Interviewed by Richard Marson for *Doctor Who Magazine* Issue 134, published in March 1988.

ON THE LENGTH OF HIS STAY IN *DOCTOR WHO*:

'Doing the first season hasn't put me off doing it for any length of time to which I'd envisaged doing it, but exactly how long I'll do it for I just don't know. I will certainly give it what I consider to be a substantial time, but I think I can safely say I don't want to break any records for duration. At the same time though, I doubt I'll be the shortest.'

Interviewed by Jeremy Bentham for *Doctor Who Monthly Summer Special*, published in June 1982.

'Well, I'm certainly doing next season, and at some point I will have to make a decision about the next year, and when that time comes I'll make the decision. I'm taking it year by year, which is what every Doctor has done after the initial two-year contract has run out.'

Interviewed by Stephen Collins in April 1983 for *Zerinza* Issue 30/31, published in August 1983.

'It seems to me that you either do it for a substantial but short amount of time, or you stay in it for life, because it does follow you around and you have to get away from it. Now, by that I don't mean that I want nothing to do with *Doctor Who*, or that I'm tired or sick of it, but you do have to work in the future. My job is acting. What happened was that when my three years were up I had the opportunity then to do it for as long as I liked, but I just felt that as I had given myself three years I should stick to that, because the temptation is always to do another year, and then another, and another...

'If you did it for endless numbers of years you could always be developing the character, but at the same time there has to come a point when you say that's it.'

Interviewed by Liam Rudden for *TARDIS* Volume 9 Issue 2, published in 1984.

'I did find it frustrating towards the end of the last year, for various reasons. I would have liked in many cases for things to have been done better. I mean, we ran out of money on lots of stories, and time. That was frustrating, because I don't think the programme is given enough time to do it.'

Interviewed by Jackie Marshall for *Space Rat* Issue 7, published in 1984.

'Obviously concern about typecasting was a factor when I said I wasn't going to do a fourth year – the fact that I felt that period was about as long as I could do it without becoming too fixed as the Doctor in people's minds. The only thing I really did to avoid typecasting was to stop playing the Doctor fairly soon. As it is, Tristan is the part I'll never quite get away from in anyone's mind. I think it's the first part in which you come to the public's attention that stays with you. So, I was "Tristan playing the Doctor"!'

Interviewed by Ben Landman in 1985 for *Starlog*

Issue 102, published in January 1986.

'I hummed and hawed for a long time. I had set myself three years, not knowing how I would feel at the end of those three years. It was touch and go – I almost did a fourth year.

'If I'd been offered *Doctor Who* when I was, say, fifty, then I would have gone on for many, many years. The fact of the matter is that I was still fairly young – still am, I hope – and there were just other things that I wanted to do. I used to have enormous fun doing *Doctor Who*. We used to rehearse at Acton, and I'd see contemporaries of mine doing other things as well, and I thought I'd do a nice stint, enjoy it and leave.'

Interviewed by Ian Atkins for *Wholook* Issue 2, published in April 1986.

'I was quite happy with my first and third seasons, but not really with the second. I had to make my decision to leave after the second season, and that was difficult. I had to gamble on the third season being quite good, because I wanted to go out on a high note. And the good thing is that the best story I did was the last story, *The Caves of Androzani*. So, I was pleased with that. I'm sure there are many things I wish I could have done differently, given different conditions. There's an anxious time when you leave, where you wonder if you're going to be stuck with nothing else but *Doctor Who*. I don't think I have been. Since I've left *Doctor Who*, I've been busy doing other things, and that's good, the security of jobs being offered.'

Interviewed by Juanita Elefante-Gordon in 1987 for *Starlog* Issue 127, published in February 1988.

'Another contributing reason why I left was that, for two of the years, I was doing *Sink or Swim* and *Holding the Fort*, and then an *All Creatures Great and Small* special during the break between seasons, but after they stopped I knew there was nothing new that someone would offer me in my three months off.'

Interviewed by Richard Marson for *Doctor Who Magazine* Issue 134, published in March 1988.

ON RECORDING THE REGENERATION SCENE FOR *THE CAVES OF ANDROZANI*:

'Of course, this regeneration scene wasn't done in the same way as the one in *Logopolis*. Most of it starred Nicola Bryant's cleavage, as I recall! I had good fun on *The Caves of Androzani*. We had a good time with Colin Baker. It was quite a jovial time, but sad as well in a way. I wanted to keep the whole thing bright but, yes, it was quite sad.'

**Interviewed by Ian Atkins for *Wholook* Issue 2,
published in April 1986.**

ON OVERSEAS LOCATION FILMING:

'We all leave *en masse* as a sort of huge coach party, and drink the plane out of booze!

'You usually get more of a sense of a unit when you're filming abroad, because there is nothing else for you to do. The filming when it's done in England is usually done within striking distance of London, so you all make your own way home, whereas when we were in Lanzarote there was a very good feeling of being a unit, very much like a company in the theatre.'

**Interviewed by Liam Rudden for *TARDIS* Volume 9
Issue 2, published in 1984.**

'It was nice to be able to film sequences abroad, because it inevitably added a bit more gloss to the look of the show. I tend to prefer location film for various reasons, because it looks better than studio-shot stuff. I was never entirely happy when we were totally studio-bound, and studio work is much more concentrated because you're recording a lot of material in the space of a very short time. Filming gives you a chance to think, to catch your breath and go into it all a bit more thoroughly. Woe betide you if you hadn't done your homework before going into the studio, because there just wasn't time for you to stop and have a quiet think about it all. Filming abroad was a different kettle of fish again. When we went to Amsterdam, I got a lot of recognition because they had *All Creatures Great and Small* running over there – but not *Doctor Who*. So I caused a lot of confusion I think, as well as some shock, wandering about with all that decaying face make-up.

'I think if anything it's harder filming abroad, because the onus is on the director to make the location work, and make it show on screen. You become very cliquey in your unit, because it's all a strange land. Socialising in the evening is very "in". I think Lanzarote looked great; it gave that story a very polished look, which was something that I felt we could be proud about. In either situation it's hard work, because you've got to get it all done within the imposed time limits. You can afford a laugh at a rubber monster or a silly line in rehearsals, but when you actually do it, if you're not concentrating 100 per cent then, as likely as not, that's what will go on tape and you'll come out of it looking silly. It can be difficult keeping a straight face in some scenes but you have to make the effort or chaos would reign.'

Interviewed by Richard Marson for *Doctor Who Magazine* Issue 106, published in November 1985.

'Lanzarote for *Planet of Fire* was great fun and generally worthwhile as far as foreign filming goes. It would have been a lot nicer to have filmed a lot more than we did – we were there for only a week. But Amsterdam for *Arc of Infinity* I had grave doubts about. I think it just interfered with the story. The trouble was that it highlighted the impossible coincidences of the programme. If it had been in London, then meeting Tegan would not have shown up as being so ridiculous as it did. That Tegan was in Amsterdam was just too absurd.'

Interviewed by Ian Atkins for *Wholook* Issue 2, published in April 1986.

ON PRODUCER JOHN NATHAN-TURNER:

'He's really very, very good because, unlike some producers, he's there all the time. He's at every day's filming that there is, every studio recording that there is. He takes a hand in everything. That's the way he wants to operate, as total overlord of everything. His dedication to the series cannot be denied.'

Interviewed by Stephen Collins in April 1983 for *Zerinza* Issue 30/31, published in August 1983.

ON PUBLIC RECOGNITION:

'After I first appeared as the Doctor in *Logopolis*, it was ages before I actually appeared in my own stories. I said to John Nathan-Turner at the start that when I did leave I would much prefer to go so that someone else had taken over, so really that thing of being the current Doctor had been lifted from me before the end of the season. If I left *Doctor Who* at the end of this season in the last story, although I would be doing other things I would still be thought of as the Doctor until the beginning of the following year. So from everyone's point of view it's really much better if one Doctor disappears and the new Doctor appears and does at least one story in the same season.'

Interviewed by Andrew M. Smith on 30 August 1983 for *The Cloister Chamber*, published in October 1983.

'People in Britain get the wrong idea about *Doctor Who* in the States. It is very big there with fans – there were 12,000 at the Chicago convention last year, too many really – but as it is shown on Public Broadcasting Service channels, not the big networks, it isn't that well known to the general public. They know me better there from *All Creatures Great and Small*, though even then I can still walk down the street unrecognised most of the time.

'I very much want to keep in touch with *Doctor Who* and all the fans. I'm not going to cut the ties with the character, but at the same time I intend to keep a low profile for a while so that I don't tread on Colin Baker's toes. It is so that Colin can become established to everyone as the Doctor. That is why it was a shame, in a way, that they didn't do the regeneration as the last few minutes of the season, as has happened before. That way, the former Doctor can sort of fade out in the time which passes to the next season, and the new Doctor has a chance to establish himself. Colin has done one story, which isn't enough to establish his Doctor to everyone, and since mine is still fresh in the memory, it is that much easier for comparisons to be made. And I think it might have been fun if they'd done the regeneration by in some way bringing in Colin's role as Maxil, the Head of Security on Gallifrey, who shot and tried to execute me in *Arc of Infinity*.

'So I don't think I'll be at conventions for a while, for Colin's sake, but after that, of course, I will when I can.'

Interviewed by Wendy Graham for *Space Voyager* Issue 12, published in December 1984.

'I couldn't go into a supermarket or walk down the street dressed as you are. At one point I took to wearing baseball hats and dark glasses. The first time I was recognised, after *Love for Lydia*, it was quite gratifying, but that was one person along a crowded street. When they all start to recognise me, I don't like it. So I look at the ground mainly.

'People's behaviour is rather strange, because they rarely come straight up to me and start talking. Mostly they stand a few feet away and say loudly, "I'm sure it's him," as if I'm on another planet or something! Even when I am not recognised, the fear that I might be is always with me. It's often said to me, "You'll be sorry when they stop recognising you," but that's not true. I won't. I'll be very happy, in fact.'

Interviewed by Terry and Andy Kerr for *Skonnos* Issue 10, published in March 1985.

'Being invited to conventions was a very new experience. It wasn't a total shock, but still very amazing. You have to accept that the fans have probably got more knowledge of the programme than you ever will have, so I never pretended to be a great authority on it, even though I played the part and also enjoyed the series before I was in it.

'Before I did the first convention, which was in America, I was fairly terrified. But when I got up there and said, "Hello, it's nice

to be here," there was spontaneous applause! It was fine after that.'
Interviewed by Ian Atkins for *Wholook* Issue 2,
published in April 1986.

'You do have some idea of what it is you're getting into before
you take on the part. I think my most immediate problem was that
I had about a year before I actually appeared on television as the
Doctor, and John Nathan-Turner was very keen to sell me beforehand. It all happened very quickly and I began to get mail and
recognition extremely quickly too, so it didn't really matter that I
was doing this personal appearance and promotion bit as well.
Even if I hadn't participated, I think press interest was still there,
and of course there's always going to be merchandise if the show
is successful.

'What I tried to do was strike a balance. I didn't mind doing all
the publicity and so on, but I didn't want *Doctor Who* to totally
take over my life. I needed time to myself, time for other projects.
Besides, if I'd have overdone it, I think the public would have got
pretty sick of my face. When I did personal appearances I wasn't
keen on going in costume – I didn't want to go in character. If
somebody asked for my autograph, it would always be signed "Best
Wishes, Peter Davison", because if you sign yourself as the
Doctor you're insulting the person's intelligence.'
Interviewed by Richard Marson for *Doctor Who Magazine*
Issue 106, published in November 1985.

'I was aware of what I was letting myself in for, which is one
reason why I hesitated when the producer, John Nathan-Turner,
offered me the part. I finally said yes in my agent's office late one
afternoon, and it was agreed we could call a press conference to
announce the fact in a couple of days.

'However, no sooner had I driven home than it was obvious
that the story had been leaked to the press, for the phone never
stopped ringing with calls from journalists.

'On the *Nine O'Clock News* that night, the first story was that
Ronald Reagan had been elected President of the United States –

while the final story was that Tom Baker was going to regenerate into me! Friends who had been watching with the sound turned down told me later that they had assumed when my photograph was flashed up on the screen that I must have died!'

Quoted by Peter Haining in *The Doctor Who File*, published in 1986.

'I'm always getting "Where's your TARDIS?" – all the time. With *All Creatures Great and Small* it was "Would you have a look at my dog?" These things people actually think no one has ever said before! With the *Doctor Who* fan thing, in a way I find it kind of sad. A lot of the fans are fine – they like the programme, know everything about it – but there's a small proportion of those fans to whom it is like a religion and who get terribly offended when you're talking about the programme.

'I remember at the first convention I ever did, they asked my philosophy of *Doctor Who*, and I said "I get the script and learn the words", and they thought that was an awful thing to say. They do care about it, as I did when I was doing it myself, but at the same time you have to laugh at it, too, or it gets very po-faced.

'I do find that with very few exceptions, you can never become friends with fans, because underneath it all they are still fans and they are in awe. I remember once I got on quite well with a couple in America, and they then asked me to sign an autograph in a particular way, and you think, "Wait a minute, if you're supposed to be friends with these people, and you invite them into your home…?" It doesn't work, though they're very friendly and very nice and we've all done a lot of conventions in America.'

Interviewed by Richard Marson for *Doctor Who Magazine* Issue 134, published in March 1988.

ON HIS 'PUBLIC SCHOOL BOY' IMAGE

'Unless you make a positive move to say "I will not play any more of these types", you are a bit stuck. It's the luck of the first part that brings you public attention. They kind of label you with that.

'I was never by nature a rebel – I never wanted to offend peo-ple, I just wanted to do what I wanted to do, so I'm quite at home being a cosy figure actually. It's quite nice to be liked by little old ladies. But I do find it disconcerting sometimes when people meet me and they expect me to be wearing blazers all the time.

'I could say, "I won't accept any similar parts, I want to play different parts," and I'm sure if I put myself out of work for six months to a year, maybe a part like that would come along. But it wouldn't necessarily be successful, and I wouldn't necessarily be any good at it, and I wouldn't necessarily enjoy doing it, which seems to me to be the most important thing. If I enjoy doing it, I'll do it. So, I've never really had a master plan.

'I find the worst thing about papers is getting them to print what you actually say. Going back to this public school thing, they have this insistence of putting everything I do say into kind of public school language. "Did you enjoy this series?" they'll ask, and I'll say "Yes", but they'll print it as, "Yes, it was jolly good fun." Loads of "goshes" flow all over the place.

'I'm a bit boring for them really, because they haven't got any dirt at the moment.'

**Interviewed by Richard Marson for *Doctor Who Magazine*
Issue 134, published in March 1988.**

ON HIS INTERESTS:

'I read a fair amount of science fiction. Either detective fiction or science fiction; mainly American detective fiction. I like Philip K. Dick, when I can understand him! Silverberg I quite like. And English science fiction; the H. G. Wells and John Wyndham school of science fiction, where it's really based on… in a way, much more normal, everyday life.'

**Interviewed by Jackie Marshall for *Space Rat* Issue 7,
published in 1984.**

'I don't find acting all-consuming at all. You do take it home with you a bit, in that if you're playing a really depressing part, then you tend to get depressed, but I never sit at home and talk about a part. Most of the friends I have are not in the business at all – most of them are school friends.

'I've never been in love with acting in the way that some people are. They love going to the theatre and seeing various shows and a lot of it is the whole thrill of showbusiness, which I don't enjoy at all. I don't object to it, but it's not me.

'There's a very stereotyped image of the business and it's generally wrong. I've never really understood the total inability of television and films to imitate themselves. When you see a thriller set in a TV studio, no one ever behaves like that in the real thing.

'My interests. Well, I don't go to the cinema much, though I ought to. I tend to watch videos! My greatest joy is actually doing absolutely nothing – not having to get up and do anything. I can just sit there and let an hour go by. Or spend hours just wandering round the house. I used to play cricket, but people expect too much of you and it ceases to be relaxing.'

Interviewed by Richard Marson for *Doctor Who Magazine* Issue 134, published in March 1988.

ON HIS CAREER AFTER *DOCTOR WHO*:

'I did a series called *L Driver* for the BBC, which was in the studio at about the same time as one of Colin Baker's *Doctor Who*s. As a bit of a joke, I went in when they were doing a scene with Pat Troughton and crept up behind Colin to give him the shock of his former lives, so to speak – but he took it all in his stride!'

Interviewed by Richard Marson for *Doctor Who Magazine* Issue 106, published in November 1985.

'Of the sitcoms I did, I didn't like *Holding the Fort* and I did like *Sink or Swim*, because one was good and one was bad. The biggest thing I'd like to do would be a film – something I haven't done before. You'd think I could get in there somewhere, wouldn't you?'

Interviewed by Richard Marson for *Doctor Who Magazine* Issue 134, published in March 1988.

'Really I guess everything I have done has been fairly visible. I went back to *All Creatures Great and Small*, left it and then went back again – Bobby Ewing style, but not via the shower… I did two series of *Campion*… I haven't, however, snuck off for years abroad or done great theatre tours.'

Interviewed by Graeme Wood, Mark Wyman and Gary Russell for *TV Zone* Issue 16, published in March 1991.

2: The Doctor

The genesis of the fifth Doctor can largely be attributed to John Nathan-Turner, who became producer of *Doctor Who* following the conclusion of work on the series' seventeenth season at the end of 1979.

Nathan-Turner had never been particularly enamoured of Tom Baker's portrayal of the Doctor. Baker had by this point completed some six years in the role, and the producer considered that his increasingly assured and flippant interpretation made the character seem too dominant and invulnerable, detracting from the dramatic potential of the stories. He also greatly disliked the slapstick-style humour that the previous production team had allowed to flourish, and the general air of jokiness that Baker now tended to inject into the proceedings. During Season 18 he therefore took steps to address these concerns, cutting down drastically on the level of humour in the series and prevailing upon his directors to keep a much tighter rein on their leading man – a policy that, at least initially, created a good deal of friction between himself and Baker. Nathan-Turner's preferences could ultimately be met only by the casting of his own, completely new Doctor, and so it was that he reached a mutual agreement with Baker that the actor would bow out of the series at the end of that year's run.

Nathan-Turner's principal requirement for the fifth Doctor was simply that he should present a complete contrast to the fourth. (And despite his teasing of the press with the notion that the series' new lead might be a 'she' rather than a 'he', he never actually contemplated casting a woman in the role.) In this he was motivated not only by his misgivings about Baker's portrayal, but also by the thought that to cast an actor who was in any way similar to the outgoing star would be to invite invidious comparisons (a consideration that had weighed similarly heavily with past producers who had overseen the Doctor's previous regenerations). He had no definite preconceptions beyond this basic desire for contrast, and initially no particular actor in mind. One candidate he thought about but then discounted was Richard Griffiths, a well-established character actor of portly build who is now perhaps best remembered for his starring roles in the series *Bird of Prey* and *The Cleopatras*.

As recounted in his 1985 book *The TARDIS Inside Out*, the producer eventually came up with a 'shopping list' of ideal characteristics that he would like to see in the new Doctor:

1. Heroism – the Doctor must be heroic
2. Youthfulness – I wanted a younger Doctor for a more youthful audience.
3. Vulnerability – we needed a Doctor who could get it wrong occasionally. This is something the series hadn't had with Tom.

At this point, I began to see that the task wasn't impossible, and my excitement mounted. Fitting together the pieces of a puzzle like this is one of the real pleasures of being a producer.

4. Straight hair – Tom's curly locks had become so famous. We needed an opposite image.

In the end, only one man was ever seriously considered for the role of the fifth Doctor: 29-year-old Peter Davison. Pinned up on the *Doctor Who* office wall were an array of stills relating to productions on which Nathan-Turner had worked, including one of Davison taken at a charity cricket match during his time starring as the country vet Tristan Farnon in the popular BBC series *All*

Creatures Great and Small. It was this that brought the actor to Nathan-Turner's mind when he happened to notice it while mulling over his choice of Baker's successor, and the suggestion was quickly approved by his BBC superiors.

'He was my first choice,' Nathan-Turner told Jeremy Bentham in a 1981 interview for *Doctor Who Magazine*. 'I had worked with him on *All Creatures Great and Small*, and he was a very talented and capable actor. He had everything I was looking for in the new Doctor.'

Nathan-Turner had realised that Davison would meet his entire list of ideal characteristics. He was younger and slighter in build than Baker and had straight, fair hair as opposed to his predecessor's dark, curly locks. He was also somewhat more reserved and easy-going in manner, and carried with him a large fan following from *All Creatures Great and Small* – a factor that the producer considered a great advantage, given that Baker had become very closely associated with the role of the Doctor and would consequently be very difficult to displace in the public's affections.

Nathan-Turner phoned Davison at his home one weekend in September 1980, told him that Baker was leaving *Doctor Who* – something that had yet to be announced to the public at that point – and asked if he would be interested in taking over. Davison was astonished, considering himself totally unsuitable for the role, and initially felt inclined to turn the offer down. He asked Nathan-Turner to phone back the following week, and then agreed to meet him for lunch one day shortly afterwards to give the producer a chance to try to change his mind.

When the meeting took place, Davison was further surprised to learn that Nathan-Turner saw him as a 'personality actor' – someone who drew to a large extent on his own personality in bringing to life the various characters that he played, and who would thus imbue the Doctor with the same boyish charm and enthusiasm as he had Tristan.

Davison himself had not previously thought in these terms. 'I'd never seen myself in a million years as a personality actor,' he admitted in a 1994 interview with Nicholas Briggs for *Doctor Who Magazine*. Rather, he took the view that he was essentially a character actor who just happened to have come to public attention in one particular type of part.

He also felt that the role of the Doctor was best suited to an older man, and that he was too young for it. Again he was left with the distinct feeling that he should decline Nathan-Turner's offer. After several further meetings and phone conversations, however, he decided to accept, almost on a whim, as he could not bear to think that someone else would be given the job instead and that he would then have to remain silent about the fact that he had been the first choice.

Keen to gain as much advance publicity as possible for his new star, Nathan-Turner ensured that the news filtered out to the press almost immediately after Davison agreed to accept the role – indeed, rather more quickly than the actor himself would have liked. An announcement was even made on the BBC's main evening news on 4 November 1980, and a hastily arranged press conference was held to give eager journalists their first chance to ask questions of the new Doctor.

Later the same month, Davison made his first substantial *Doctor Who*-related television appearance, on the popular BBC children's show *Blue Peter*. Then, on 3 December 1980, he guested on the lunchtime magazine programme *Pebble Mill at One*, discussing with presenter Donny McLeod a number of costume ideas sent in by viewers, ranging from a 'college boy' look, complete with yellow striped blazer, to an outfit consisting of a 'tinfoil suit' and a red bow tie. Davison, although reacting diplomatically to these ideas, found little amongst them to spark his interest. There was, however, a panel of fans on hand in the studio to offer further advice, and a young man named Stuart Unit drew a favourable response when he suggested that the fifth Doctor should be 'like Tristan Farnon, but with bravery and intellect'. The actor was later to cite this as having been one of the most influential ideas in his early thinking about the role.

Nathan-Turner himself offered Davison relatively little advice or guidance as to how he should approach his characterisation of the Doctor – perhaps not surprisingly, given his view that the newcomer was a personality actor who would bring to the series his own distinctive personal qualities and traits.

'I don't think John had much in mind about what he wanted the part to be,' Davison told journalist Ben Landman in a 1985 interview for *Starlog*, 'except for casting me in it. I mean, he didn't say, "I'm offering you the part, and I want you to play it like this." The trick of a good producer is to cast someone who is right for the part in the way that they see it, and then let them do it. Which is really what he did. I was very much thrown in and told, "You're the Doctor – now do it!"'

The producer did, however, have some lengthy discussions with the actor as to the type of costume that he should wear. Both men were agreed that it should have, in the tradition of the previous Doctors' images, an air of old-fashioned and slightly eccentric Englishness about it. A sporting motif was also thought to be a good idea. Polo jodhpurs were at one point considered but, in the end, period cricketing attire was decided upon as being a better choice – a suggestion made by Davison, who was himself a keen cricketer, and possibly again inspired in part by the photograph of him on the *Doctor Who* office wall. A test costume fitting was held around the end of the year, in which Davison tried on various cricketing outfits from stock to assess their effectiveness.

Work was meanwhile in hand on scripts for the forthcoming season. A character summary sent out to freelance writers in the closing months of 1980 gave a general description of the Doctor's background but offered little hint as to the newcomer's intended personality.

The intention at this point was that the new season should open with a four-part story entitled *Project Zeta-Sigma*, the scripts for which had been commissioned from John Flanagan and Andrew McCulloch on 7 October 1980 under the working title *Project '4G'*, and that this should also be the first of the new block in production order. This would then be followed, both on transmission and in production, by another four-parter, Terence Dudley's *Day of Wrath*. By the beginning of 1981, the writers had been briefed to include cricketing references in their scripts. A considerable degree of uncertainty was still apparent, however, as Flanagan recalled in an interview conducted by John C. Smith and Michael McLester in September 1981 for the fanzine *Definitive Gaze*:

'We wrote a scene in which Tegan Jovanka, who is Australian, is saying that the Doctor looks like a cricketer, because of his costume. And Adric says, "That's an Earth insect, isn't it?" "Yes, but it's also a game." "Well, how do you play it?" And we had this thing where the Doctor tries to explain cricket to him. If you've ever tried to explain cricket to an American, you'll know it's virtually impossible, so the more the Doctor explains about it, the more ludicrous it becomes. The whole idea behind cricket is that it's so absurd. We had quite a long section on that. Plus a lot of rather bad punny jokes – sort of like "How's that?" Cricket imagery all the way through.

'Peter had his own ideas, the producer had his own ideas, everyone else had their own ideas. There was quite a lot of discussion about the character, especially the costume. We were phoned up halfway through writing the cricket scene and told, "Forget every reference to cricket; he's not wearing cricket gear at all; we're going for something else."

'Then, later that afternoon, another call came saying, "Don't scratch it altogether." Two days later, "Look, he's possibly going to wear a morning suit." There was a problem.'

The man charged with the task of giving substance to the costume ideas worked out by Nathan-Turner, Davison and others was Colin Lavers, who had been assigned as costume designer for *Project Zeta-Sigma*. Nathan-Turner gave him the following instructions in a memo dated 10 February 1981:

Literally about to depart to the USA for a few weeks for a holiday and wanted to give you some information about the new Doctor's image.

As you probably know, Peter Davison and I have been discussing various ideas for several months now, namely as follows:

That the basic costume would be period cricket outfit (all the Doctors have reflected Earth's history). I enclose some photos of Peter which we took at a 'stock' fitting some time ago. I do feel the *Doctor Who* shirt with the '?' mark on the lapels is worth hanging onto. Similarly, I am committed to a cricket jersey in terms of *Doctor Who* annuals and other merchandise.

Anyway, here are the latest thoughts – I'm sure you can vastly improve them…

Doctor Who shirt, cricket pullover, white cricket shoes, period baggy pants – possibly some colour introduced here, e.g. stripes?, with an optional top coat and hat. One idea we tossed around was a morning suit jacket and collapsible topper.

I shall be returning to the office on 4 March and I wonder if you and I and Peter Davison could have some sort of experimental session on the afternoon of Friday 6 March (Peter Davison is not available any other time and leaves the country around 11 March).

If you would like to come and see me either on 4 or 5 March with any drawings or further thoughts I'd be delighted to see you.

A major change of plan for the new season occurred shortly after this when Nathan-Turner, apparently while on holiday in the USA, decided to drop *Project Zeta-Sigma* from the schedule, possibly with a view to moving it back to a later slot. (Ultimately it was abandoned altogether, although some pre-production work had been carried out on it.)

A replacement first story was hastily sought from Christopher H. Bidmead, who had until recently been the series' script editor – a post now held on a caretaker basis by newcomer Antony Root (see Chapter 5). An outline entitled *The Visitor* was commissioned from him on 9 March, shortly after Nathan-Turner's return from holiday, and a full set of scripts under the revised title *Castrovalva* on 8 April.

One consequence of this change of plan was that Davison's first transmitted story could no longer be the first into production, for the simple reason that recording was due to start in mid-April and the scripts for *Castrovalva* could not possibly be completed in time. Consequently *Day of Wrath*, which in late February had been retitled *Four to Doomsday*, was moved forward to fill the production slot previously held by *Project Zeta-Sigma. Castrovalva* was meanwhile scheduled to be made fourth in line, after *Four to Doomsday* and two other stories, *The Visitation* and *Kinda*, which would be transmitted fourth and third respectively. Making a virtue of this necessity, Nathan-Turner considered it a positive advantage that Davison would now have a little time to settle into the role before having to record the story that would introduce his Doctor to the public – particularly as the plot of *Castrovalva* would see him experiencing a confused state of post-regeneration trauma, presenting a considerable challenge to the actor. This was a view with which Davison concurred. He still felt somewhat unsure about his approach to the role, and continued to seek advice from Nathan-Turner, executive producer Barry Letts and others, including *Four to Doomsday*'s director John Black.

Recording of *Four to Doomsday* began on schedule in mid-April, at which point a photocall was also held to unveil the Doctor's costume to the press – and, through them, to the public. The design drawn up by Lavers and approved by Nathan-Turner had a highly stylised, uniform look. This was something that Nathan-Turner had particularly favoured – in line with the redesign of the fourth Doctor's costume that he had instigated for the previous season – as he considered that it would give the character a readily marketable image and help to boost interest amongst toy and other manufacturers in producing spin-off items. Davison himself was not entirely happy with this aspect of the costume; as he would later admit in interviews, he would have preferred a more 'off-the-peg' look, giving the impression that the Doctor had simply picked up an assortment of clothes found in the TARDIS wardrobe, much as his previous incarnations had done.

The finishing touch to the outfit (although this was removed for the purposes of the initial photocall) was a prop stick of celery affixed to the lapel of the coat – another idea hit upon by Nathan-Turner, although he has never revealed the inspiration behind it.

For *Four to Doomsday*, Davison adopted a style of performance that he would later describe as 'bland', his intention being to avoid doing anything that could conceivably clash with his eventual interpretation of the role, once he had refined this to his full satisfaction. By this stage he had already formed some quite firm views as to how he should approach the part, as he explained in an early press interview quoted by Peter Haining in the 1983 book *Doctor Who – A Celebration*:

'For a start, I will be a much younger Doctor and I'll be wearing a kind of Victorian cricketing outfit to accentuate my youth. I would like him to be heroic and resourceful. I feel that, over the years, the Doctor has become less vital, no longer struggling for survival, depending on instant, miraculous solutions to problems.

'The suspense of "Now how is he going to get out of this tight corner?" has been missing. I want to restore that. My Doctor will be flawed. He will have the best intentions and he will in the end win through, but he will not always act for the best. Sometimes, he will even endanger his companions. But I want him to have a sort of reckless innocence.'

Davison drew a certain amount of inspiration for his performance from the earlier Doctors – particularly the first and second, as played by William Hartnell and Patrick Troughton respectively. He had been an avid viewer of the Hartnell and Troughton stories as a teenager, and had recently watched a number of them again (along with several Jon Pertwee and Tom Baker stories) after borrowing videotape copies from Nathan-Turner. Some fan commentators would later suggest that his portrayal most closely resembled Troughton's, but he himself felt that it drew more heavily on Hartnell's, as he explained in a 1982 interview with David Hirsch for *Starlog*:

'I was given a completely blank page to do with as I liked. But at the same time, I didn't have the advantage I would have with another part, where I could create the character by saying, "His parents were like this," or, "This is his background." So I thought about what the other Doctors had done and I picked up ideas. I didn't want to dive in with a totally down-the-line character. I think my character has more than I intended to do with that of William Hartnell's Doctor. My Doctor gets cross sometimes, as Hartnell's did. Very gruff. He always has the best intentions in the world but, because of this... He doesn't always make mistakes, but he sometimes causes them. When he gets into a dangerous situation, he gets into trouble.'

Perhaps providing some support for this view, Hartnell's widow Heather would later comment that Davison strongly reminded her of her husband as a young man, and that she saw a number of parallels between their respective portrayals of the Doctor (although she also thought that the fifth Doctor's alien qualities were insufficiently emphasised, making him too similar to an ordinary human being).

One major difference between Davison and his four predecessors was that he was already very well known for other TV work at the point when he first appeared on screen as the Doctor – a fact that in the opinion of some critics made it more difficult for viewers to suspend their disbelief and accept him in the role. Not only was he still recognised from *All Creatures Great and Small*, but he was also gaining exposure in two current situation-comedy series: LWT's *Holding the Fort* and the BBC's own *Sink or Swim*. *Sink or Swim* would indeed remain in production during the first two years of Davison's time in *Doctor Who*, obliging Nathan-Turner to release the actor between *Doctor Who* stories to work on that series.

The first televised pictures of the fifth Doctor in costume came not in *Doctor Who* itself but in the BBC's outside broadcast coverage of the annual Lord Mayor's Show in London on 14 November 1981, during the course of which Davison and a group of assorted monsters (fans wearing largely home-made costumes) were seen waving to the crowds from a float devoted to the series. After a further round of publicity appearances, including a guest spot on *Boxing Night at the Mill* when Davison was, amongst other things, required to demonstrate his prowess at making chocolate milk shakes, transmission of the new season began with the first episode of *Castrovalva* on Monday 4 January 1982, finally getting the fifth Doctor's era underway on the screen.

This first story saw the Doctor making a gradual recovery from his aforementioned state of post-regeneration trauma His behaviour was initially confused and erratic, coloured by occasional reversions to the mannerisms of his previous incarnations – Davison essaying brief impressions of his predecessors in explicit recognition of the inspiration that he was drawing from them. He became progressively more stable, however, as the events of the story unfolded in the supposedly healing environment of *Castrovalva* and as his true character started to emerge.

Many of the qualities that had led Nathan-Turner to cast Davison were immediately evident to the viewer – particularly his relative youthfulness. One early idea, particularly favoured by Bidmead, was that he should give the impression of being an old man in a young man's body, and this also was reflected in the story. It quickly became apparent, too, that the fifth Doctor was to be a less overtly eccentric and off-the-wall character than the fourth. This was partly a consequence of Nathan-Turner's determination to cut down the level of humour in the series – or, as he put it, to concentrate on 'wit rather than slapstick' – but partly also a reflection of Davison's own natural disposition, in keeping with the producer's appraisal of him as a personality actor.

'I'm not a wacky, eccentric person,' noted Davison in a 1988 interview conducted by Richard Marson for *Doctor Who Magazine*. 'If they had wanted a wacky, eccentric person, John would have cast one. He did not want me to do that. I went along with what he wanted – he was the producer – and he wanted me to play it in a certain way. I'm sure if he had wanted me to be wacky and eccentric, I could have done it, but I could never have played the part in the way Tom Baker did. I'm not by nature like that.'

Expanding on this theme, Davison told Ben Landman in his 1985 *Starlog* interview: 'I don't think you ever think too consciously – especially if you're playing someone from Gallifrey, someone 750 years old – exactly what parts of yourself you're putting into it. I wanted to change the direction of *Doctor Who* a bit, to make it more believable. The fact of the matter is that it was me playing the part. Therefore, bits that are me came over.'

As Season 19 continued, so further aspects of the new Doctor's character began to become familiar. The heroism that had been one of the producer's original requirements was very much to the fore, as was the vulnerability – a quality demonstrated perhaps most vividly in the fact that the Doctor was unable to prevent the death of Adric in a space freighter crash at the end of *Earthshock,* a story written by the series' new permanent script editor, Eric Saward.

The thinking behind this vulnerability was a subject on which Nathan-Turner elaborated when interviewed by David Hirsch in 1982 for *Starlog*: 'I opted for a more fallible Doctor, a more vulnerable character who wasn't always on top of every situation. I felt that, in the past, some of the Doctors had been too dominant. There really had been no threat. Every cliffhanger ending had left the Doctor in jeopardy of some kind, and we had all known that he was going to get out of it and be back next week. I think that if the role is played infallibly, then, in a way, that's undercutting the drama. If you've got a Doctor who is fallible, I think, hopefully, the viewers can get more involved and seriously believe he might not be back next week.'

The combined qualities of heroism and vulnerability meant that the fifth Doctor was sometimes seen to act rather recklessly, rushing breathlessly into new situations with an air of innocent curiosity and failing to consider all the risks.

'I think he has a certain amount of tunnel vision!' opined Davison in a 1982 interview with Jeremy Bentham for *Doctor Who Magazine*. 'He's not always the wisest of men. Maybe when he sits back and ruminates on the way things have gone he is wise, but I think that he's headstrong and he makes more of a mess of things in the short run until he's sorted out his own problems. He doesn't always act for the best. Quite often he'll land in a certain situation and, obviously, the common-sense thing to do would be simply to leave – to get out of there because it's dangerous to everyone. But he doesn't get out, he wants to find out what's going on, he's got to explore... and thus he gets embroiled in the story.'

Like all his predecessors, the fifth Doctor was a resolute champion of the cause of good against evil, invariably standing up for the underdog and combating tyranny and oppression wherever he encountered them. He also had a considerable degree of moral courage.

Davison was considered by BBC management to have made a great success of his debut season as the Doctor. Nathan-Turner's superior, Head of Series and Serials David Reid, wrote to him in glowing terms on 29 March 1982:

> Sadly we have only said a fast 'Hello' to each other in the BBC Club but then your schedule doesn't leave you much free time. I wanted simply to congratulate you at the end of your first season of *Doctor Who* and to express my admiration for the way in which you have taken the part and made it your own. I am delighted with the response from the audience and I hope very much that you are.
>
> It is, I know, a very demanding schedule and the confidence and expertise achieved is remarkable – so thank you also for the enormous amount of energy, concentration and work that you have put into the series.
>
> What more can I say except to say that the season has been a great pleasure and a success largely due to you and I greatly look forward to the next season.

Season 20 revealed little more about the fifth Doctor's character than had been established in Season 19. This may have been due in part to the fact that Saward, although acknowledging Davison to be a very good actor, considered him miscast in the role and consequently, as he would later admit, felt uninspired to devote much attention to the character's development. Davison, for his own part, was understandably perturbed at this situation and felt that he was being less well served than he should be by the series' scripts. One thing that he was especially keen to do was to inject some elements of flippant humour into his portrayal, but any such suggestions were generally vetoed by Nathan-Turner in what the actor regarded as an overreaction against the perceived excesses of Tom Baker in this regard. Davison was also rather dissatisfied with his own performance during the course of this season.

Quite apart from these concerns about his own role, the actor harboured a number of misgivings about the general direction in which the series was moving at this point. In particular, he thought that the stories were becoming too reliant on familiar monsters and characters from *Doctor Who*'s past; he felt that there was an increasing tendency for stylish production values to take priority over good plotting; he disagreed with Nathan-Turner's decision to have Nyssa written out in *Terminus*, the fourth story of the season, as he considered her to be the companion best suited to his Doctor; and he disliked the producer's policy of casting 'guest star' celebrities, often best known for comedy or light entertainment work, in supporting roles (see Chapter 6).

'I was actually very unhappy with the second season, script-wise and concept-wise,' admitted the actor in his 1988 interview with Richard Marson for *Doctor Who Magazine*. 'I just felt that it didn't go anywhere and John couldn't quite decide if he was having old monsters back or bringing in new ones. And I wasn't very happy with me in it.

'It was then – in the second year – that I had to decide if I wanted to do a fourth year, because of the way it works. But I just wasn't sure about the programme.

'John and I have always got on very well, but we did have a creative difference over the direction in which he wanted *Doctor Who* to go, and the direction in which I thought it should go. We talked it through and I decided I would be better off if I left.

'As far as companions went, I thought there should be one companion, who was a fairly nice person, to work with the Doctor – preferably Nyssa, although I wasn't insisting on her. I also thought it needed to get away from turning into a sort of variety show in space.

'If you look back to the very first season of *Doctor Who*, I know it looked very tacky – sets that wobbled and all that – but it had a kind of mystical quality in it, an atmosphere which was disappearing when I did it, and which I think has completely disappeared now. It was that atmosphere which made the need to compete with special effects unnecessary. Certain effects we did fine, but you've got to know your limitations and you can't expect to compete with *Star Wars* in BBC Television.

'It wasn't a row at all – indeed, I didn't decide until about two months after our discussion that maybe I should leave. It was kind of frustrating coming to the BBC rehearsal rooms every day as well, and seeing people doing other things.'

'I used to meet Peter from time to time for chats and so on,' noted Saward in a 1993 interview, 'and he always used to have this thing at the end of each season: was he going to come back? I know that he felt a little uncomfortable playing the part, and I think he felt it wasn't working as he would have liked. As I recall, before the end of the second season, he was saying more frequently, "I don't know if I'm going to do it again. I don't know if I'm going to do it again." Really he was just saying out loud what he was feeling. So when John came in and said, "Peter isn't doing it again," I wasn't surprised. I don't think anyone was surprised, as he'd been saying it for so long.'

Davison was in fact much happier with Season 21 than he had been with Season 20, and even had second thoughts about his decision to leave. By this point, however, steps had already been taken to write him out and to cast a replacement, so it was too late for a rethink. Thus it was that the fifth Doctor bowed out with the transmission on 16 March 1984 of the final episode of Robert Holmes's *The Caves of Androzani*, bringing to an end an era of the series' history that, for the actor's many fans, had been all too brief.

'The press were all looking for a behind-the-scenes row,' recalled Davison in his 1988 interview for *Doctor Who Magazine*. 'Indeed the *Daily Mail* printed that I'd been given the elbow because I was too boring! Unfortunately for them, there was no row – in fact John Nathan-Turner tried very hard to keep me on for another season. However, I remembered, when I joined, meeting Patrick Troughton in the BBC car park, and him saying, "Congratulations. Don't stay longer than three years though." And I think he was right. You see, as an actor I've lived for a long time with the terror of expecting a day to come when there's no work for me. The temptation with doing *Doctor Who* was that I could just have stayed for season after season. But I was risking an association that could have been very damaging career-wise. It was a decision I made through attempting to further my career. It wasn't a happy decision, as in "Thank God that's over". I just wanted to do other things after my time. *Doctor Who* was a lot of fun to do. We had some terrific guest artists, and I wouldn't have missed it for anything. It was very demanding, and strikes delayed my last story so I was too tired to feel sad when it was all finally over, but, yes, one does suffer the odd pang.'

PART TWO – FICTION

3: The Stories

'So he was the Doctor all the time…'

As the newly regenerated Doctor struggles to his feet, the sound of alarms rings out. Nyssa, Tegan and Adric help the Doctor towards the safety of the TARDIS. Before they can reach it, however, they realise that the Master has not yet finished with them.

Note: In the following listings, the technical details are as follows: 'Time' refers to the starting time, rounded to the nearest minute, of the original transmission of an episode in England; 'Durn' indicates the exact duration of the episode on the master tape (where known) or otherwise the duration of the original transmission; 'Viewers' gives the official viewing figure in millions; 'Chart Pos' is the position of the episode in the top 200 programmes for that week. Where a dash appears in the 'Viewers' or 'Chart Pos' column, this signifies that no information was collected by the BBC for the transmission in question.

SEASON NINETEEN

Castrovalva (5Z)

EP	DATE	TIME	DURN	VIEWERS	CHART POS
1	04.01.82	18.55	24'14"	9.1	54
2	05.01.82	19.02	24'13"	8.6	84
3	11.01.82	18.55	23'35"	10.2	47
4	12.01.82	19.06	24'12"	10.4	46

PRODUCTION DETAILS
Location Filming: 01.09.81–04.09.81.
Studio Recording: 15.09.81–16.09.81 in TC3 and
29.09.81–01.10.81 in TC6.

Chased by the Pharos Project's security chief (Dallas Cavell) and
two guards (Harry Fielder, Kenneth Lawrie), Nyssa, Tegan and
Adric help the newly regenerated Doctor towards the TARDIS.
The Doctor collapses and they are caught as a Sussex Area Health
Authority ambulance drives up. The ambulancemen (David Ellis
[not seen on screen], Derek Matt, Peter Roy) load the Doctor into
the back of the vehicle. While Adric distracts the guards, Tegan
and Nyssa drive off in the ambulance. They arrive at the TARDIS
and get the Doctor inside. Watching on the TARDIS's monitor,
Nyssa sees the Master's TARDIS appear, still in the shape of an
Ionic column. Force rays are emitted from it which knock everyone out. Then it dematerialises, leaving Adric behind. Nyssa and
Tegan help Adric into the Doctor's TARDIS.
   The Doctor is wandering the TARDIS's corridors and comes
across a room full of cricket paraphernalia. He changes his clothes
into cricketing whites and an Edwardian beige coat and a hat that
he finds hanging by a mirror outside the room. His regeneration
is, however, failing and he enlists Nyssa's and Tegan's help to find

the zero room, described as a neutral environment cut off from the rest of the universe.

Once inside the zero room, the Doctor levitates and settles down to sleep. Suddenly an image of Adric appears on the wall. He warns Nyssa and Tegan that they are plunging into a trap.

The trap has been set by the Master who is holding the real Adric captive while a false image of the boy is loose on the TARDIS. The image has sent the ship plunging back to Event One – the hydrogen in-rush that preceded the big bang at the creation of the universe. The Doctor recovers sufficiently to show Tegan how to eject rooms from the TARDIS and thus create thrust which will push them away from the explosion. She jettisons the rooms and they escape unscathed. Unfortunately, one of the jettisoned rooms was the zero room and all that remains of the stable environment is the doors. Nyssa fashions these into a coffin-like casket in which to carry the Doctor.

Tegan meanwhile has found an entry in the TARDIS data bank describing the 'dwellings of simplicity' on Castrovalva, a place that has properties similar to those of the missing zero room. It is a small planet of the Phylox Series in Andromeda.

Arriving on the planet, Nyssa and Tegan transport the Doctor towards the dwellings, which are on top of a massive cliff. There they meet Ruther (Frank Wylie), Mergrave (Michael Sheard) and Shardovan (Derek Waring), who offer them rooms and hospitality. They also meet the Portreeve, a person of importance and wisdom who seems to know who the Doctor is, despite the fact that the Doctor isn't sure himself.

The Portreeve is, in fact, the Master (Anthony Ainley), who has engineered Castrovalva using Adric's skill at mathematics and the power of block transfer computations. The entire place is a trap for the Doctor, who eventually realises the deception through study of the Castrovalvan history books, which are 500 years old but tell the planet's history up to the present day.

The Doctor reveals the trapped Adric behind an apparently magical tapestry which shows changing images. The boy is held in a web of hadron power lines but Shardovan, exercising his free will, swings down on a chandelier and smashes the web. As

Castrovalva starts to fold in on itself, the Master tries to escape in his TARDIS, now disguised as an ornamental fireplace, but cannot. The Doctor, Nyssa and Tegan are led to safety by a recovered Adric who, as the creator of the world, can see the way out. Mergrave stays behind to impede the Master's escape.

The doors close behind the Doctor, Tegan, Nyssa and Adric, trapping the Master beneath a pile of fighting, struggling Castrovalvans.

The quartet of time travellers return to the TARDIS where the Doctor places a stick of Castrovalvan celery on his coat lapel.

WHO FAX

- Novelised as *Doctor Who – Castrovalva* by Christopher H. Bidmead in 1983.
- Story released on BBC Home Video in 1992.
- Working title: *The Visitor*.
- **Locations:** Crowborough WT Station, Duddleswell (on B2026), nr Crowborough, East Sussex; Buckhurst Park, Withyham, East Sussex; Harrison's Rocks, Birchden Wood/Nettons Wood, nr Groombridge, Sussex.
- For the first time, *Doctor Who* was transmitted not in a Saturday teatime slot but on Mondays and Tuesdays. This was to be the case for all the stories of Season 19. For Season 20, the days would change to Tuesdays and Wednesdays (except for the first episode of *Arc of Infinity*, transmitted on a Monday). The anniversary special *The Five Doctors* was transmitted on a Friday. Then, for Season 21, the transmission days changed again to Thursdays and Fridays (except for *Resurrection of the Daleks*, the two episodes of which went out on consecutive Wednesdays).
- During the course of the story, several past companions – including Jamie, Jo and the Brigadier – and several established monster races – including the Daleks, the Ogrons and the Ice Warriors – are mentioned by the Doctor. The Doctor also uses the phrase 'Reverse the polarity of the neutron flow', more commonly associated with the third Doctor.
- A smoke effect was overlaid on the picture during the scenes in

the TARDIS as it approaches the Event One explosion.

● To preserve the surprise that the Portreeve was actually the Master, the part was credited as being played by 'Neil Toynay' – an anagram of Tony Ainley – in the *Radio Times* listing and on the closing titles of part three.

● For the first time in *Doctor Who*'s history, a pre-title sequence was used. This was for the story's opening episode and recapped the conclusion of *Logopolis*. Although the sequence was not re-recorded for *Castrovalva*, the flashback of the Doctor's old companions was omitted and the dialogue spoken by Nyssa was altered from 'He was the Doctor all the time' to 'So he was the Doctor all the time'. In addition, the music was re-recorded by Paddy Kingsland to lend the scene a more optimistic tone.

● Sound effects for the jungle/forest in parts two, three and four were taken from a BBC effects record and were of a jungle in Sri Lanka at dawn in the year 1945. Other sound effects included a canary singing, a Tibetan horn, wind effects and an open fireplace.

The story originally planned to launch the fifth Doctor on screen

● was *Project Zeta-Sigma* (working title: *Project '4G'*) by John Flanagan and Andrew McCulloch, which would also have been the first to be made. However, this was abandoned at a late stage, necessitating the commissioning of a hasty replacement and the rejigging of the season's production order.

● Although *Castrovalva* was the first transmitted story to feature Peter Davison as the Doctor, it was actually recorded fourth, after *Four to Doomsday*, *The Visitation* and *Kinda*.

● On 27 July 1981 the BBC's Head of Series and Serials, David Reid, sent a memo to producer John Nathan-Turner after reading through Christopher H. Bidmead's initial scripts. He asked if a recap was going to be included to explain the change of Doctor, and also commented that the end of part three was unclear. Nathan-Turner replied that a recap was indeed going to be included at the start, and that the end of part three would be altered accordingly.

● The story was inspired in part by two prints by the Dutch artist

Maurits Cornelis Escher (1898–1972) hanging in the office of the then Controller of BBC1, but the title was taken from that of an unrepresentative lithograph by the same artist of a castle set atop a mountainside. Works by Escher that more accurately represent the flavour of the story include *Up and Down* (1947), *House of Stairs* (1951), *Relativity* (1953), *Belvedere* (1958), *Ascending and Descending* (1960) and *Waterfall* (1961).

● The first episode actually had its first transmission in the BBC Scotland area on 4 January 1982 at around 15.30.

● A selection from Paddy Kingsland's incidental music for this story was released on an audio-cassette called *The Corridor of Eternity* by Julian Knott in October 1990.

QUOTES

● 'I realised that the Doctor had to be the central part of it, but at this vulnerable stage I saw him being placed in a box – making him the focus of interest. The unstable regeneration was a wonderful, inherited idea and it was logical to go on exploring the TARDIS. I poured over an Escher book for a long time but the *Castrovalva* print is not typical of his work. It was just a castle at the top of a hill, but it was the first idea to really fall into place. The web was a kind of science-fiction icon which really came alive for me – the Master's elaborate trap made me think of spiders, which gave me the web, and what better than to tangle Adric up in it? However, I took John Nathan-Turner's advice of making Adric appear a lot more than he was going to. Those visionary appearances in the TARDIS and in Castrovalva were quite frightening.

'We'd got Tegan into the TARDIS because she was excited about this kind of super aircraft, so it was a natural development of that idea that she should think she was steering the ship.

'The Castrovalvans didn't know they were illusory – they were as real to themselves as you are to you. What interested me in this idea was that we may all be illusions ourselves. I got tremendous mileage out of the marginal awareness of Shardovan and this very much reflected my own childhood thoughts about human existence. A lot of children spend a lot of time thinking in this existential way.' Writer Christopher H. Bidmead interviewed by Richard Marson for *Doctor Who Magazine* Issue 109, published in February 1986.

COMMENT

DJH: Castrovalva *concludes the battle against the Master that was started in* Logopolis *at the end of the previous season, and as such provides a good bridge for the change-over of Doctors. There is much to commend the story: the sets are particularly effective and capture well the paintings of M. C. Escher on which the story was based, the acting is of a generally high standard with Anthony Ainley providing a startling portrayal of the aged Portreeve before he reveals himself as the Master, and the location work around Harrison's Rocks in East Sussex also stands out.*

Unfortunately there has to be a downside, and in this case it is that the plot – and in particular the Master's plan to trap the Doctor – is illogical. The Master was fully expecting the Doctor to have been destroyed in Event One, and yet at the end he claims that Castrovalva was his real trap – despite the fact that Tegan finds out about Castrovalva from the TARDIS's data bank before the Master realises that the Doctor has escaped from the explosion. Other cringe-worthy aspects include Nyssa losing most of her clothes and jewellery en route *to the dwellings of simplicity and the complete lack of any acting ability displayed by Matthew Waterhouse as Adric. Overall the story is interesting but bland, and is not the best start that a new Doctor could have been given. (5/10)*

SJW: Unlike the previous Doctors' debut stories, Castrovalva *makes the aftermath of the regeneration its principal focus. This is particularly the case in the first two episodes, set largely within the TARDIS, which are somewhat reminiscent of (though considerably less effective than) the two-parter* Inside the Spaceship *from the series' first season. It is only after the action moves to*

Castrovalva itself that the story really starts to take off. There are some interesting concepts and characters here, and the whole thing is well handled by director Fiona Cumming. All in all, though, this is a rather low-key and uneventful start to the fifth Doctor's era. (4/10)

Four to Doomsday (5W)

EP	DATE	TIME	DURN	VIEWERS	CHART POS
1	18.01.82	18.57	23'36"	8.4	66
2	19.01.82	19.05	24'11"	8.8	61
3	25.01.82	18.57	24'09"	8.9	63
4	26.01.82	19.07	24'52"	9.4	53

PRODUCTION DETAILS
Studio Recording: 13.04.81–15.04.81 and 28.04.81–30.04.81 all in TC6.

The date is 28 February 1981 when the TARDIS materialises on board a massive spaceship *en route* for Earth. As the travellers leave the TARDIS to investigate, putting on space helmets with air supplies, their progress is monitored by hovering monopticons – mobile cameras.

Adric and Nyssa are separated from the Doctor and Tegan, and the latter meet up with their hosts – the frog-like Urbankan Monarch (Stratford Johns), and his ministers Persuasion (Paul Shelley) and Enlightenment (Annie Lambert). Monarch explains that they are all headed for Earth – their first visit in 2500 years – and offers the Doctor his hospitality for the journey. Tegan, meanwhile, sketches the latest fashions for Enlightenment to see.

Adric and Nyssa have been exploring and meet up with the Doctor and Tegan in their rest room. There all of them meet Bigon (Philip Locke), an Athenian; Villagra (Nadia Hammam), a Mayan of the Americas; Lin Futu (Bert Kwouk), a Chinese; and Kurkutji (Illarrio Bisi Pedro), an Australian Aborigine. All these people are travelling back to Earth.

Monarch's ministers also enter the rest room but their appearance has changed to that portrayed in Tegan's sketches. Enlightenment explains that Urbanka's sun, Inokshi, collapsed into a black hole a thousand years ago and that the population – all three billion of them – are on board the space ship awaiting a new start on Earth.

The Doctor decides to explore and deactivates the monopticon in their quarters. The time travellers become separated: Nyssa and Adric find themselves in areas of the ship tended by zombie-like Aborigines, Chinese and Greeks while the Doctor and Tegan attend a recreational – dance and music from the different ethnic groups on board. Bigon quietly tells the Doctor that he must speak with him and when they have returned to the rest room, he reveals himself to be an android.

Nyssa and Adric are brought before Monarch who explains that he intends to bring the benefits of an android existence to Earth. Adric seems convinced but Nyssa is horrified. She is hypnotised by Enlightenment and then taken to the mobiliary where her personal history will be placed on a microchip.

Bigon tells the Doctor that Monarch caused the destruction of Urbanka and he now intends to strip the Earth of its silicon, carbon and other minerals in order to achieve his great plan, which is to travel faster than light and thus return to the creation of the Universe where he believes he will meet himself as he thinks he is God. He intends to use a poison, produced by the Urbankans to shrink matter, to subdue humanity.

Tegan decides to get away and enters the TARDIS, inadvertently moving it into a position just outside the ship. Meanwhile the Doctor and Bigon manage to rescue Nyssa. Monarch is about to have the Doctor executed when Adric intervenes on his behalf. Monarch agrees to stay the execution as he hopes to learn more about the TARDIS from the boy. Bigon is scheduled to be reprogrammed.

The Doctor manages to warn Adric and the pair convince Lin Futu to help them. Bigon is also rescued. The Doctor manages to get to the TARDIS by space-walking between the ships – with the aid of a carefully thrown cricket ball when he becomes stranded in space – and returns his ship to the recreational hall. Persuasion and Enlightenment – both of them androids – are disabled and their circuits thrown into space.

Monarch orders that the life support systems be shut down to stop the time travellers, but Bigon sets the ship on a return course to Urbanka. The Doctor takes the Urbankan poison to analyse but, returning to the TARDIS, the travellers are confronted by Monarch. The Doctor throws the poison at the Urbankan who shrinks away to nothing.

The Doctor, Tegan, Nyssa and Adric bid farewell to Bigon, Villagra, Kurkutji and Lin Futu and leave in theTARDIS. Once on their way, Nyssa suddenly collapses…

WHO FAX

- Novelised as *Doctor Who – Four to Doomsday* by Terrance Dicks in 1983.
- Working title: *Day of Wrath*.
- Urbanka is revealed to be in the solar system Inokshi in Galaxy 1489.
- Several facts about the Doctor are revealed in this story. He claims that he once took five wickets for New South Wales. It is discovered that he can withstand sub-zero temperatures for six minutes and can put himself into a trance which reduces the need for oxygen (possibly referring back to the Tom Baker story *Terror of the Zygons*).
- The story features elaborate dance sequences for each of the main civilisations represented. The choreographer brought in to handle this aspect was Sue Lefton. A fight arranger, B. H. Barry, was also contracted to supervise a mock battle between two Trojan warriors.
- *Four to Doomsday* replaced the abandoned *Project Zeta-Sigma* in the production schedule.
- The didgeridoo music played during theAborigine recreationals was the signature tune of a BBC programme called *Quest Under Capricorn* first transmitted in the early sixties.
- John Nathan-Turner requested that the space suits designed for the Doctor, Adric, Tegan and Nyssa be retained for future use following the end of production on this story.

QUOTES

- 'Stratford Johns took a little bit of persuading to play the King Frog, but the part was pivotal and I think that's what finally led him into doing it. He wasn't terribly happy about the idea that he was going to be covered up in this enormous costume. He had probably realised, from his long experience, that it had the potential of being exceedingly uncomfortable – and it was!' Director John Black interviewed for *In-Vision* Issue 56, published in March 1995.

- 'The cricket ball sequence was interesting for me as a director... I story-boarded it right out in total detail and we had endless meetings with technical people about it... It all had to be done rather carefully, and was difficult to do credibly. Of course, it did eat away at studio time, and it was fairly nail-biting at times! There were endless hold-ups and delays while they tried to improve the lighting to avoid all the usual problems involved with Colour Separation Overlay, such as "fringing". I think we managed it quite successfully, though.' Director John Black interviewed for *In-Vision* Issue 56, published in March 1995.

COMMENT

DJH: Four to Doomsday was no doubt on paper a good idea but unfortunately it ended up being perhaps one of the weakest stories of the Peter Davison era. While Stratford Johns is very good as Monarch, the rest of the cast seem to be going through the paces, perhaps taking the fact that they were playing androids to heart. There is a great deal of aimless corridor-wandering as well, and the ultimate revelation that Monarch is not an android comes as no real surprise. There are some nice touches, however. The model work of the Urbankan ship is particularly good, and the space-walk sequence in which the Doctor throws a cricket ball against the side of the ship to propel himself towards the TARDIS is a nice idea, albeit somewhat unbelievable in practice. The whole story unfortunately has a very flat feel to it. (5/10)

SJW: Four to Doomsday *is a visual treat. The sets, costumes and make-up are all highly effective; the Urbankans are well-realised aliens; and the regular 'recreationals' are very colourful and spectacular. Where the story falls down, though, is in its scripting. There are a number of major plot holes, and the recent departure of Season 18's technically-minded script editor Christopher H. Bidmead is readily apparent from the inclusion of some very dodgy science. The concepts are interesting, certainly, but – as with so many other stories of this period – style ultimately wins out over content. (5/10)*

Kinda (5Y)

EP	DATE	TIME	DURN	VIEWERS	CHART POS
1	01.02.82	18.57	24'50"	8.4	78
2	02.02.82	19.04	24'58"	9.4	45
3	08.02.82	18.57	24'17"	8.5	67
4	09.02.82	19.06	24'28"	8.9	56

Repeat					
1	22.08.82	18.24	24'50"	4.2	96
2	23.08.82	18.27	24'58"	4.3	91
3	24.08.82	18.35	24'16"	3.9	103
4	25.08.82	18.32	24'29"	5.0	70

PRODUCTION DETAILS

Studio Recording: 29.07.81–31.07.81 and 12.08.81–14.08.81 all in TC8. Additional scenes recorded during the first studio recording of *Earthshock*, 10.11.81 in TC8.

The Doctor prescribes some augmented D-sleep for Nyssa and constructs a delta wave augmentor to ensure that she gets it. The TARDIS has arrived on the planet Deva Loka and, while Nyssa sleeps inside the ship, the Doctor, Adric and Tegan decide to look around. They find, hanging from some trees, a set of wind chimes which seem to have a strange effect on Tegan. The Doctor and

Adric are distracted when they find an armoured suit – a Total Survival Suit (TSS) – elsewhere in the jungle. Tegan, feeling sleepy, settles down to rest by the chimes.

The suit is activated when Adric slams shut its door, and it herds the Doctor and Adric to a dome-shaped base. There they meet Sanders (Richard Todd), Todd (Nerys Hughes) and Hindle (Simon Rouse), the remaining members of an expedition aiming to classify planet S14 – as they term it – as to its suitability for colonisation. Hindle has captured two of the native Kinda (Michael Mungarven, Barney Lawrence) for study and he discovers that, by using a mirror, he can hypnotise them and then telepathically order them to do his will. Already slightly unstable, Hindle slips into madness. When Sanders leaves in the TSS to look for Roberts – a missing crew member – Hindle places all the others under arrest.

Meanwhile, the natives drape Tegan's sleeping form with garlands and other offerings. In her dreams, Tegan meets a strange man (Jeffrey Stewart) with a snake tattooed on his arm, who wants to take over her body. The stranger confuses her with multiple images of herself and then leaves her totally alone in her own mind. Terrified, she capitulates to his demand. She wakes up back in the forest, but is now possessed by an alien force.

Sanders has met up with the blind wise woman Panna (Mary Morris) and her young telepathic acolyte Karuna (Sarah Prince). Panna gives Sanders the Box of Jhana, which he opens. Light floods his face.

Back at the dome, Hindle is planning to raze a 50-mile area around the dome with fire as protection against the plants and trees. The Doctor and Todd have been locked up and Adric is pretending to be on Hindle's side in order to get the electronic key to the cell. When Sanders returns he gives Hindle the Box but Hindle orders the Doctor to open it. The Time Lord does so and sees an image of Panna and Karuna beckoning him.

The possessed Tegan meets another Kinda, Aris (Adrian Mills), and offers to help him. The snake mark moves from her arm to his and he is possessed. The creature within Tegan reveals itself to be a Mara.

The Doctor and Todd escape from the dome only to come across a group of Kinda. Aris arrives and orders that the pair be restrained. Karuna suggests that Aris's speech – he was previously mute, as are all Kinda males – fulfils a prophecy and that he must be obeyed. She takes the Doctor and Todd to see Panna. The old wise woman speaks of the cycle of life, of great wheels turning and civilisations rising and falling. She shows the Doctor and Todd a vision – time running out as the Kinda despair. When they return to reality, Panna appears to be dead, but Karuna is revealed to be her reincarnation. The Doctor and Todd find Tegan in the jungle and wake her. She seems fine, if puzzled by her bad dreams.

Aris, meanwhile, is exhorting the Kinda to attack and destroy the dome. They have built a TSS-like structure out of sticks with which to battle the real TSS. This machine now attacks, and the Kinda are scattered. Adric is trapped inside the machine and the Doctor releases him. Hindle has wired the dome with bombs and is planning to blow it up. The Doctor and Todd rush back to try to stop him. Hindle has reverted to a child-like state, and Todd tricks him into opening the Box of Jhana. The light floods his mind.

The immediate danger over, the Doctor realises he must deal with the Mara and plans to use a circle of mirrors to trap it. Karuna acts as bait to draw Aris into the circle. Trapped, the Mara leaves Aris's body and grows into a giant snake (operator: Stephen Calcutt). Then it weakens and vanishes.

Later, Todd recommends that the planet is unsuitable for colonisation. The Doctor bids the expedition team farewell.

A recovered Nyssa greets the Doctor, Tegan and Adric and they leave in the TARDIS.

WHO FAX

- Novelised as *Doctor Who – Kinda* by Terrance Dicks in 1983.
- Working title: *The Kinda*.
- Story released on BBC Home Video in 1994.
- Christopher Bailey's script was heavily influenced by Buddhist teachings and philosophy. Many words and names are taken from Buddhism: *Anatta* meaning egolessness; *Anicca* meaning

impermanence; *Dukkha* meaning pain, suffering, sorrow and misery; *Panna* meaning wisdom; *Karuna* meaning compassion; *Jana* or *Jhana* meaning meditation; and *Mara* meaning temptation.

- The characters and situations that Tegan encounters in her own mind are deliberate distortions of events that she has recently experienced. For example, she encounters two characters (named Anatta (Anna Wing) and Anicca (Roger Milner) in the credits) playing draughts beside a strange metal structure, described in the script as a 'caravan', just as at the start of the story Adric and Nyssa were playing draughts beside the TARDIS. The stranger who taunts her is named on the closing credits as Dukkha – which apart from its Buddhist meaning is also a play on the word 'Doctor'.

- During recording it was realised that episode four was running under length and so Christopher Bailey was asked to provide some further material. The additional scenes featured Adric and Tegan discussing the situation while the Doctor and Todd try to persuade Hindle not to destroy the dome. They were recorded during the first studio session for *Earthshock*.

- The reason for Sarah Sutton's non-appearance in much of this story was that she had been contracted for only 24 of the season's 26 episodes and therefore had to drop out for the making of two episodes. (See Chapter 6.)

- The large snake prop was made by an external special effects company, Stephen Greenfield Construction.

- Barnaby's Picture Library supplied a transparency for the establishing shots of the forest. The photographer was Keith N. Radford.

- The making of this story was featured in the media studies book *Doctor Who – The Unfolding Text* by John Tulloch and Manuel Alvarado, published by Macmillan in 1982.

- Peter Howell created the Mara's screech by running a violin bow down a cymbal and loading the sound into a Fairlight computer synthesiser. The sound of the wind chimes had previously been used in a movement of his track 'Through a Glass Darkly – A Lyrical Adventure' on side one of the album

'*Through A Glass Darkly*'.

QUOTES

● 'If as an academic, you were going to investigate a story, you couldn't have chosen a better one than *Kinda*. It had to be made to work for the audience; if the writer goes into philosophical conceptions, that's fine ... but one's got to weave them into the story, otherwise people will have switched off, and it doesn't work on any level. It certainly worried me that we'd lost the Doctor's point of view entirely – that's not to say that I'm going in as a barbarian saying "we mustn't have any intellectualising", it's just getting the balance.' Director Peter Grimwade interviewed by Mark Wyman for *Opera of Doom* Issue 1, published in February 1985.

● 'As well as the philosophical side of the story, *Kinda* was problematic because despite its internalised drama, it had to be seen in a visually externalised plane. There were the pure technical problems of getting a large alien landscape in the studio. If we'd gone to shoot it in the South Sea Islands, all on film, it would have been less troublesome – but I suppose you'd have lost the rehearsal element for characters.' Director Peter Grimwade interviewed by Mark Wyman for *Opera of Doom* Issue 1, published in February 1985.

COMMENT

DJH: Kinda is one of the most imaginative and thought-provoking stories to have been presented in the Doctor Who *format. Christopher Bailey's script is rich in Buddhist theory and iconography and yet this does not obscure what is a ultimately a simple tale of good versus evil. There are practically no downsides to this story. The acting, in particular from Janet Fielding and Simon Rouse, is superb, the music complements the action, and the sequences set inside Tegan's mind are both unsettling and frightening. After a shaky start, the season is well on form. (8/10)*

SJW: The highlights of this story are, once again, its images and concepts – particularly the Buddhist influences with which writer

Christopher Bailey has infused his scripts. The downside is that little concession is made to the more casual viewer in terms of plot exposition and clarity. On the production front, Deva Loka is one of the less convincing alien environments presented in Doctor Who, probably the worst aspect of all being the very plastic-looking tree from which the possessed Tegan drops apples on Aris. On the whole, though, the commendable intelligence and sophistication of the scripts and the quality of the performances from an excellent cast – Janet Fielding being particularly outstanding on this occasion – easily outweigh any less positive features. (6/10)

The Visitation (5X)

EP	DATE	TIME	DURN	VIEWERS	CHART POS
1	15.02.82	18.57	24'11"	9.1	54
2	16.02.82	19.06	24'26"	9.3	48
3	22.02.82	18.58	24'24"	9.9	41
4	23.02.82	19.05	23'32"	10.1	40

Repeat					
1	15.08.83	18.25	24'11"	4.3	85
2	16.08.83	18.32	24'26"	4.6	79
3	17.08.83	18.26	24'30"	3.6	104
4	18.08.83	18.26	23'32"	4.8	75

PRODUCTION DETAILS
Ealing Filming: 01.05.81 Stage 2
Location Filming: 05.05.81–08.05.81
Studio Recording: 20.05.81–21.05.81 in TC3 and 3.06.81–5.06.81 in TC6

Strange lights in the sky are witnessed by a young girl called Elizabeth (Valerie Fyfer) from the window of a seventeenth-century manor house. She tells Squire John (John Savident), Charles (Anthony Calf) and their servant Ralph (John Baker) what she has seen. Subsequently all the house's occupants are killed by a mysterious alien intruder.

The TARDIS is behaving erratically and the Doctor blames the fault on the lateral balance cones. He tries to return Tegan to Heathrow in 1981, half an hour before she first entered the TARDIS, but although the ship arrives at the right location it is some 300 years too early. Villagers are burning potassium and sulphur in the woods to ward off the plague. The Doctor, Tegan, Adric and Nyssa meet up with Richard Mace (Michael Robbins), an unemployed actor, who leads them to the safety of a barn. The Doctor notices an ornament made from polygrite around Mace's neck and recognises it as part of an alien bracelet from a prison planet. When Mace speaks of a comet falling to Earth a few weeks earlier, the Doctor surmises that this might have been a spaceship crashing and that there might be survivors. Lending weight to his theory, Nyssa finds some power packs in the barn.

The barn is owned by Squire John, and Mace takes the travellers to the Squire's house. The place is deserted, so they decide to have a look around. The Doctor finds a laser mark on a wall by some stairs, but the base of the staircase is apparently blocked by another wall. The Doctor realises that the latter is in fact an energy barrier, and he breaches it. He recognises the smell of soliton gas. The travellers are surprised by an android (Peter Van Dissel), which renders Tegan and Adric unconscious. The Doctor, Nyssa and Mace manage to escape.

The android takes Adric and Tegan to its master, a Terileptil (Michael Melia). The Terileptil questions them.

The Doctor suggests that a sonic booster and frequency modulator might vibrate the android to pieces. Meanwhile the Terileptil orders the local poacher (Neil West) and a group of villagers, all of whom are enslaved to his will by control bracelets worn on their wrists, to capture the Doctor and find the TARDIS.

Mace, Nyssa and the Doctor locate the crashed space shuttle. Its internal lighting is powered by vintaric crystals and still operates. Under attack from the controlled poacher, axeman and wood collector, they escape. Nyssa returns to the TARDIS to construct the sonic device with which to attack the android. The Doctor and

Mace meanwhile go to see the miller (James Charlton). He is also under Terileptil control, however, and the two friends are captured by the villagers and held in the barn.

The Terileptil fits Tegan with a control bracelet, but Adric escapes and heads for the TARDIS. The Terileptil then sends the android to get the Doctor and Mace, and they are brought to the Squire's house. The Terileptil reveals that he and the others in his group are escapees from the tinclavic mines on the planet Raaga. Terileptil law states that imprisonment on Raaga is for life, so the Doctor cannot return them home. Their ship was badly damaged in an asteroid storm, and all but four of them perished in the crash. One of the four who survived has also since died. The Terileptil leader now plans to try to wipe out humanity.

The Doctor and Mace are put in a cell. When the Doctor checks through his pockets to try to find a means of escape, the Terileptil catches him and destroys the sonic screwdriver. The Terileptil then reveals that he plans to infect black rats with a genetically-engineered plague, intended to augment the Black Death that is already spreading across the country. When the Terileptil has gone, the Doctor rescues Tegan and Mace. They are unable to return to the TARDIS, however, as they find that all the exits from the house are sealed.

Nyssa has meanwhile completed the sonic device, which proves its effectiveness after Adric inadvertently allows the android access to the TARDIS. Adric then pilots the ship to the house and rescues the Doctor's party. They then all go to London, following a trail of electrical emissions from the Terileptil's equipment.

The travellers discover the Terileptil leader and the other surviving Terileptils (Michael Leader, David Summer) in their base in a small bakery. Mace despatches one of the creatures but, in the struggle, a flaming torch sets fire to the shop. The Terileptil leader's gun explodes in the heat and the remaining two Terileptils perish in the blaze. The Doctor, Mace, Tegan, Nyssa and Adric throw the plague serum into the fire. The Doctor then gives Mace, as a keepsake, the control chip that he removed from the Terileptil equipment at the house.

The time travellers leave as the fire rages on. As the TARDIS dematerialises, a street sign reveals that the bakery is situated in Pudding Lane.

WHO FAX

- Novelised as *Doctor Who and The Visitation* by Eric Saward in 1982.
- Working titles: *Invasion of the Plague Men*, *The Plague Rats*.
- Story released on BBC Home Video in 1994.
- Locations: Black Park, nr Iver, Slough; Tithe Barn, Hurley.
- The three Terileptils all had different colours featured on their costumes. The leader had a green tint, and the other two had blue and red respectively.
- The mask for the Terileptil leader was the first example in *Doctor Who* of animatronics. Remote controlled by radio, the mouth moved, the lips curled and the gills on the side of the head opened and closed as the creature 'breathed'. The head was constructed by Peter Wragg of the BBC's Visual Effects Department, while the heads of the other two Terileptils, and all three bodies, were made by Richard Gregory of the specialist effects company Imagineering who were to create many of the monsters and special props for the Davison years.
- The making of this story was the subject of Alan Road's book *Doctor Who – The Making of a Television Series* published by Andre Deutsch in 1982.
- The name Terileptil was derived by writer Eric Saward from 'territorial reptile'.
- The character of actor/amateur detective Richard Mace had originally been developed by Saward for a number of one-off BBC radio dramas: *The Assassin* (01/06/1974), *Pegasus* (21/05/1975) and *The Nemesis Machine* (13/08/1976). In these dramas the part was played by Geoffrey Matthews.
- This story saw the final appearance in *Doctor Who* of the Doctor's sonic screwdriver. It had first been seen in the Patrick Troughton adventure *Fury from the Deep* and had made numerous appearances since then.
- Stock footage of fireworks exploding was used at the begin-

ning of episode one to simulate the lights seen by Elizabeth when the Terileptils' capsule arrived on Earth.

● John Nathan-Turner sent a note to the BBC's presentation department around the time of this story's transmission requesting that if at all possible there should be no spoken trails over the end titles of *Doctor Who*.

QUOTES

● 'A girlfriend, who is a student, was writing an essay on architecture in the seventeenth century, the influence of the Fire, and how London radically changed afterwards with Wren and so on. During her researches she came across this fact that the black rat more or less died out in this country after the Great Fire of London, the reason being it had been subject to its own disease and had died of the Plague. I thought, Wouldn't it be nice to think around something more imaginative as to why it might have died. Then I thought, We really don't know how the Great Fire started – there are so many theories – and so I devised a way of entwining those ideas into a *Doctor Who* story.

'The reason *The Visitation* was an old-fashioned story was that I hadn't watched *Doctor Who* in years, so I tended to recall things from when it had started and I had been 17 watching it. I remembered the bits I had liked then and the elements that I thought made a good story, and turned out *The Visitation* from that.' Writer Eric Saward interviewed by Jeremy Bentham for *Doctor Who Monthly* Issue 69, published in October 1982.

COMMENT

DJH: One of the things in The Visitation*'s favour is the sumptuous location work, something that also marked out* Castrovalva. *It also marks a return to the traditional* Doctor Who *monster story, with aliens from space attempting to take over the world. In this instance, there are only three aliens and one android, but, as with* The Time Warrior *back in Season 11, the counterpointing of the modern with the historical works well. Of the period characters, Michael Robbins's Richard Mace takes all the awards. This is a part that Robbins could almost play in his sleep, and it works well* *in small doses. The other 'yokels' are somewhat faceless and seem to be there only to pad out the story.*

Michael Melia's Terileptil leader is a little wooden. It is unfortunate that the costume would allow neither for very much bodily movement nor for any of the actor's features to be seen. Instead it was reliant on radio control and animatronic movement to provide the expression, which, as these techniques were in their infancy at this time, leant the creature a static quality that might otherwise have been avoided. The story is bog standard, and enjoyable for it, but again Matthew Waterhouse's Adric lets the side down with a performance that veers from the barely acceptable to the unwatchable. (7/10)

SJW: The Visitation *is essentially a traditional* Doctor Who *monster story, and it works very well on that level. The Terileptils are in fact probably the best new monsters introduced during the fifth Doctor's era, and it is surprising – and a little disappointing – that they were never accorded a proper return appearance. An added bonus is the story's rare historical setting – the first since that of* Horror of Fang Rock *over four years earlier. The quality of the production matches that of the scripts, ensuring a very entertaining result. The only real drawback for me is Michael Robbins's excessively mannered performance as Richard Mace, which detracts somewhat from the story's credibility. (7/10)*

Black Orchid (6A)

EP	DATE	TIME	DURN	VIEWERS	CHART POS
1	01.03.82	18.57	24'56"	9.9	57
2	02.03.82	19.04	24'41"	10.1	55

Repeat					
1	31.08.83	18.34	24'56"	4.4	94
2	01.09.83	18.27	24'41"	5.0	79

PRODUCTION DETAILS
Location Filming: 05.10.81–09.10.81
Studio Recording: 20.10.81–21.10.81

The TARDIS arrives on Earth, at a railway station called Cranleigh Halt at 3.00 p.m. on 11 June 1925. The Doctor's party are taken aback to be met by Tanner (Timothy Block), Lord Cranleigh's chauffeur, and driven to a cricket match. Lord Cranleigh (Michael Cochrane) and his family assume that the Doctor has come from Guy's Hospital and inform him that there is to be a ball that night in aid of a hospital for sick children.

Everyone assumes that Nyssa much be a Worcestershire Talbot as she is the spitting image of Ann Talbot (Sarah Sutton/Vanessa Paine), Charles's fiancée. The ball is to be a masque and the costumes are chosen: Tegan is to be a rose; Nyssa and Ann have identical butterfly costumes; and the Doctor chooses a Harlequin outfit. While the Doctor is taking a bath, a stranger enters his room via a secret passage. The Doctor fails to see the stranger but notices the open door to the passage and goes through it. The stranger meanwhile makes off with the Harlequin costume.

At the ball, Nyssa and Ann are having great fun confusing everyone as to their true identities. The only way to tell them apart is that Ann has a mole on her left shoulder. Lady Cranleigh (Barbara Murray) is taken to one side by an Indian named Dittar Latoni (Ahmed Kahlil), who explains that Digby (David Wilde), one of the servants, has gone.

They go to investigate, leaving Tegan dancing the Charleston and Adric eating. A character in a Harlequin costume appears, entices Ann/Nyssa to dance with him and then approaches her threateningly in the hallway. A footman who tries to intervene is killed.

The Doctor, meanwhile, has found a dead body – Digby – in a cupboard. He shows it to Lady Cranleigh and Latoni, who have just arrived. The Harlequin costume is returned to the Doctor's room by the stranger, who then goes to another room and puts the unconscious Ann to bed there.

Ann soon recovers and runs out to Lady Cranleigh. At that moment the Doctor appears on the stairs in the Harlequin costume and Ann accuses him of attacking her. The Doctor tries to explain but Lady Cranleigh will not corroborate any of his stories of secret passages and dead bodies. Sir Robert Muir (Moray Watson), the local police chief, arrests the Doctor on suspicion of having killed the footman, James (Derek Hunt). Charles receives a call from a man named 'Smutty' who tells him that the replacement cricketer for whom the Doctor has been mistaken actually missed his train.

On the way to the police station, the Doctor gains Sir Robert's permission to stop off at the railway station. To his dismay, the TARDIS has gone. Luckily it has just been moved to the police station. There, the Doctor takes Sir Robert, Sergeant Markham (Ivor Salter) and Constable Cummings (Andrew Tourell) inside.

Back at the Hall, Lady Cranleigh admits all to Charles. She and Latoni have been secretly looking after his brother, George Cranleigh (Gareth Milne), who was presumed dead after apparently failing to return from an expedition he made up the Orinoco river two years earlier in search of the Black Orchid. He has been hideously scarred – both physically and mentally – by the natives to whom the flower is sacred.

Latoni is knocked unconscious by George but, by hiding the key between two floorboards, prevents him from escaping from the room in which he is being held. George then starts a fire to burn through the door. The Doctor transports everyone back to the Hall in the TARDIS. There, Nyssa is snatched by George as he escapes from the burning room and taken up onto the roof. Lady Cranleigh explains that the Kajabi Indians disfigured George and cut out his tongue. Latoni was the chief of another tribe who rescued him and brought him home.

The Doctor persuades George to let Nyssa go. Charles then steps forward to hug his brother, but George backs away and falls from the roof to his death.

The Doctor and his companions stay for the funeral, and when they leave they have some souvenirs. Tegan is presented with the rose dress from the ball, and the Doctor is given George Cranleigh's book *The Black Orchid*.

WHO FAX

● Novelised as *Doctor Who – Black Orchid* by Terence Dudley in 1986.

● Story released on BBC Home Video in 1994.

● Working title: *The Beast*.

● Locations: Quainton Railway Station, Quainton Road, nr Aylesbury; Quainton Road between Quainton and Waddesdon; house and yard at 99 Quainton Road, Waddesdon; Buckhurst Park, Withyham, East Sussex; Buckhurst House, Buckhurst Park, Withyham, East Sussex.

● Other locations considered for this story but not ultimately used included: New Lodge, Drift Road, Windsor; Missenden Abbey, Great Missenden; Pennyhill Park, Bagshot, Surrey; Berkshire College of Agriculture, Burchett's Green, Berkshire; Taplow House Hotel, Berry Hill, Taplow, nr Maidenhead; Nether Winchendon, Aylesbury, Bucks.

● Stock footage of a steam train was used in episode one to simulate the arrival of a real train at the station. The footage came from a programme called *God's Wonderful Railway*.

● To preserve the mystery of his identity, George Cranleigh was referred to as simply 'the Unknown' in the *Radio Times* cast lists and on the closing credits of episode one.

● The following period songs were played during the story: 'Lazy' by Irving Berlin, 'Show Me The Way To Go Home' by Irving King, 'Pasadena' by Warren, 'Charleston' by Mack-Johnson, 'Gentlemen Prefer Blondes' by Irving Berlin, 'Dinah' by Feldman, '5' 2" Eyes of Blue' by Henderson and 'When Erastus Plays His Old Kazoo' by Coslow-Fain-Spier.

● Sarah Sutton played both Nyssa and Ann Talbot in this story. Vanessa Paine doubled for Sarah Sutton for certain scenes when both characters were in shot together; other scenes were achieved using a split-screen effect.

QUOTES

● 'We had a minor dispute with our technicians over lighting in the studio and so we never got the lighting exactly as I wanted it. There is basic lighting and fine lighting, and in the event we only has the basic, so the drawing room and hall sets weren't picked out as well as I wanted. It's the kind of thing I expect we, as a production, agonise over more than the viewer would.' Director Ron Jones interviewed by Richard Marson for *Doctor Who Magazine* Issue 101, published in June 1985.

● 'I knew as soon as I saw the script that it wasn't going to be a fantasy-based programme, but the lovely challenge was to create 1920s fancy dress costumes. Finding things that would have been seen as fancy dress at that time. It was a very enjoyable show to do... In the twenties, fancy-dress parties were very popular but there was a definite twenties interpretation of what period costume was, particularly if it was meant to be fancy dress. I tried to get that sort of look to it... Nyssa's costume had to have a mask. That was a requirement of the script. The butterfly idea was very popular at the time and as I had to have a head-dress that could incorporate a mask very easily, it seemed obvious to make it an insect head.' Costume designer Ros Ebbutt interviewed by David J. Howe for *The Frame* Issue 10, published in May 1989.

● 'The weather was frightful when they staged that cricket match. In the end they had to curtail it because the weather was so poor. It was a great pity because a lot of work had gone into those costumes. We had all the spectators as well as the cricketers, and we had found two teams' worth of period cricket gear! There was a lot of time spent on it, and really, the weather was so awful that we didn't get good value from the cricket match. During the buffet scenes, too, the wind was freezing. We were shooting those scenes in Tunbridge Wells in October. It could have been mild, but we had an absolutely biting wind.' Costume designer Ros Ebbutt interviewed by David J. Howe for *The Frame* Issue 10, published in May 1989.

COMMENT
DJH: If The Visitation *is a traditional monster story, then* Black Orchid *is anything but. This is clever counterpointing, placing a purely historical story after a historical monster story, and* Black Orchid *works well at cleansing the palate in preparation for what*

is to follow. Once again the guest cast are first rate, and the settings lend this tale of revenge and mistaken identity a very authentic air. Sarah Sutton is given a chance to shine in the twin roles of Ann and Nyssa, but she doesn't quite manage it with the same aplomb as Janet Fielding in Kinda. *Adric is again forgettable, but Peter Davison is at last coming to terms with the character of the Doctor. This is the sort of experimental story that* Doctor Who *does well, and it is a shame that* Black Orchid *ended up being the last of the purely historical stories for the Doctor on television. (7/10)*

SJW: Black Orchid *marks a very welcome return for the pure historical story, and constitutes a pleasant and enjoyable interlude from the more serious fare of the rest of the season. It is pleasing to see the fifth Doctor's supposed interest in cricket being fully exploited in the plot for once. It is good, too, to find Sarah Sutton being given a little more to do than usual in her dual role as Nyssa and Ann. The BBC has always excelled at making period drama, so it is perhaps no surprise to note that* Black Orchid *has uniformly high production values. The costume ball is particularly effective in this regard. The only pity is that the success of this experimental two-parter did not in the end lead on to further pure historical stories in later seasons. (6/10)*

Earthshock (6B)

EP	DATE	TIME	DURN	VIEWERS	CHART POS
1	08.03.82	18.56	24'22"	9.1	45
2	09.03.82	19.06	24'23"	8.8	50
3	15.03.82	18.58	24'24"	9.8	32
4	16.03.82	19.03	24'28"	9.6	40

Repeat (Two-part omnibus edition)

1	09.08.82	19.39	45'49"	4.9	83
2	16.08.82	19.22	46'45"	5.2	79

PRODUCTION DETAILS
Location Filming: 29.10.81
Studio Recording: 10.11.81–12.11.81 and 24.11.81–26.11.81 in TC8

At the entrance to a largely uncharted cave system on Earth, a party of troopers prepares to descend. Professor Kyle (Clare Clifford) is the only survivor of a group of palaeontologists and geologists who have been surveying a cave full of fossils. The troopers, led by Lieutenant Scott (James Warwick), enter the caves. As they do so, two black figures (Carolyn Mary Simmonds, Barney Lawrence), follow them. Outside, Walters (Steve Morley), the soldier in charge of a tracking scanner device, notices the screen flare.

After a heated argument with Adric, who wants to return to E-Space, the Doctor brings the TARDIS to Earth in the year 2526 and exits into a dark underground cave full of fossils. He discusses the fate of the dinosaurs with Tegan and Nyssa and postulates that their demise was due to a massive asteroid crashing into the Earth. They move elsewhere in the caves and Nyssa finds a metallic door hidden behind a rock fall.

Meanwhile the troopers suffer casualties. Trooper Bane (Anne Clements) hurts her leg and has to turn back, and she and her helper are then killed by the black figures. Snyder (Suzi Arden), waiting outside with Walters, decides to find out why the scanner trace of the wounded party has stopped moving. She too ends up reduced to an organic puddle on the ground. Another group of troopers, Mitchell (Ann Holloway), Carter (Mark Straker) and Bailey (unknown), who have also gone to investigate, suffer the same fate.

Scott's main group arrive at the main cave and confront the Doctor, Tegan and Nyssa. Suddenly they are all attacked by the two black figures, who turn out to be androids with laser weapons set into the palms of their hands. The troopers try to fight back, but to no avail. Watching the action through a camera placed in one of the androids' heads are three Cybermen (David Banks, Mark Hardy, Jeff Wayne). The Cyber Leader (Banks) orders that the people in the cavern be destroyed.

With the Doctor's assistance, and also that of Adric who has left the TARDIS to see where the others have got to, the androids are destroyed. Investigating the hatchway, which the androids were programmed to protect, the Time Lord finds a bomb. He deactivates it just as the Cybermen send a signal to try to detonate it.

Following the signal back to its source in the TARDIS, the Doctor and his companions take the troopers and Kyle to an area referred to as Sector 16, where a massive freighter is about to leave a space station and head back to Earth under the command of Captain Briggs (Beryl Reid) and her deputy Berger (June Bland). Earth is on red alert due to an interstellar conference being held there, but Briggs has been given clearance and is determined to deliver her cargo on time and gain the bonus for doing so.

The Doctor and Adric investigate the freighter's hold, leaving Scott and the troopers on the TARDIS. They are observed on monitor screens by the Cyber Leader, who has identified the Doctor and determined that he must suffer for the Cybermen's past defeats. Two crew members, Vance (Mark Fletcher) and Carson (Christopher Whittingham), are killed, and the ship's security officer, Ringway (Alec Sabin), arrests the Doctor and Adric.

The two prisoners are taken to the bridge, where they watch as a power surge is detected. This has been caused by the Cyber Leader activating his personal guard. Briggs orders the guards to position themselves around the hold to contain whoever is down there. The Cyber Leader's guards meanwhile stir in their cocoons and break out into the hold. Scott, Tegan and the troopers have ventured out of the TARDIS, and they find themselves surrounded by awakening Cybermen (Graham Cole, Peter Gates-Fleming, Steve Ismay, David Bache, Norman Bradley, Michael Gordon-Browne).

The freighter's crew (David Melbourne, John Towns, Tim Goodings, Val McCrimmon) are unable to stop the advancing Cybermen and fall back. Ringway reveals that he is in league with the Cybermen and holds Briggs, Berger, the Doctor and Adric hostage. They overpower him and close the doors just as the Cybermen appear. The Cyber Leader orders the door to be burnt through, but the Doctor rigs up the ship's anti-matter stabilising container and temporarily prevents the machine-creatures from breaking in. However, the Cybermen then detonate an explosive and blast their way onto the bridge. Ringway is killed and the Cyber Leader informs the Doctor that the Cyber-race wishes to destroy the Earth. More Cybermen have been revived to deal with the remaining humans.

In the hold, Scott and his party find themselves facing more Cybermen than they can comfortably deal with, and try and return to the TARDIS. Two Cybermen await them there and they try to force their way through to the ship. The Cybermen are destroyed, but Kyle is killed and Tegan is captured and taken to the bridge. Scott and two troopers again leave the TARDIS, armed with the Cybermen's own weapons.

The Cybermen incorporate a machine into the flight controls of the freighter. The Cyber Leader reveals that the purpose of the conference on Earth is to unite the planets in a war against the Cyber race. Its destruction will be a psychological victory for the Cybermen.

The Cyber Leader forces the Doctor and Tegan to take him and his Lieutenant (Hardy) on board the TARDIS, leaving Adric, Briggs and Berger on the bridge of the freighter. Adric decides that he must try to decipher the three logic codes that are locking the freighter on a collision course with Earth.

Scott and the troopers arrive on the bridge and all decide to get away in an escape pod. Adric, having solved two of the codes, is reluctant to leave, and at the last moment leaps back onto the bridge to continue his task.

Partially freed from Cyber control, the freighter is now travelling back through time, watched from the TARDIS by the Doctor, Tegan, Nyssa and the Cyber Leader. The Cyber Lieutenant is searching the TARDIS.

The Doctor jumps the Cyber Leader and rubs the gold edge of Adric's badge for mathematical excellence against his chest unit. The creature writhes in agony and the Doctor then snatches its gun and fires nine times into its chest unit, killing it.

Adric is interrupted in his attempt to solve the last code as a wounded Cyberman blasts the console before dying. Adric stands and watches helplessly as the image of prehistoric Earth grows larger on the screen.

Nyssa despatches the Cyber Lieutenant when it returns to the TARDIS console room. The Doctor, Tegan and Nyssa then watch in silence as the scanner shows the freighter explode on impact with Earth.

WHO FAX

- Novelised as *Doctor Who – Earthshock* by Ian Marter in 1983.
- Working title: *Sentinel*. (The titles *Sentenial*, *Cenenal* and *Sentinal* also appear on BBC paperwork, but these are almost certainly simply misprints and misspellings.)
- Story released on BBC Home Video in 1992.
- Locations: Springwell Lock Quarry, off Springwell Lane, Rickmansworth, Herts.
- John Nathan-Turner was anxious to preserve the surprise of the Cybermen's appearance in this story and so made sure that this aspect was given no advance publicity. He had the studio observation galleries closed for the duration of the recording and even turned down the *Radio Times* when they offered to feature the Cybermen in a cover photograph and article to mark the start of the story. The Cyber Leader and Cyber Lieutenant were referred to as simply 'Leader' and 'Lieutenant' in the *Radio Times* listings for the first two episodes.
- Clips from three previous Cyberman stories appear on the Cybermen's monitor in episode two. These are from: *The Tenth Planet* episode two, *The Wheel In Space* episode six and *Revenge of the Cybermen* episode three. All are shown in monochrome.
- Seven Cybermen and one Cyber Leader (distinguished by having black tubes on the side of his head) were constructed by the Imagineering firm for this story.
- Adric dies at the end of the story and the closing titles for episode four were rolled in silence over a picture of his broken badge for mathematical excellence. This was the first time since episode ten of *The War Games* in 1969 that the credits had been rolled as opposed to presented as static captions.
- Gareth Hunt was originally considered for the part of Scott.

● Following the story's transmission, letters of complaint were received from viewers concerned about seeing Cybermen with plastic bags over their heads, and also about the death of Adric.

● This story was a last-minute replacement for Christopher Priest's *The Enemy Within* which also saw Adric being killed off.

QUOTES

● 'I watched all the old Cyberman tapes still existing and, noting that the Cybermen had physically changed from story to story, and that there were inconsistencies anyway with their history, it was a matter of trying to make sense out of what I could and what was there. It was quite deliberate that *Earthshock* was such a collation of everything from *The Tomb of the Cybermen*. It was said that I'd studied that one in particular, which was not true – I hadn't even read the script. In fact, I saw in *Doctor Who Monthly* a selection of photographs from and a synopsis of the story and I liked so much the image of them breaking out of their tombs that I wanted to try to incorporate that sort of element into *Earthshock*. It was a conscious effort on my part to try to bring back the impact I thought the Cybermen had. Of all the old monsters, the Cybermen are my favourites. They are very menacing as a concept, being physically so large, so militaristic and so ruthlessly dedicated, that I found it challenging to try to control.' Writer Eric Saward interviewed by Jeremy Bentham for *Doctor Who Monthly* Issue 69, published in October 1982.

COMMENT

DJH: Earthshock *is a somewhat typical story from the pen of script editor Eric Saward. Driven and inspired by producer John Nathan-Turner's desire for gloss, Saward turned in a story which, on the surface, is a masterpiece of atmosphere, horror and everything that* Doctor Who *has traditionally done well. However, if the surface is scratched, there is little substance to the plot, and even a couple of holes large enough for Briggs to drive her freighter through.*

Again, the cast are superb, with Beryl Reid coming out as a surprise success. The return of the Cybermen was well timed, and their traditional redesign for the eighties worked very well indeed. Of particular note are the set pieces of the Cybermen breaking out of their storage tubes and a Cyberman becoming trapped in the fabric of the bridge door, and also the sequence where the Cyber Leader threatens Tegan's life to gain the Doctor's co-operation. In a shock ending, Adric is killed, yet I cannot find it in my heart to mourn him. He was easily the worst companion to have travelled with the Doctor up to the point when Earthshock *was made, and it is unfortunate that he was played by an actor with relatively little television experience. (8/10)*

SJW: Earthshock *is probably the best story of Season 19. True, it is relatively undemanding action-adventure fare, and the plot doesn't bear very close scrutiny, but it is great fun and has a lot going for it. It certainly succeeds in restoring the reputation of the Cybermen as one of the series' most impressive monster races – a particularly welcome development after their rather disappointing last appearance in Season 12's* Revenge of the Cybermen. *One factor contributing greatly to their effectiveness is their sleek new design, although unfortunately the distinctive feature of the chest unit is largely lost in this version. Peter Grimwade's direction is excellent, and the early cave scenes are particularly noteworthy in that they convey a real sense of menace and recapture some of the much-missed 'behind the sofa' quality of old. The production team's decision to kill off Adric was a brave and somewhat unexpected one, and the dramatic final minutes add considerably to the story's impact. (8/10)*

Time-Flight (6C)

EP	DATE	TIME	DURN	VIEWERS	CHART POS
1	22.03.82	18.57	24'56"	10.0	26
2	23.03.82	19.06	23'58"	8.5	48
3	29.03.82	18.57	24'29"	8.9	46
4	30.03.82	18.52	24'30"	8.1	64

PRODUCTION DETAILS
Location Filming: 06.01.82–08.01.82, 11.01.82
Studio Recording: 19.01.82–20.01.82 and 01.02.82–03.02.82 in TC8

Speedbird Concorde 192 from New York vanishes on its approach to London Heathrow.

Having returned the crew of the freighter to their own time and with the Cyberman fleet dispersed, the Doctor heads for Earth in 1851, hoping to visit the Great Exhibition in Hyde Park. Due to spatial convergence, however, he has to materialise more quickly than intended and finds that the ship is on the same flight path as the vanished Concorde. He activates the co-ordinate override and the TARDIS appears on the concourse at Terminal One, Heathrow. When the airport police arrive, the Time Lord suggests that they speak to Department C19 – and specifically to Sir John Sudbury of UNIT. When they do this, they are given instructions to brief the Doctor on the disappearing plane.

The TARDIS is loaded onto another Concorde, which is crewed by Captain Stapley (Richard Easton), First Officer Bilton (Michael Cashman) and Flight Engineer Scobie (Keith Drinkel). The plane takes off on the same flight path as the first one, and it too vanishes from the skies. On board, the occupants at first notice nothing wrong as the plane apparently arrives back at Heathrow. Then Nyssa sees decaying corpses. They all concentrate and, breaking the perception induction, find that they are actually in a different time zone, around the Pleistocene era, 140 million years ago. Tegan sees the other Concorde in the distance and sets off for it.

Events are being controlled by a being called Kalid, who resembles an oriental sorcerer. He calls into being Plasmatons (Martin Grant, Chris Holmes, Mykel Mills, Nigel Tisdall, Giles Melville) – protein agglomerates made from the atmosphere – to restrain the Doctor and to bring Bilton and Scobie to him. The TARDIS is carried off by a group of hallucinating passengers from the first Concorde.

From within a Plasmaton bubble cocoon, the Doctor hears someone calling for help. The cocoon then vanishes and the Doctor, Nyssa, Tegan and Stapley meet Professor Hayter (Nigel Stock), a passenger from the first plane who is able to resist the hallucinations. They all head for a citadel-like building in the distance. Nyssa is overcome and possessed by some force which speaks to her (Andre Winterton) and tries to warn the group off. Kalid sends another cocoon to prevent Nyssa from talking.

Having reached the citadel, Stapley and Hayter try to free the other passengers from their hypnotically induced hallucinations. The Doctor finds the TARDIS and meets Kalid. Nyssa, freed from the cocoon when Kalid redirects the force to stop Stapley and Hayter, is prompted to find the centre of the citadel. With Tegan, she penetrates the structure and enters the inner sanctum, even though Kalid throws up a number of images – Adric (Matthew Waterhouse), the Melkur (Graham Cole) and a Terileptil (Chris Bradshaw) – to try to dissuade them from going on. Kalid threatens the Doctor with a conjured snake creature, but Nyssa throws a rock at the centre of the sanctum and thereby causes the power to drain away. Kalid is revealed to be the Master (Anthony Ainley). He has escaped from Castrovalva and has since used components from his TARDIS to build a focusing device and capture the Concordes.

The Master removes components both from Kalid's control sphere and from the Doctor's TARDIS, unaware that Stapley has interfered with the latter after realising what he was doing. He sends Stapley and Scobie off in the Doctor's TARDIS on their own.

The passengers are trying to break into the inner sanctum from outside. When they succeed, the Doctor and Hayter enter. Within stands a sarcophagus containing an intelligence at the centre of a psychic vortex. Hayter finds some miniaturised figures and the Doctor identifies them as Xeraphin, creatures whose planet Xeriphas was devastated by the Vardon-Kosnax war. The Time Lord realises that the entire Xeraphin race is a single organism and that the Master intends to use this as a dynamorphic generator in his TARDIS.

Two Xeraphin creatures materialise by taking power first from Nyssa and then from Hayter. One of them, Anithon (Hugh Hayes), is good, but the other, Zarak (Andre Winterton), is evil. Anithon explains that the Xeraphin travelled to Earth but had radiation sickness. They collected together into a single entity to wait for the sickness to pass, but the Master arrived at the moment of their regeneration and destroyed the first of the new race of Xeraphin. He then contacted the base element of the race and caused them to become divided. The evil side intends to take over the universe and now tries to call forth other evil Xeraphin. Tegan, Nyssa and the Doctor will the dark Xeraphin not to appear, and they are successful. Hayter, however, has apparently been killed, absorbed into the Xeraphin. Suddenly the sarcophagus vanishes. The Master has completed his induction loop and transferred the Xeraphin to the centre of his TARDIS.

Hayter appears in the Doctor's TARDIS and pilots it back to the sanctum before vanishing again. The Doctor picks up Bilton and they all return to their Concorde. Stapley prepares the plane for take-off while Tegan and the Doctor check that the Master has taken everyone else with him. The Doctor explains that the other Concorde is in fact the Master's TARDIS, which has been materialised around the crashed plane. However, due to Stapley's fiddling with the components taken from the Doctor's ship, the Master is now trapped.

The Doctor bargains with the Master, offering him a temporal limiter in return for the freedom of the passengers and the return of his own components. The Master agrees, and the exchange is made. The Master then leaves in his TARDIS, but the Doctor assures the others that their adversary will arrive after they do owing to the way the limiter is programmed.

The Concorde arrives safely back at Heathrow, as does the Doctor's TARDIS. The Master's TARDIS cannot materialise as the Doctor's is already occupying the co-ordinates for which it is programmed. It is knocked back into space to the planet Xeriphas, where the Doctor hopes that the Master will stay for good.

To avoid awkward questions, the Doctor and Nyssa quickly leave in the TARDIS. Tegan, however, arrives back from a nostalgic wander round the airport terminal just too late to go with them.

WHO FAX

- Novelised as *Doctor Who – Time-Flight* by Peter Grimwade in 1983.
- Working titles: *Zanadin, Xeraphin.*
- Locations: Heathrow Airport, Middlesex.
- Kalid was credited in the *Radio Times* as being played by 'Leon Ny Taiy' – an anagram of 'Tony Ainley'.
- The snake-like Plasmaton creature that threatens the Doctor in episode three was a hand puppet. It was operated against a CSO background by Richard Gregory of the Imagineering company which supplied it.
- David Reid, the BBC's Head of Series and Serials, sent a note to John Nathan-Turner after seeing the scripts. He commented: 'Be very careful with all the disintegrating bodies – it can be very frightening. Make sure it's not too frightening.' He added: 'Are you really going to be able to get Concordes to play around with?'
- Two of writer Peter Grimwade's original character names, Captains Irvine and Rathbone, were changed before the story went into production as checks had revealed that there were real British Airways pilots with those names.
- On 25 January 1982, Grimwade was asked to write an additional seven minutes for episode three as that episode was running under time.

QUOTES

- 'I don't think it worked on screen. The writer's own concept of the story means you'll invariably feel some disappointment. Certainly what I'd imagined didn't come out on screen whether for financial reasons or whatever.' Writer Peter Grimwade interviewed by Mark Wyman for *Opera of Doom* Issue 1, published in February 1985.
- 'I think at one time in its history we could have liked to have done all that heath stuff on location, but it would have required at least two weeks filming which was out of the question. That said, to recreate an entire heath in the studio is very difficult. We had a perspective set to try and give some idea of scale, but

that meant that the actors were limited in their movement and the overall impression was too static. I tried to be a bit more interesting by using that rocky outcrop and setting some scenes up against it, some slightly away from it and so on.' Director Ron Jones interviewed by Richard Marson for *Doctor Who Magazine* Issue 101, published in June 1985.

● 'The Plasmatons came out of our pre-planning meeting when we all agreed the problem with monsters was that because you usually have a man inside, it's difficult to get away from the basic human shape. As a kind of amorphous glob, the Plasmatons were a desire to break away from that, although unfortunately I don't think they worked as well as they could have done had they been more mobile.' Director Ron Jones interviewed by Richard Marson for *Doctor Who Magazine* Issue 101, published in June 1985.

COMMENT

DJH: As the season started on a low, so it ends on a low, with a muddled tale of time-travelling Concordes, mysterious oriental mystics, the Master and blobby monsters. Peter Grimwade just has too much material to work with here, and the result is a mess. The inclusion of the Master was unnecessary, particularly as it is not explained how he escaped from Castrovalva at the start of the season. Ainley plays the oriental Kalid with far more conviction than he gives to the Doctor's arch enemy. The Concorde crew are also pretty bland, and the story, involving some sort of gestalt organism splitting into two factions and being used by the Master to power his TARDIS, just doesn't make a lot of sense. Janet Fielding and Sarah Sutton are pretty good, however, and the surprise of Tegan getting left behind at the end works well. (4/10)

SJW: Time-Flight suffers from the same problem as many of the other stories of this period – a difficult-to-follow and hole-ridden plot. Worse still, the scripts make totally unrealistic demands of the production. Scenes involving Concorde crash-landing on the barren plains of prehistoric Earth would be difficult enough for an epic cinema film to achieve convincingly, let alone a series

with the modest resources of Doctor Who. *How the production
team ever thought that this story could be made to work is a complete mystery. The realisation of its requirements was always going to be an uphill struggle, and in the final analysis the whole
thing is a bit of a shambles. Particularly unsuccessful is the ill-
fated attempt to mix stock footage of Concorde aircraft with shots
of a studio-bound 'landscape'; and the Plasmatons must surely be
just about the worst monsters ever to appear in the series. (2/10)*

SEASON TWENTY

Arc of Infinity (6E)

EP	DATE	TIME	DURN	VIEWERS	CHART POS
1	03.01.83	18.46	24'37"	7.2	74
2	05.01.83	18.47	24'42"	7.3	66
3	11.01.83	18.52	24'37"	6.9	89
4	12.01.83	18.46	24'28"	7.2	82

PRODUCTION DETAILS
Location Filming: 03.05.82–07.05.82
Studio Recording: 17.05.82–18.05.82 and 31.05.82–02.06.82 in
TC1

A conspirator on Gallifrey informs his unknown master that he
has made his selection. Because of time, present location and personality, the Doctor has been chosen. The unknown master is
pleased with the choice. A physical imprint of bonding is required,
and the creature intends to obtain it.

The Doctor is completing some repairs to the TARDIS – adding an audio link on the scanner – when an ethereal force invades
the TARDIS. The unknown creature appears to merge with the
Doctor, much to Nyssa's consternation. The Doctor and Nyssa
realise that they are near Rondel, the location of a collapsed Q-
star which shields anti-matter. This area is otherwise known as the
Arc of Infinity.

A TARDIS arrives in a crypt wherein Colin Frazer (Alastair Cumming) and Robin Stewart (Andrew Boxer), two tourists in Amsterdam, have decided to sleep for the night. A creature (Malcolm Harvey) emerges from the TARDIS, which looks like an ornate tomb, and fires a gun at Colin. Colin vanishes screaming.

On Gallifrey, the High Council of Time Lords – President Borusa (Leonard Sachs), the Castellan (Paul Jerricho), Cardinal Zorac (Max Harvey), Chancellor Thalia (Elspet Grey) and Councillor Hedin (Michael Gough) – are told of the recent events. An anti-matter creature has tried to bond with the Doctor. It has partially succeeded and so is still in this universe. Borusa checks with the Matrix but cannot supply any further information. The High Council orders that the Doctor's TARDIS be brought to the security area on Gallifrey. Commander Maxil (Colin Baker) requests sole access to the ship.

On board the TARDIS, the Doctor notices that the ship has changed course and comments that the recall circuit has been used only twice before.

When the TARDIS arrives on Gallifrey, the Doctor and Nyssa try to find the computer room but are confronted by Maxil. The Doctor is shot, but only stunned. Maxil then removes the main space-time element from the TARDIS, and the Doctor and Nyssa are confined there.

On Earth, meanwhile, Tegan arrives at Schipol Airport in Amsterdam at 10.59 a.m. to meet up with her cousin Colin. She is instead met by Robin who tells her that Colin is missing.

Borusa sentences the Doctor to death to prevent the anti-matter creature from fully bonding with him. Damon (Neil Daglish), a worker in the computer centre whose colleague Talor (John D. Collins) has been killed by the traitor, is suspicious of the Castellan. He and Nyssa approach Councillor Hedin to see if he can help. The Doctor later manages to ask Damon – an old friend of his – if he can get another space/time element for the TARDIS, and Damon builds one.

The Doctor is placed in the termination machine even as the anti-matter creature prepares to bond with him.

At the moment of termination, the creature appears in the Doctor's place. The Doctor finds himself floating in the space-time dimension of the Matrix, where he finally meets the creature – it is Omega (Ian Collier).

Commander Maxil finds that the termination was rigged and that it did not complete itself. He advises the Castellan, who determines to locate the Doctor.

Robin and Tegan find Colin in a trance-like daze in the crypt, tending some alien equipment. Tegan and Robin are captured by the alien creature that earlier attacked Colin. It fires the gun device at them, causing them to vanish. They come round inside Omega's TARDIS, where the creature – the Ergon – scans Tegan for future use. In this way Omega discovers that she knows the Doctor. He then uses her to warn the Doctor off interfering with his plans. The Doctor soon reappears in the termination machine on Gallifrey. The Castellan discovers the identity of the Gallifreyan traitor, and summons the High Council to reveal all.

It is revealed that the Lord President's codes were used to access the Doctor's bio-scan and also to transmit to Earth a fusion booster element which can convert water into power. However, it is not the President who is the traitor: it is Hedin.

Hedin wants the President to isolate the Matrix and threatens him with a gun. The Doctor and Nyssa enter and Hedin reveals that the threat is Omega. The Castellan then arrives and shoots Hedin down. The Doctor asks that the Matrix be shut down, but he is too late – Omega appears on the Matrix screen.

The Doctor enters the Matrix and obtains from Tegan some clues as to the location of Omega's TARDIS: 'JHC' … Holland … Amsterdam. The Doctor and Nyssa leave in the Doctor's TARDIS, a pulse loop being used to allow them to go undetected. The Doctor builds a device to knock Omega's fusion booster out of phase.

The Doctor arrives with Nyssa in Amsterdam and finds 'JHC' in the telephone directory – it is a youth hostel chain. He has no money and so cannot telephone the hostels; the only option is to check them all on foot.

Omega's power meanwhile continues to build until he has

enough to achieve a transference. His head starts to melt.

The Doctor discovers from a hostel receptionist (Maya Woolfe) that Tegan is at Frankendahl, and he and Nyssa rush there. He realises that Omega is in Amsterdam because it is below sea level and this maintains the water pressure for the fusion generator. The Ergon tries to prevent the Doctor and Nyssa from entering Omega's TARDIS but Nyssa uses its own gun to make it vanish. The Doctor explains that it was a psycho-synthesis being. The Doctor attaches his device to the fusion generator.

Omega is dissolving, but when the fusion generator explodes he is unscathed. He reveals his face, which is now identical to the Doctor's, and then leaves the crypt. The Doctor takes the Ergon's gun – a matter converter – as he cannot destroy Omega without it. Outside, Omega (Peter Davison) has killed a gardener and taken his clothes.

The Doctor, Tegan and Nyssa chase Omega through the streets of Amsterdam as there will be a massive explosion if they don't stop him. Omega's body is slowly starting to decay as he runs through the streets.

Eventually cornered, Omega taunts the Time Lord that he lacks the courage to kill him. He then wills his own destruction, but the Doctor fires the matter converter at him and he fades away.

Back on Gallifrey, Damon reports that the anti-matter has gone. Omega has been destroyed.

WHO FAX

● Novelised as *Doctor Who – Arc of Infinity* by Terrance Dicks in 1983.
● Working titles: *Time of Neman*, *Time of Omega*.
● Story released on BBC Home Video in 1994
● Locations: all locations are in Amsterdam, Holland: Schiphol Airport, arrivals hall; Muntplein (Mint Tower Square); flower market, Muntplein; Schiphol Airport runway; Bob's Youth Hostel and adjacent streets, NZ Voorburgwal 92; police station and adjacent streets, Lijnbaansgracht 219; Hoopman Bodega, Leidsplein 4; Vondelpark Youth Hostel, Zandpad 5; Amstelveld and adjacent streets; flower stall, Prinsengracht/Utrechtestraat;

'Huis Frankendael', Middenweg 72; Amstel Lock and adjacent streets (south of Skinny Bridge); Central Station forecourt (telephone); Dam Square; Damrak.

● To preserve the mystery of his identity, Omega was referred to as 'the Renegade' in the *Radio Times*.

● The tune played on the barrel organ in part four of this story was 16 seconds of a traditional piece called 'Canal Song'. The episode also featured one minute 10 seconds of an organ playing 'Tulips From Amsterdam'. Both pieces were recorded on location.

● The use of an overseas location attracted much interest from the British press with no fewer than five newspapers, as well as the Press Association, sending journalists to cover the filming.

QUOTES

● 'When we went to Amsterdam for *Arc of Infinity* – and I'm sure Johnny Byrne won't mind me saying this – I virtually plotted the whole of the end action. With a week's filming we wanted to get some sort of value out of it, and a chase on foot has to be very carefully constructed to make it exciting. I added things like the bridge being pulled up just as they wanted to cross it, as a way not only of prolonging the suspense but also of saying, "Look everybody, this is the locale at its most dramatic". My locating of the final moments on the lock gates was another change from the original script. I thought it pointed out rather nicely that Omega had nowhere to run any more." Director Ron Jones interviewed by Richard Marson for *Doctor Who Magazine* Issue 101, published in June 1985.

● 'I think *Arc of Infinity* falls into the mainstream of *Doctor Who* stories and I liked it. I was concerned to bring back Omega as someone who was not so terribly black and white and ranting. I saw the first one he was in and although he was good he was completely over the top. I tried to convey that an injustice had been done. I also wanted to involve the characters on Gallifrey, rather than using the place as simply a setting. The final playout in Amsterdam was decently shot and it did have a few moments of the almost Frankenstein idea of returning to life.'

Writer Johnny Byrne interviewed by Marcus Hearn for *Doctor Who Magazine* Issue 169, published in January 1991.

COMMENT

DJH: As the opener to a season in which the producer had promised 'an old enemy every story', Arc of Infinity is something of a disappointment. All the elements are there – the plot is reasonable; the cast are pretty good; the effects and costumes are well up to standard – but somehow the whole is less than the sum of the parts. Perhaps it is because the plot is contrived to bring in the Amsterdam location, itself not a particularly good idea as that city lacks the landmarks that make Paris or London instantly recognisable. The return of Omega is also a bit of a damp squib as is all the nonsense about bonding. There is a pretty nasty looking monster, the Ergon, who turns out to have nothing to do with anything, and Andrew Boxer's acting ability is also absent. Even the scenes set on Gallifrey lack mystery and suspense, with ceremonially garbed Time Lords sitting in what appears to be a Gallifreyan coffee shop. The motivations of many of the characters are unclear, and the return of Tegan seems contrived as well. Not a good start to the season. (4/10)

SJW: Arc of Infinity is another instance of style winning out over content. The location filming in Amsterdam; Omega's new costume; the new outfit for Tegan; the glitzy new designs for Gallifrey. It all looks very nice, but the glossy visuals tend to overshadow the plot – particularly in the extensive location sequences, which at times seem more appropriate to a travelogue than to a science fiction drama series. There is also rather too much emphasis placed on the build-up to the surprise revelation of Omega's involvement. Although this is fine for the fans who actually know who Omega is, it must have fallen very flat for the general viewing audience. It also meant that the character's identity had to be rather clumsily disguised for most of the story. There are, however, some redeeming features to Arc of Infinity. Tegan's initial absence gives Nyssa a chance to shine, and her character is particularly well handled – perhaps not surprisingly, given that the writer is her creator

Johnny Byrne. Omega is also well characterised, and Peter Davison gives an excellent performance in his dual role in the fourth episode. It's not a bad story exactly, but it could have been much better. (4/10)

Snakedance (6D)

EP	DATE	TIME	DURN	VIEWERS	CHART POS
1	18.01.83	18.50	24'26"	6.7	95
2	19.01.83	18.47	24'35"	7.7	75
3	25.01.83	18.50	24'29"	6.6	98
4	26.01.83	18.44	24'29"	7.4	78

PRODUCTION DETAILS
Ealing Filming: 31.03.82
Studio Recording: 12.04.82–14.04.82 and 26.04.82–28.04.82 in TC6

In the TARDIS, Tegan sleeps as the Doctor and Nyssa discover that they are not where they expected to be – and that there are traces of anti-matter present. They have arrived on Planet G 139901 KB, otherwise known as Manussa – a type 314S planet in the Scrampus system and part of the Federation of Three Worlds. The Doctor realises that it was Tegan who set the co-ordinates to bring them here.

In her room, Tegan dreams of a cave-mouth shaped like a snake. She awakens screaming at what she has seen. The Doctor is interested and tries to recover Tegan's dream by hypnotising her. This attempt fails, however, so he then constructs a device to limit the production of brain waves associated with dreaming, his aim being to try to protect Tegan from whatever is in her mind. The three friends leave the TARDIS to investigate Manussa.

Also on Manussa is Lon (Martin Clunes), the Federator's son, and his mother Tanha (Colette O'Neil). Lon is a bored young man and craves excitement, while his mother is concerned that the affairs of state should be seen to be carried out. Preparations are being made for a pageant which is held every ten years to celebrate the destruction of the Mara 500 years earlier. Tanha and Lon go with Ambril (John Carson), the planet's Director of Historical Research, to see the nearby cave systems. There, the history of the Manussan empire and the earlier Sumaran empire is told in a series of pictograms on the walls.

Tegan, confused and effectively deaf while wearing the Doctor's device, becomes separated from her two friends and ends up in a barker's hall of mirrors, wherein she is tempted by the Mara. She is possessed by the creature and a snake tattoo appears on her arm. She sends the barker, Dugdale (Brian Miller), to get Lon, who is then also possessed.

The Doctor meanwhile tries to find out more about the Mara, first from the Director and then from looking at the pictograms in the caves. He realises that the legend revolves around the Great Crystal – the Great Mind's Eye – which collected energy from living minds and focused it. Chela (Jonathon Morris), one of Ambril's attendants, gives the Doctor a smaller version of the Crystal, a Little Mind's Eye, and by experimenting with it he discovers that it has the power to turn thought into matter. The Doctor realises that the Mara is planning to recreate itself in the ceremony at the conclusion of the pageant, but he is locked up when he tries to warn Ambril.

Ambril is tempted by Lon and Tegan, who reveal to him numerous 'lost' artefacts from the ancient Sumaran civilisation. They instruct him that the 'real' Great Crystal will be used in the ceremony. When Lon and Ambril leave to arrange this, the snake on Tegan's arm starts to come alive and she destroys Dugdale's mind with a look.

Chela gives the imprisoned Doctor the diary of Dojjen, the Director before Ambril, who wrote of the Mara's rebirth before he wandered off into the wilderness and disappeared. Through the diary, the Doctor realises that the Manussans brought the Mara into being themselves when they created the Crystal. With Chela's help, he and Nyssa – who has been captured and imprisoned with him – escape and head off to try to contact Dojjen.

The Doctor summons the old man via the small Crystal. Using

the venom from a small snake, the pair telepathically commune. Dojjen (Preston Lockwood) states that fear is the only poison and that, in order to defeat the Mara, the Doctor must find the still point within himself. Recovering, the Doctor returns to the caves with Nyssa and Chela to try to stop the ceremony.

In the cave, Lon plays out his role and ritually challenges the snake. There is a triple temptation: fear in a handful of dust delivered from a skull; despair in a withered branch; greed in the hidden depths of the Crystal. Lon suddenly breaks from the established litany and smashes the fake Crystal. He shows the real Crystal to the assembled Manussans and opens a hidden door to reveal Tegan clutching a snake. Lon places the Great Crystal in the allotted space in the carved design on the cave wall. Lines of power then radiate from it and, except for Lon, Tegan and the mindless Dugdale, everyone present collapses and writhes in mental agony. Tegan drops the snake she is holding and it starts to grow. The Doctor, Chela and Nyssa rush in, but they too are assaulted by the power from the Crystal. The Doctor warns them not to look – not to believe – as the Mara is creating itself from their fear. The Doctor concentrates on his smaller Crystal, trying to find the still point. Tegan merges with the giant snake, but the Doctor manages to hold off the final becoming. The real Tegan then starts to reassert herself as the Doctor concentrates on Dojjen and the Crystal. The Mara orders Lon and Dugdale to destroy the small Crystal but they are repelled. The Doctor snatches the Great Crystal from the wall and the power drain stops. The Mara and Tegan split apart once more and, robbed of power, the snake dies.

As the Manussans recover, the Doctor tells a tearful Tegan that she is now free of the Mara forever.

WHO FAX
● Novelised as *Doctor Who – Snakedance* by Terrance Dicks in 1984.
● Story released on BBC Home Video in 1994.
● The BBC designer for this production, Jan Spoczynski, wanted to have the studio settings made by an outside contractor but was initially refused permission. Then, at a very late date, it

was decided that half the work should after all go outside. This resulted in a rushed job, with which Spoczynski was dissatisfied.

● For the scenes involving snakes, two garter snakes and one tree snake, all of them non-poisonous varieties, were hired from a specialist company called Janimals run by Jan Gray. For the scenes where the snakes are to bite Dojjen and the Doctor, a replica garter snake head was created by the Visual Effects Department.

● This story featured two actors who would later find fame in sitcoms. Jonathon Morris, playing Chela, went on to star in *Bread*, while Martin Clunes as Lon starred in *No Place Like Home* and *Men Behaving Badly*.

● Writer Christopher Bailey provided a detailed design of what the carved picture on the cave wall, into which the Great Crystal would be inserted, was to look like.

● Brian Miller, who played the hapless Dugdale, is married in real life to actress Elisabeth Sladen, who had played the Doctor's companion Sarah Jane Smith from 1973 until 1976.

QUOTES

● 'We filmed the snake stuff at Ealing, also the walking across the top of the caves. We were shooting it in March and the idea of having Preston [Lockwood] sitting in a claypit with rain pouring down and snakes didn't appeal, so we put it where we could control the temperature and give it this really solid, harsh light.' Director Fiona Cumming interviewed by Richard Marson for *Doctor Who Magazine* Issue 129, published in October 1987.

COMMENT

DJH: After Kinda, *this sequel was awaited with anticipation, and it was worth the wait. Some flawless performances, superb art direction and an excellent plot combine in a story that manages to improve and add to the myth of* Kinda.

As usual the casting is interesting and works because of this. Martin Clunes is excellent as the laconic and bored Lon, and John

Carson presents a believable Ambril. Janet Fielding again steals centre stage as the possessed Tegan and proves that she is an actress of no small ability. Even the supporting cast do well. The main disappointment of Kinda *was the unconvincing giant snake at the end, but this time the creature is well handled, appearing in various rubber guises during the story and then in a giant version at the end. This is one of the best stories of the Peter Davison era. (9/10)*

SJW: *Like all good* Doctor Who, Snakedance *is a story that works on a number of different levels. The script, another Buddhist parable by Christopher Bailey, matches the intelligence and sophistication of his earlier* Kinda *but goes one better by presenting a reasonably accessible plot for the benefit of the more casual viewer. Fiona Cumming's direction is superb, and there are some excellent performances both from the regular cast and from the guest artists – particularly Colette O'Neil as Tanha and Martin Clunes as Lon. The production values are also very high, with some fine sets and costumes to complement the drama. The best story of Season 20. (8/10)*

Mawdryn Undead (6F)

EP	DATE	TIME	DURN	VIEWERS	CHART POS
1	01.02.83	18.51	24'03"	6.5	103
2	02.02.83	18.46	24'33"	7.5	83
3	08.02.83	18.50	24'32"	7.4	84
4	09.02.83	18.47	24'33"	7.7	78

PRODUCTION DETAILS
Location Filming: 24.08.82–27.08.82
Studio Recording: 08.09.82–09.09.82 in TC6 and 22.09.82–24.09.82 in TC8

At Brendon School in England, two boys, Turlough (Mark Strickson) and 'Hippo' Ibbotson (Stephen Garlick), make off with the Brigadier's 1929 Humber 1650 Open Tourer Imperial model motor car. Turlough takes the wheel and, in avoiding a collision with a white van, manages to crash the vehicle. As teachers and police converge on the scene, Turlough finds himself floating in a void, watching the events on the ground. A black-robed figure (Valentine Dyall) appears and offers to get Turlough away from the school – if he undertakes to murder the Doctor. Turlough agrees and fades from the void, awakening in his own body.

Later, back at the school, Turlough finds that he has a small glass crystal which glows and allows him to speak with the man in black, otherwise known as the Black Guardian.

The TARDIS, meanwhile, collides with the warp ellipse field of a giant spacecraft in a fixed orbit in time and space. The Doctor is forced to make an emergency materialisation on board. He and his companions explore the craft, which is lushly decorated and appears to have been in orbit for 3,000 years. They find an empty transmat bay and the Doctor notes that the capsule left for Earth six years earlier.

The travellers return to the TARDIS but discover that it is unable to leave the craft as the beam from the transmat is interfering with its operation. The capsule has now returned to its bay, and the Doctor uses it to travel to Earth and disconnect the beam. In doing so he meets Turlough, who was responsible for sending the capsule back to the craft.

The TARDIS, now free of the beam's interference, brings Nyssa and Tegan to Earth – but unknown to them it has travelled six years back in time to 1977, so they are now separated from the Doctor and Turlough.

In 1983, the Brigadier (Nicholas Courtney) arrives and takes Turlough back to the school. Strangely, though, he professes no knowledge of the Doctor.

Tegan and Nyssa see the capsule arrive and, venturing inside, find a bloody and injured humanoid (David Collings) whom they assume to be the Doctor. They help him into the TARDIS and Tegan goes to find Turlough. Instead she finds a younger Brigadier (Nicholas Courtney). At the mention of the TARDIS, the Brigadier realises that the Doctor is in trouble. Tegan meanwhile realises that she is in the wrong time zone.

The Doctor manages to jog the memory of the Brigadier, who explains that he had a nervous breakdown some time ago. He left UNIT in 1976 and joined the staff of Brendon as a maths teacher. The Doctor mentions Tegan, and the Brigadier recalls meeting her on 7 June 1977 – the Queen's Silver Jubilee.

Tegan decides that the person in the TARDIS is not the Doctor. She and the younger Brigadier hurry back there, guided by a TARDIS homing device. The Brigadier subsequently appropriates this device from Tegan.

The creature in the TARDIS has changed his appearance, and it is now clear that he is an alien.

On learning more of the Brigadier's memories, the Doctor realises that he can use the capsule to return to the orbiting spacecraft. When he tries to do so, however, the homing beacon explodes. The Brigadier mentions that he has a homing device for the TARDIS, so the Doctor uses that as a substitute. The Brigadier is certain that he didn't travel to the craft with Nyssa and Tegan.

The alien in the TARDIS identifies himself as Mawdryn and implores Nyssa and Tegan to return him to the craft. They agree, and the Brigadier insists on going with them.

It transpires that Mawdryn and seven similar beings (David Cole, Ian Craig, Mitchell Horner, Michael Leader, Richard Olley, Peter Walmsley, Brian Darnley) have been condemned to endless mutation by the elders of their planet. They exist on this craft, which every 70 years comes close to a planet where they can attempt to find help. They want the Doctor to help them die by giving up the power of his remaining regenerations, but insist that he must do so of his own free will. The Doctor at first declines. He later changes his mind, however, when he realises that Nyssa and Tegan have been contaminated by the mutation and will die if they leave in the TARDIS.

The Brigadier from 1977 and the Brigadier from 1983 have meanwhile been wandering around the spaceship, narrowly missing each other. This is fortunate, as the Doctor has warned of dire consequences should they meet.

The Doctor links up himself, Nyssa and Tegan to a metamorphic symbiosis regenerator (a machine used by Time Lords to help them through difficult regenerations) which Mawdryn has on board the ship. When the machine is operated, the power will kill the eight Mutants and 'cure' Nyssa and Tegan – but the Doctor will forfeit his remaining regenerations and cease to be a Time Lord. The elder Brigadier activates the equipment, but Turlough – under orders from the Black Guardian – disregards the Doctor's instructions to prevent the younger Brigadier from entering the same room. At the moment of power transfer, the two Brigadiers touch and there is a massive discharge of energy.

The Brigadiers are unharmed. Nyssa takes the elder of the two to the centre of the TARDIS. The Doctor explains that, at the moment of transfer, the energy came not from him but from the discharge caused by the Brigadiers meeting. Mawdryn and the Mutants are dead, Nyssa and Tegan are no longer infected and the Doctor is still a Time Lord. The ship is also dying, however, so the Doctor hurriedly returns the Brigadiers to their respective time zones.

Turlough asks if he can join the Doctor on his travels and the Doctor agrees. They all watch as Mawdryn's ship explodes.

WHO FAX

- Novelised as *Doctor Who – Mawdryn Undead* by Peter Grimwade in 1983.
- Story released on BBC Home Video in 1992.
- Locations: Middlesex Polytechnic, Trent Park, Cockfosters; 'obelisk' at Trent Park, Cockfosters.
- When the Doctor jogs the Brigadier's memory in episode two, it is revealed that Sergeant Benton left the Army in 1979 and now sells second-hand cars and that Harry Sullivan was seconded to NATO to work on a secret project at Porton Down. Prior to a short sequence of clips, the Doctor mentions Jo Grant, Sarah Jane, Liz Shaw, Yeti and Colonel Lethbridge-Stewart. The clips are from the following episodes: *The Three Doctors* part two, *The Web of Fear* part one, *The Invasion* part five, *The Claws of Axos* part four, *Day of the Daleks* part four, *Spearhead from Space* part three, *Robot* part two, *Terror of the Zygons*

part two and *Terror of the Zygons* part four.

- The effects of the Mutants' disease on Tegan and Nyssa were represented in two ways: first by ageing Janet Fielding and Sarah Sutton with make-up as the TARDIS travelled forward in time; then by substituting two child actresses – Sian Pattenden for Tegan and Lucy Baker for Nyssa – as it travelled backward in time.
- The record to which the Brigadier listens in his room is a track called 'Lilliburlero' from an LP called *Bandstand*.
- Nick Gillard (stuntman and stunt arranger) doubled for Mark Strickson and Paul Heasman doubled for Stephen Garlick in the scene where the car crashes. The van driver was played by stuntman Mark McRide.
- Richard Sheekey doubled for Nicholas Courtney when the two Brigadiers were called to be in the same shot together and split-screen effects could not be used.
- The Brigadier's moustache was retained in the BBC's 'wig store' for future use following the completion of this story.
- A selection from Paddy Kingsland's incidental music for this story was released on an audio-cassette called *The Corridor of Eternity* by Julian Knott in October 1990.

QUOTES

- '[The return of the Brigadier] was entirely my idea. Because of the plot it had to be someone who had known the Doctor; the only brief was to include the Black Guardian and Turlough. I'd had the idea of a schoolboy character already, so when Turlough was given to me certain characteristics that I had in mind were amalgamated.' Writer Peter Grimwade interviewed by Mark Wyman for *Opera of Doom* issue 1, published in February 1985.
- 'There was a scene where David Collings as Mawdryn had lost all his strength and was crawling along the ship's floor. The make-up girl provided him with some revolting looking sick, which he threw up all over the floor. I didn't like it so we re-corded it again without the sick, and I used the second version. It was unnecessary.'Director Peter Moffatt interviewed by Richard Marson for The *Doctor Who Winter Special*, published in 1984.

COMMENT

DJH: Mawdryn Undead *is a very complex story, and yet somehow the elements come together into something that is coherent and enjoyable. The main thing about the story that everyone picks up on is the major continuity gaffe over the dates – the Brigadier could not have been retired in 1977 as the UNIT stories were set in the eighties – but if you can ignore this, then the story works well. Nicholas Courtney manages to bring both versions of the Brigadier a dignity and believability so that you feel that they really are separated by six years, and Mark Strickson turns in a superlative performance as Turlough, one of the best companions we have seen. The re-appearance of the Black Guardian was unexpected, but it is not explained why he has a dead bird on his head. David Collings is as good as ever in his portrayal of the tragic and doomed mutant Mawdryn, and with lush sets and a rock music score courtesy of Paddy Kingsland, the story works on numerous levels. (8/10)*

SJW: Although not reaching the heights of Snakedance, Mawdryn Undead *is another good story. Peter Grimwade's scripts are multilayered but comprehensible and contain some nice ideas and imagery. Production standards are again high, and Mark Strickson gives an outstanding performance in his debut as Turlough. The return of the Brigadier is well handled and, although some commentators have expressed doubts about him becoming a maths teacher, I would rather see him credited with some intelligence than treated as a complete buffoon as he was in some of the later third Doctor stories. The return of the Guardians is rather more unexpected, but nevertheless welcome. On the downside, the plot relies rather too much on convenient pseudo-science for its resolution, and I personally find Paddy Kingsland's rock-influenced incidental music too intrusive. On the whole, though, a promising start to the Guardian trilogy. (6/10)*

Terminus (6G)

EP	DATE	TIME	DURN	VIEWERS	CHART POS
1	15.02.83	18.55	24'58"	6.8	86
2	16.02.83	18.46	24'40"	7.5	75
3	22.02.83	18.55	24'39"	6.5	97
4	23.02.83	18.46	24'49"	7.4	80

PRODUCTION DETAILS
Ealing Filming: 29.09.82–30.09.82 on stage 3B
Studio Recording: 11.10.82–12.10.82 in TC6, 25.10.82–27.10.82
in TC8, remount 16.12.82 in TC1

Under instruction from the Black Guardian (Valentine Dyall),
Turlough operates some blue switches hidden behind a roundel in
a corridor of the TARDIS. He then goes to the console room and
the Guardian tells him to rip out the 'heart' of the TARDIS. He
tries to remove the piece of equipment indicated, but it gets stuck.
A wall of shimmering light starts to encroach upon the interior of
the ship, trapping Nyssa. Hurrying to the console room, the Doctor notes that the time rotor is jamming and activates the cut-out.
By refocusing the scanner monitor on the interior of the ship he is
able to see and speak to Nyssa. A door emblazoned with a skull
pattern appears in the wall of Nyssa's room. The Time Lord tells
her to go through it, and she does so.

The Doctor, Tegan and Turlough then rush to her room. The
strange door starts to close, but the Doctor jams a chair in the gap.
He goes after Nyssa. Turlough and Tegan also pass through the
door, which closes behind them and then vanishes.

The Doctor finds Nyssa and together they locate a control room.
They are on a ship that appears deserted aside from two space
pirates, Kari (Liza Goddard) and Olvir (Dominic Guard), who take
them captive. The ship's motors suddenly start up as it begins a
docking procedure. The computer announces via a tannoy voice
(Martin Muncaster) that they are arriving at Terminus Inc. Skull-
patterned doors open all over the ship and diseased humanoids

emerge to shuffle to the exits. Olvir realises that they are on a plague ship. To avoid the crush of people, Tegan and Turlough open a hatch in the floor and hide in the air vent beneath. When the coast seems clear they try to emerge but find that they cannot reopen the hatch. They decide to go along the venting instead. The Doctor meanwhile discovers that Terminus is at the exact centre of the known universe.

On Terminus, the Vanir are in charge of operations. They unload the diseased humanoids into holding cells and prepare to sterilise the ship in which they arrived. Nyssa is found by one of the service robots and, as she has contracted lazar's disease, is placed in a cell along with the others.

There is unrest among the Vanir. Eirak (Martin Potter), the leader, controls the supplies of the drug hydromel which they need to survive the effects of radiation. Valgard (Andrew Burt) and Sigurd (Tim Munro) are unhappy with the situation. The company seems intent on cutting back to the extent of making their working conditions intolerable. Another Vanir, Bor (Peter Benson), wanders off into the forbidden zone to try to locate the source of the rising radiation levels. The Garm (R. J. Bell), a huge dog-headed alien, is summoned from the zone by the others and told to locate Bor and bring him back. The Doctor and Kari also enter the zone, and Eirak offers Valgard a deal: if Valgard brings back the two strangers, who are assumed to be from the company, Eirak will stand down in his favour. Valgard agrees.

The Doctor and Kari find Bor. He is trying to block the radiation, which is coming from a damaged engine. He is delirious and says that he followed the control cables. The Doctor and Kari do likewise and find the long-dead pilot of Terminus. The place was once capable of time travel, and the Doctor postulates that an ejection of fuel from one damaged engine could have created the universe. The second engine is also unstable and will soon explode, bringing the universe to an end.

Tegan and Turlough are still trapped in the conduits. The Black Guardian directs Turlough to what he says is an emergency bypass switch. As Turlough pulls out the wires on the switch, Terminus begins the procedure to jettison the fuel. The Doctor cannot prevent the jettison lever from moving and so recruits the Garm to help. The creature manages to push the lever back and prevent a catastrophe. By way of thanks, the Doctor releases the Garm from the Vanir's service by smashing the device with which they summon and control him.

Nyssa, meanwhile, has been exposed to the radiation and left in a room to recover. She realises that the cure Terminus promises for lazar's disease can actually be made to work. The Doctor and Kari return with Valgard, and Eirak is deposed peacefully. Nyssa explains that she can synthesise hydromel and free the Vanir from the company's control.

Tegan finally emerges from the ship – Turlough has made his way back to the TARDIS without her – and meets up with the Doctor and Nyssa. Nyssa decides to stay on Terminus to help the Vanir perfect the cure for lazar's disease, and they say their farewells.

In the TARDIS, the Black Guardian gives Turlough a final ultimatum. He must kill the Doctor.

WHO FAX
- Novelised as *Doctor Who – Terminus* by John Lydecker (a pseudonym for Stephen Gallagher) in 1983.
- Story released on BBC Home Video in 1993.
- Kari and Olvir were not originally intended to be seen wearing their space helmets, but this plan was changed when the story was recorded. As they had not been designed to be worn, the masks steamed up, making it difficult for the actors to see, speak and breath. Small holes were drilled in the front of them to try to alleviate this problem.
- There were two drone robots constructed for the story, but only one was seen on screen.
- The fight arranger for the story was John Waller.
- Following transmission, the production office received a letter from Peter Osborne, the Marketing Sales Manager of Tannoy Ltd, complaining about the use of the credit 'tannoy voice' for the voice of the ship's computer. He pointed out that 'Tannoy' was not a generic term but a registered trade-mark referring to products manufactured by Tannoy Ltd.

- A letter of complaint was also received from David Stevenson MD, a senior lecturer at the Liverpool school of tropical medicine, regarding the depiction of leprosy in the story.
- Episode one of *Terminus* was first transmitted on 14 February 1982 at 18.45 on BBC Wales.

QUOTES

- 'The misery was based very much on medieval iconography of death and suffering. The costumes that the sufferers wore were all based on shrouds that were used around the time of the Black Death. The costume designer, Dee Robson, went into that quite deeply, and the costumes of the Vanir, who were the guardians of Terminus, were based on *memento mori* sculpture of the Middle Ages, which you get in Westminster Cathedral. The Garm's from Scandinavian mythology, just as are the Vanir, but they have a medieval image. A wonderful kind of stirred up mixture of stew in there!' Writer Stephen Gallagher interviewed by Paul Travers for *Doctor Who Magazine* Issue 139, published in August 1988.

COMMENT

DJH: Following on from Mawdryn Undead *and continuing the plot of the Black Guardian trying to get Turlough to kill the Doctor,* Terminus *doesn't quite live up to the promise of the first episode. The scenes of the skull door appearing in Nyssa's room, and the eerie emptiness of the lazar ship are excellently handled, as is Kari and Olvir's introduction. The Vanir look like walking skeletons and the plot is again interesting. However there are some less than satisfactory elements. The Garm is an interesting character who does nothing, says little, and whose costume is too obviously a costume to work well, and as Tegan and Turlough spend most of the story crawling around in cable ducts, one wonders how they escaped the sterilisation gas that flooded the rest of the ship. Nyssa's departure is also hasty and seems ill conceived. She has shown little desire to help others in previous stories, and no interest whatsoever in bioengineering. Despite this, the story is not bad, and provides for a diverting, if slightly tedious, time. (6/10)*

SJW: Terminus *is a story that I enjoyed very much on its original transmission, although it has palled somewhat on repeated viewing. The idea that the universe was created due to the actions of a time-travelling spaceship is an ingenious and appealing one, reflecting writer Stephen Gallagher's hard science-fiction influences. The Vanir are interesting characters, and the Garm an unusual and well-realised 'monster'. Kari and Olvir, on the other hand, are less impressively portrayed. What really lets the story down, I suppose, is its shortage of incident and its unremittingly grim atmosphere. It doesn't make very good use of Tegan and Turlough, either, as they seem to spend an inordinate amount of time trapped under a grating. It still provides a good exit for Nyssa, though. (5/10)*

Enlightenment (6H)

EP	DATE	TIME	DURN	VIEWERS	CHART POS
1	01.03.83	18.55	24'12"	6.6	89
2	02.03.83	18.46	24'23"	7.2	76
3	08.03.83	18.55	24'38"	6.2	99
4	09.03.83	18.46	24'34"	7.3	68

PRODUCTION DETAILS
Ealing Filming: 03.11.82–05.11.82 Stage 3B
Studio Recording: 16.11.82–17.11.82, 30.11.82–02.12.82 (original dates, cancelled due to strike); 17.01.83–18.01.83, 30.01.83–2.02.83 (remount dates) in TC1

While Turlough and Tegan occupy themselves playing chess, the Doctor tries to discover the cause of a power drain that is affecting the TARDIS. He realises that someone is trying to contact them and increases the power.

The White Guardian (Cyril Luckham) appears and tells him that the balance of power is at risk and that there is extreme danger. He then fades away once more. The Doctor keeps the power up, causing smoke to pour from the console, and the Guardian reappears just long enough to deliver some co-ordinates – galactic north six degrees, 9-0-7-7 – and instruct him to go to the indicated location immediately. The Black Guardian (Valentine Dyall) then appears and gloats that the Doctor cannot succeed and will soon be dead.

After the two Guardians have vanished, the TARDIS materialises. The Doctor surmises that the time-override locking must have been in the co-ordinates. The Doctor and Turlough check outside, leaving Tegan behind in case the White Guardian tries to make contact again. They seem to have arrived on a ship, and they make their way to the crew room. There, the crew, including Jackson (Tony Caunter) and Collier (Clive Kneller), accept them as new arrivals – 'Doctor' is the slang name for the ship's cook. They discover that they are on an Edwardian sailing ship called *SS Shadow*, which is taking part in a race. Curiously, however, none of the crew can remember joining the ship.

Meanwhile the White Guardian has delivered another message to Tegan: winner takes all. She sees the face of a man looking in through the TARDIS's scanner and leaves the ship when he appears to fall. The stranger, who seems to be able to move from one place to another instantaneously, seizes her and takes her to meet her friends.

The Doctor is reunited with Tegan in the dining room and she delivers the Guardian's message. Captain Striker (Keith Barron) then enters. His first mate, Marriner (Christopher Brown), is the stranger who escorted Tegan. The whole party sit down to dinner but Tegan falls seasick and Marriner offers to lead her to a cabin.

The Captain orders the rum rations broken out, and the crew prepare to go aloft. Tegan, on the way to her cabin, sees some modern wet-suits and realises that all is not as it seems. The Doctor, Tegan and Turlough discover that they are indeed on a sailing ship – but it is in deep space, floating alongside several others.

The ships are racing around the solar system using the planets as marker buoys. As *SS Shadow* approaches Venus, the Doctor sees on the scanner an image of Critas the Greek (Byron Sotiris), the captain of one of the other ships, and notes that the only thing out of place is the Greek's jewelled ring – it is from seventeenth-century Spain. Striker explains that the ships' crews are collected from different time zones. Reading the Doctor's mind, he discovers that he is a Time Lord. This fails to impress him, however, as he himself functions in eternity. The Greek's ship is destroyed as the race takes it close to Venus, but Turlough is suspicious. The only other ship nearby was the *Buccaneer*. Striker reveals that the ships' officers are all Eternals and that they need the minds of 'Ephemerals' – as he terms all living beings – to exist.

Once alone, Turlough tries to contact the Black Guardian. The Guardian appears and throttles him, warning that he will never leave the ship. The Doctor goes to talk to Tegan, who is much recovered due to a remedial drink proffered by Marriner. Striker 'listens in' on their conversation using his telepathic abilities, and is intrigued to hear of the TARDIS. When the Doctor and Tegan subsequently try to return to the ship, they find it has vanished.

The Doctor, Tegan and Turlough all get suited up and go aloft with Marriner. Turlough, who keeps hearing the Black Guardian's threats ringing in his ears, throws himself overboard. He is picked up in a net by the *Buccaneer*. There he meets Captain Wrack (Lynda Baron), who orders that a sword with a jewelled handle be sent to Captain Davy and that invitations be sent to Striker for a social function. When she turns her attentions to Turlough, he claims that he wishes to serve her. The race passes through an asteroid storm and Wrack enters an ion room on the lower deck of her ship, leaving Turlough outside. Davy's vessel explodes, apparently hit by an asteroid.

The Doctor, Tegan and Marriner arrive on board the *Buccaneer* to attend a party in its stateroom. The Doctor, following directions given to him by Marriner, sneaks off to find Turlough. The boy has been trapped in the ion room by one of the crew members, and the Black Guardian has again appeared to taunt him. Wrack meanwhile takes Tegan into a private room and freezes her in time. She places a new jewel in her tiara before unfreezing her and returning to the party. The Doctor and Turlough are captured by Wrack's number two, Mansell (Leee John), when they leave the ion room. Turlough remains on board the *Buccaneer*, but Wrack sends all the others back to *SS Shadow*.

The two ships are now approaching the Enlighteners – represented by a giant crystalline structure in space – and the race is nearly over. The *Buccaneer* comes level with *SS Shadow* and the Doctor realises that it is about to launch an attack. As with the Greek's ring and Davy's sword, a crystal must have been brought on board to act as a point of focus. Tegan remembers her tiara and the Doctor smashes the new crystal with a fire axe. This just multiplies its power, however, so he then hurls the shards overboard just before they can explode. The explosion has been brought about by Wrack, who has used the ion chamber to summon the Black Guardian's powers and focus them on the crystal.

The Doctor persuades Striker to release the TARDIS, which has been hidden in his own mind, and then uses it to travel to the *Buccaneer*, which has taken the lead in the race. Tegan watches from *SS Shadow* as two humanoid forms fall from Wrack's ship. It seems that the Doctor and Turlough have failed.

On each of the ships, the human crew members fade from sight. The Black and White Guardians then appear in the *Buccaneer*'s state room and place a glowing artefact on the table. They are joined there by the Doctor and Turlough: it was they who brought the ship in to dock, while Wrack and Mansell were ejected from the ion chamber. The Doctor turns down the prize of Enlightenment, however, saying that none should have it. The White Guardian agrees, and returns the Eternals to the void. The White Guardian then offers a portion of Enlightenment to Turlough. The Black Guardian reminds the boy of his agreement and demands that he give the Doctor over to him in exchange for a huge diamond within the glowing artefact. Turlough makes his choice: he sweeps the crystal from the table to the Black Guardian, who vanishes in flames. The boy is now free, as Enlightenment was not in fact the crystal but the choice. Even so, the White Guardian cautions continued vigilance; while he still exists, so too does his Black counterpart, until they are no longer needed.

Tegan wants to get away from this place, and Turlough asks if they can go to his home planet. The Doctor agrees.

WHO FAX

- Novelised as *Doctor Who – Enlightenment* by Barbara Clegg in 1984.
- Story released on BBC Home Video in 1993.
- The story's working title was *The Enlighteners*. This was changed at the suggestion of the production team.
- Leee John was the lead singer with the pop group Imagination at the time this story was recorded.
- The Black and White Guardians were both played by the same actors as in the sixteenth (Key to Time) season.
- Dolore Whiteman, who played Tegan's Aunt Vanessa in the fourth Doctor's final story *Logopolis*, was hired for a special photocall on 18 October 1982 to provide the photograph that Tegan finds in her cabin on *SS Shadow*.
- Striker and Mansell were originally to have been played by, respectively, Peter Sallis and David Rhule, who did actually start rehearsals. The making of the story was then delayed by industrial action, however, and as they were unable to make the new dates Keith Barron and Leee John were brought in instead.
- The incidental music used for Wrack's party was originally written by Malcolm Clarke for *Borges at 80* and can be found on the Radiophonic Workshop's *Soundhouse* LP. The track is called 'The Milonga'.
- The story was found to be running short during rehearsals, so an additional one and a half minutes was written for episode one and an additional two minutes for episode two.
- Striker's ship was unnamed in the original scripts, but a name had to be created for use on the crew's jerseys, uniforms and life belts.

QUOTES

- 'I wanted Striker and his Edwardian officers all to have a "look" that would set them apart, for they were the Eternals who would occupy most of the first two episodes. Keith Barron, Christopher Brown and James McClure all cultivated a bland demeanour, which the non-speaking Officers picked up very quickly. I find people who don't blink quite unnerving, so this seemed a good starting-off point. Christopher then used it to very good effect when he blinked as Marriner asked Tegan, "What is Love?".'Director Fiona Cumming writing in *Doctor Who Magazine* Issue 186, published in May 1992.

● 'In rehearsal we had the most difficulty with the scenes in the hold of the yacht. The perimeter of the set was marked out but we knew that the shape would be determined by the boxes and ropes stowed, and that the pools of darkness which lighting director Fred Wright was planning would create the right atmosphere. Even so it was difficult to stop the giggling setting in, when the cast were all negotiating non-existent hurdles at non-existent levels in broad daylight.'Director Fiona Cumming writing in *Doctor Who Magazine* Issue 186, published in May 1992.

COMMENT

DJH: Concluding the Guardian trilogy, Enlightenment *contains a superb idea at its heart, and one that is done full justice when an Edwardian sailing ship is seen floating through space, racing against other tall-masted vessels. The concept behind the Eternals is also good; and, barring Wrack, they are all believably acted and, ultimately, quite tragic. I say 'barring Wrack' because the casting of Lynda Baron in this part was a mistake. If the character had truly been a larger-than-life pirate captain, then Baron would have been perfect for it. In fact, however, the Eternals are inherently lonely creatures, and not only does she fail to convey this but her constant cackling and pirate mannerisms become annoying. The hasty replacement choice of pop singer Leee John was also a mistake, as he displays no acting ability whatsoever! This is a shame as Keith Baron and Christopher Brown are quite excellent. A patchy story, then, and one that only just manages to resolve the battle for Turlough's soul. (7/10)*

SJW: Enlightenment *is a similar sort of story to* Snakedance, *in that it successfully combines some deep and complex themes – again, heavily influenced by Buddhist philosophy – with a relatively straightforward and accessible plot. It is almost as good as that earlier story, too, being very well written and made. The final confrontation between the two Guardians makes for a effective climax to the trilogy. The only really negative points are the poor performance of Leee John as Mansell and the rather tacky design work for the entrance to and interior of the ion chamber on board Wrack's ship. (7/10)*

The King's Demons (6J)

EP	DATE	TIME	DURN	VIEWERS	CHART POS
1	15.03.83	18.55	24'48"	5.8	107
2	16.03.83	18.47	24'27"	7.2	66

Repeat

1	06.07.84	18.55	24'48"		
2	13.07.84	18.55	24'27"		

PRODUCTION DETAILS
Location Filming: 05.12.82–07.12.82
Studio Recording: 19.12.82–20.12.82 and remounted on 16.01.83 in TC1

King John (Gerald Flood), recently arrived at Castle Fitzwilliam, accuses his host Ranulf (Frank Windsor), of insulting him with his lack of generosity towards the crusade. The King's champion, Sir Gilles Estram (Anthony Ainley), challenges Ranulf to a duel, but Ranulf's son, Hugh (Christopher Villiers), accepts in his place.

The following morning, villagers and knights gather to watch Hugh and Sir Gilles joust for the King's honour. As the jousters' horses make their second pass, the TARDIS appears alongside the field and the contest is temporarily halted.

The Doctor is mystified as to why the TARDIS has arrived at this point – England on 4 March 1215 – as he didn't set those co-ordinates. The travellers go outside, and are taken aback to be greeted by the King as his 'demons'. They watch the remainder of the joust, which Sir Gilles wins. The Doctor intercedes to plead for Hugh's life, and the youth is spared. Everyone repairs to the castle, where Turlough becomes separated from the Doctor and Tegan. The Doctor thinks there is something afoot – King John is supposed to be in London at this time, taking the crusader's oath.

Turlough is captured by a disgruntled Hugh – in sparing his life, the Doctor denied him honour – and taken to the dungeon. Sir Gilles likewise imprisons Ranulf's wife, Lady Isabella (Isla Blair), to ensure Ranulf's good behaviour. He also has Hugh himself chained up alongside Turlough and Isabella.

Ranulf decides to trust the Doctor and voices grave concerns about the King's behaviour. The Doctor suggests that the King here is an impostor, but Ranulf finds this hard to believe.

Two riders approach the castle and are met by Sir Gilles. The lead rider is Geoffrey de Lacey (Michael J. Jackson), just returned from attending the King in London. Sir Gilles has him taken prisoner.

At the next meal, the King plays the lute and sings a song in praise of war. Sir Gilles then brings in an iron maiden and prepares to have Geoffrey placed inside it. The Doctor again intercedes, claiming that Sir Gilles has behaved outrageously in even attempting to follow the King's fine performance. Sir Gilles challenges the Doctor and they fight with swords. The Doctor wins, but Sir Gilles pulls out a familiar weapon and his face transforms into that of the Master. Tegan throws a knife at the Master, but he catches it and offers the Doctor the choice of weapons: the knife or his tissue compression eliminator. The Doctor snatches the eliminator but the Master merely laughs: he knows his adversary would never use it. The King then orders the Master placed in the iron maiden, and the Doctor is unable to prevent this. The Master is held inside the device and the door closed.

Suddenly the maiden fades from sight – it was the Master's TARDIS all along. The King knights the Doctor as his new champion. The Doctor then makes a pretence of placing Geoffrey under arrest in order to gain access to the dungeons. The Master gets there first, however, and releases Hugh and Isabella, claiming that the Doctor is plotting to topple the King from the throne. After they have gone, the Doctor arrives with Tegan and Geoffrey and releases Turlough. He also rigs up the Master's eliminator at the back of the iron maiden.

The Master turns the whole castle against the Doctor and has Geoffrey shot in the back as he tries to leave for London to warn the real King. The Doctor and Tegan are captured, but Tegan gets inside the Doctor's TARDIS and dematerialises it, allowing the Doctor to slip away in the confusion.

The Doctor makes his way to the King's chamber, where he finds a sophisticated android playing the lute and singing in the King's voice. The Master appears and explains that he used the android – Kamelion – to escape from Xeriphas, the planet on which the Doctor trapped him at the end of their previous encounter. The tool of an earlier invader of Xeriphas, Kamelion was designed as a decoy weapon, capable of infinite form and personality, all controlled by concentration and psychokinetics. The Master is now using Kamelion to discredit King John and thereby ensure that the Magna Carta is not signed.

Ranulf and his men burst into the King's chamber and there ensues a battle of wills between the Master and the Doctor for control of Kamelion. This is won by the Doctor when Tegan materialises the TARDIS in the chamber, distracting the Master and the watching men. The Doctor, after causing Kamelion to adopt Tegan's form, hustles the android and Turlough into the TARDIS.

The Master makes his escape in his own TARDIS, unaware that the Doctor's tampering with the tissue compression eliminator will have affected its dimensional control.

Kamelion, who has a mind of his own, asks if he may travel with the Doctor. Tegan is suspicious, but Turlough agrees. The Doctor welcomes the creature aboard and sets the ship's co-ordinates, heading for the Eye of Orion.

WHO FAX
- Novelised as *Doctor Who – The King's Demons* by Terence Dudley in 1986.
- Released on BBC Home Video in 1995.
- Working title: *The Android*.

- Locations: Bodiam Castle, Bodiam, East Sussex.
- Following the second episode of *The King's Demons*, a special advertising trailer was transmitted for the forthcoming *Doctor Who* celebration at Longleat House in Wiltshire. The trailer consisted of a voice-over and the following clips: Hartnell title sequence from *100,000 BC*; Troughton title sequence from *The Krotons*; first Pertwee title sequence from *Carnival of Monsters*; second Baker title sequence from *Logopolis*; Davison title sequence from *Castrovalva*; and the *Doctor Who* logo from the Davison title sequence. This was actually a combination of two pre-existing trailers: one for *The Five Faces of Doctor Who* repeat season of 1981 and one for *Castrovalva*.
- To conceal the fact that the Master appeared in the story, producer John Nathan-Turner had the *Radio Times* credit the part of Sir Gilles Estram – whose surname was itself an anagram of 'Master' – as being played by 'James Stoker' – an anagram of 'Master's Joke'.
- Peter Howell was originally to have composed all the incidental music for this story but, due to commitments on the BBC's radiophonic drama *Inferno Revisited*, he was in the end able to complete only the lute music, which was played in studio by Jakob Lindberg. The rest of the story's incidental music was composed by Jonathan Gibbs, a newcomer to the Radiophonic Workshop staff. A musician named Tim Barry was hired to play the drums for this.
- The sword fight between the Doctor and the Master was performed by Peter Davison and Anthony Ainley themselves, with no stuntmen involved. The fight was choreographed by John Waller.
- The stuntmen in the joust scenes were Brian Bowes and Nick Wilkinson.
- The song in praise of war had lyrics by Terence Dudley and music by Peter Howell and was sung by Gerald Flood. Both verses featured in part one, and the first was also sung in part two. The lyrics were as follows:

  We sing in praise of total war
  Against the Saracen we abhor

To free the tomb of Christ the Lord
We'll put the known world to the sword
There is no glory greater than
To serve with gold the son of Man
No riches here on Earth shall see
No scutage in Eternity

● Kamelion was a computer-controlled, sound-activated, animated robot created by software designer Mike Power and computer hardware expert Chris Padmore. Padmore was a colleague of freelance designer Richard Gregory and during recording of *Earthshock*, for which Gregory had supplied the newly designed Cyberman costumes, Gregory approached John Nathan-Turner to see whether he would be interested in featuring the robot in the series. Nathan-Turner agreed and the robot was introduced in Terence Dudley's *The King's Demons*. Unfortunately Kamelion's limitations quickly became apparent: it reportedly took nearly two weeks to program in the speech for each episode; it was unable to walk; and it became subject to numerous internal BBC union demarcation disputes. Unfortunately, Mike Power was killed in a boating accident shortly after it had been decided to include the robot in the series, and no one else had the technical knowledge to build and maintain the software to run it. As a result, Kamelion was effectively written out of the series until *Planet of Fire*, when the Doctor destroyed it for good.

QUOTES

● 'Richard Gregory had this robot Kamelion, and for a long time he'd been trying to promote to us the idea of using it. He submitted some material and John liked the look of the thing, so with Terence Dudley, who was to write our two-parter that year, we went down to see it at Richard's studio. We asked Terence to include it in his original storyline. He agreed, went away and incorporated the Kamelion plot into what became *The King's Demons*.' Script editor Eric Saward interviewed by Richard Marson for *Doctor Who Magazine* Issue 94, published in November 1984.

● 'What happened with *The King's Demons* was, because of the difficulties with staff refusing to do overtime, we had to have a remount, so I had to be paid again which I was very happy about. Just a few scenes … the ones in the King's bedchamber where they were trying to gain control over Kamelion. For one thing, the robot had gone wrong, but they got it right in the end. The actual filming took four days, the rehearsal period is a week for every half hour and the remount took two or three days.' Actor Gerald Flood interviewed by David Richardson for *Frontier Worlds* issue 18, published in February 1984.

COMMENT

DJH: The King's Demons *is a curiosity. As a two-parter it fulfils its purpose, managing to entertain while bringing the Master back for a return appearance. It is a historical tale with an SF twist, rather like Season 11's* The Time Warrior, *and in that respect has a similar feel. The historical characters are very well cast and played, with Frank Windsor stealing the honours but the others adding to the authentic atmosphere. Unfortunately the story's major failing is in the Master, who once again returns with only the sketchiest of explanations as to how he escaped from his last predicament. Anthony Ainley's portrayal of Sir Gilles is dreadful, with a cod French accent adding to the embarrassment. Kamelion itself is little more than a curiosity, allegedly included in the show only because John Nathan-Turner thought it was a good idea. That the android didn't work properly and wasn't therefore used again until the story in which it was written out was a shame, but somewhat inevitable. Despite all this, the story is very enjoyable, and at only two episodes does not overstay its welcome. (7/10)*

SJW: Again, this is a story that is all style and very little content. The period settings and costumes as usual look wonderful, and the excellent cast give uniformly good performances. The location work is also extremely effective and pleasant on the eye. Unfortunately the central premise of the story is less than inspiring. Leaving aside the question of its rather dubious historical accuracy, why should the Master be interested in preventing the signing of the Magna Carta? Even the Doctor is moved to com-

ment that this is small-time villainy by his standards, which is almost tantamount to giving an on-screen admission of the story's limitations. On one level this is just an introductory vehicle for Kamelion but, as the android is hardly one of the most welcome or successful additions ever made to the series, this isn't really enough to satisfy. (5/10)

TWENTIETH-ANNIVERSARY SPECIAL

The Five Doctors (6K)

EP	DATE	TIME	DURN	VIEWERS	CHART POS
1	25.11.83	19.20	90'23"	7.7	54

Repeat

1	14.08.84	18.15	24'15"	4.7	88
2	15.08.84	18.16	25'11"	4.5	93
3	16.08.84	18.17	24'16"	3.7	107
4	17.08.84	18.15	24'51"	4.0	102

PRODUCTION DETAILS

Location Filming: 05.03.83, 07.03.83–11.03.83, 13.03.83–15.03.83, 17.03.83
Ealing Filming: 18.03.83
Studio Recording: 29.03.83–31.03.83 in TC6

The fifth Doctor and his past incarnations (Richard Hurndall, Patrick Troughton, Jon Pertwee, Tom Baker) are taken out of time by Time Lord President Borusa (Philip Latham) using a forbidden time scoop device. They find themselves, together with some old companions (Elisabeth Sladen [Sarah Jane Smith], Carole Ann Ford [Susan], Nicholas Courtney [the Brigadier]) in the Death Zone on Gallifrey, facing a Dalek (John Scott Martin; voice: Roy Skelton), a Yeti (Lee Woods), a deadly Raston Warrior Robot (Keith Hodiak) and a troop of Cybermen (David Banks [Cyber Leader], Mark Hardy [Cyber Lieutenant], Lee Woods, Richard Naylor, Mark

Whincup, Gilbert Gillan, Emyr Morris Jones, Graham Cole, Alan Riches, Ian Marshall-Fisher, Mark Bassinger, Myrddin Jones), as well as the Master (Anthony Ainley), who has been summoned by the High Council of Time Lords (Dinah Sheridan [Flavia], Paul Jerricho [Castellan]) to help the Doctor.

Borusa aims to use the Doctors to breach the defences of the Dark Tower – Rassilon's tomb – so that he can enter the place and claim immortality. When he does so, however, he is condemned by Rassilon (Richard Mathews) to eternal existence in the form of a living statue.

WHO FAX

- Novelised as *Doctor Who – The Five Doctors* by Terrance Dicks in 1983.
- Working title: *The Six Doctors*. The outline version with this title was written by Robert Holmes.
- Story released on BBC Home Video in edited form in 1985, unedited form in 1990 and in an extended re-edited form in 1995.
- Locations: Plasbrondanw, Llanfrothen, Penrhyndeudraeth, Gwynedd; Carreg Y Foel Gron, off B4407, nr Ffestiniog; Manod Quarry, Cwt Y Bugail, Ffestiniog; Cwm Bychan, nr Llanbedr, Gwynedd; Tilehouse Lane, Upper Denham, Bucks; MOD/YMCA Hostel, Hayling Lane, off Tilehouse Lane, Upper Denham, Bucks; West Common Road, Uxbridge, Middlesex.
- The following companions (or hallucinatory images) also made cameo appearances in this story: K-9 (voice: John Leeson), Jamie (Frazer Hines), Zoe (Wendy Padbury), Liz Shaw (Caroline John) and Captain Mike Yates (Richard Franklin).
- Because Tom Baker had declined to appear in the story, his Doctor and Romana II (Lalla Ward) were included by way of clips from the abandoned Season 17 story *Shada*.
- There was a pre-title sequence featuring William Hartnell as the first Doctor in a scene from the final episode of *The Dalek Invasion of Earth*.
- See Chapter 7 on the making of this story for further information.

QUOTES

● 'The main problem was that there were five leading men plus companions and so it was a matter of giving them all something to do that contributed to the story, advanced the plot and so on. The other thing was that we didn't want to bring them together too soon because we wanted the fun, enjoyment and nostalgia of them doing their own bit with their old companions. This proved difficult simply through sheer numbers – there were so many characters that we had to have five strands leading to a final conclusion. Tom Baker, of course, dropped out, which necessitated a rapid rewrite, but overall Terrance rose to the occasion admirably. We'd had a long meeting one afternoon with John, and out of that came a lot of what became *The Five Doctors*.' Script editor Eric Saward interviewed by Richard Marson for *Doctor Who Magazine* Issue 94, published in November 1984.

COMMENT

DJH: When the brief for a story includes featuring all five Doctors, numerous old companions, Daleks, Cybermen and as many other old monsters as can be fitted in, then it is obvious that in many respects plot will be sacrificed to nostalgia. It is therefore refreshing to find that Terrance Dicks has managed to achieve the near impossible and developed a plot that embraces all these elements in a scenario that makes sense. The Five Doctors is perfect as a celebration of some of what Doctor Who is all about. Unfortunately, some of the other elements – including terror, suspense and characterisation – are missing. The cast are fine, with Richard Hurndall turning in a passable first Doctor, Troughton and Pertwee playing their Doctors with deftness and Anthony Ainley going through the motions as the Master (with no explanation as to how he escaped from the Doctor's trap at the end of The King's Demons, *assuming that these stories are chronological from his point of view). Even Philip Latham's Borusa is passable. A nice celebration for the 20th year. (7/10)*

SJW: The Five Doctors is great fun, and strikes just the right anniversary note. Few people could be more experienced at writing Doctor Who *than Terrance Dicks, and here he does an expert job in coming up with a plot that enables him to weave in all the various returning characters and cameo appearances while still telling an entertaining story. There is no hidden meaning or deep subtext here, but that's not what's required for a special occasion like this. Instead, what we have is a celebratory romp with a suitably nostalgic feel. Gallifrey still has the overly glitzy look it acquired in* Arc of Infinity, *but otherwise the production delivers everything that's required of it.*

The performances are all fine, too, although in truth Richard Hurndall bears little more than a passing resemblance to the late, great William Hartnell. (7/10)

SEASON TWENTY-ONE

Warriors of the Deep (6L)

EP	DATE	TIME	DURN	VIEWERS	CHART POS
1	05.01.84	18.41	24'48"	7.6	51
2	06.01.84	18.41	24'04"	7.5	52
3	12.01.84	18.41	24'02"	7.3	74
4	13.01.84	18.41	24'25"	6.6	87

PRODUCTION DETAILS

OB Recording: 28.06.83
Shepperton (OB) Recording: 29.06.83–30.06.83 stage A
Studio Recording: 23.06.83–24.06.83 and 13.07.83–15.07.83 in TC6

Turlough has changed his mind about going home, and the Doctor plans to show Tegan something of Earth's future.

The TARDIS materialises in space where it is intercepted and attacked by Sentinel Six (voice: unknown), a robot weapons system. The Doctor manages to avoid the ship's destruction by performing a materialisation flip-flop.

The TARDIS then materialises in an underwater base, Sea Base 4, around the year 2084. The base is being monitored from a nearby battle cruiser by a group of three Silurians – Icthar (Norman Comer), sole survivor of the Silurian Triad; Tarpok (Vincent Brimble); and Scibus (Stuart Blake) – who later revive the Sea Devil warriors of Elite Group One (Steve Kelly, Chris Wolfe, Jules Walters, Mike Braben, Dave Ould), led by Sauvix (Christopher Farries).

The Sea Base is commanded by Vorshak (Tom Adams), with Bulic (Nigel Humphries) as his second in command.

There is a cold war in progress, and the Base goes through frequent practice missile runs for which a sync operator is required to link with the computer and thereby control the firing of the missiles. Maddox (Martin Neil), the temporary sync operator, is uncertain of his skill at the job.

In charge of the Base's medical lab is Doctor Solow (Ingrid Pitt) who is in truth an enemy agent in league with Nilson (Ian McCulloch). They plan to program Maddox to destroy the computer circuitry. To do this they ask Vorshak to release Maddox's duplicate program disk under the pretext of helping the sync operator cope with his job. Vorshak does so, and Maddox is programmed in the Base's psycho-surgery unit.

The Doctor's presence on the Sea Base is detected when Turlough summons an elevator. The Time Lord programs the base's reactor to overload in an attempt to avoid capture. This fails, however, and the time travellers are all taken prisoner. The Base's security officer, Preston (Tara Ward), also finds the TARDIS.

The Silurians launch an attack on the base and the Doctor, recognising their ship on the monitor screen, tries to prevent Vorshak from firing on them. Vorshak ignores him, however, and the Base's defences are neutralised as the Silurians deflect its fire. The Silurians then unleash a huge reptilian creature called the Myrka (William Perrie, John Asquith). While this is attacking Airlock 1, the Sea Devils launch an assault on Airlock 5.

Using the attacks as a diversion, Solow and Nilson activate Maddox, who starts tampering with the equipment. Karina (Nitza Saul), another of the Base personnel, is suspicious, and Nilson makes Maddox kill her.

The Myrka forces its way into the base, temporarily trapping the Doctor and Tegan until Turlough gets the inner airlock door open to save them. The creature starts making its way towards the bridge, killing people by electrocution. Meanwhile the Silurians make ready a device called the manipulator and prepare to enter the base themselves. The Sea Devils break through Airlock 5 and start the push for the bridge, killing any crew that stand in their way.

The Doctor attacks the Myrka using an ultra-violet light generator which blinds and then kills it. However, this comes too late to save Doctor Solow, who was foolish enough to try to engage the creature in kung fu on her way to an escape pod.

Nilson, who has been unmasked as a traitor by Vorshak, takes Tegan hostage. The Doctor blinds him with the ultra-violet device, and a group of Sea Devils appear and kill him. The Doctor and Tegan are taken as prisoners to the bridge, which is now under the control of the Silurians. The Doctor knows Icthar of old and thought he had been killed. The Silurians' plan is now revealed: they intend to get mankind to destroy itself by triggering a global war. They fix Maddox's tampering and connect the manipulator to the systems.

The Doctor escapes from the bridge and tries to find something to use against the reptiles. He discovers some cylinders of hexachromite gas, which is lethal to them. Sauvix kills Preston before being sprayed with gas and killed by Bulic.

As the Silurians prepare to fire the missiles, the Doctor bows to pressure from Bulic, Tegan and Turlough (who have also got free) and agrees that they should feed the gas into the ventilation system. Bulic stays in the chemical store to ensure that the gas keeps flowing, while the Doctor and his companions leave for the bridge to try to stop the Silurians.

The reptiles collapse under the effects of the gas and the Doctor tells Tegan and Turlough to give the Silurians oxygen to keep them alive. Meanwhile, aided by Vorshak, he tries to stop the missiles by linking himself into the equipment as sync operator. The

Doctor succeeds, but Vorshak is killed by one of the Silurians before the Silurian itself is killed by Turlough. The Doctor and his companions have won through, but everyone bar themselves and Bulic is dead. The Doctor is left to muse that there should have been another way.

WHO FAX

● Novelised as *Doctor Who – Warriors of the Deep* by Terrance Dicks in 1984.

● An abridged version of the novelisation read by Peter Davison was released on audio tape by BBC Worldwide Publishing in 1995.

● Location: Royal Engineers Diving Establishment, McMullen Barracks, Marchwood, nr Southampton, Hants.

● The Myrka was played by two actors who also played the pantomime horse in the BBC children's programme *Rentaghost*.

● Stuntman Gareth Milne doubled for Peter Davison when the Doctor fell into a tank of water at the end of episode one.

● In Johnny Byrne's original scripts, Icthar was the only Silurian to be named. The other two Silurians were referred to simply as 'First Companion' and 'Second Companion'.

QUOTES

● 'My script for *Warriors of the Deep* always hinged on the Doctor's sympathies for the Silurians. The first draft was indeed overlong, but not unusually so. What is true is that my script was massively rewritten by Saward and the director without any reference to me. If I had been involved, the end result might have done justice to a story that merited enhancing, not the crude thrashing that ultimately showed up on screen. I certainly couldn't have done worse.' Writer Johnny Byrne contributing to a 1995 Internet discussion on the story.

● 'I remember the Myrka as menacing, unstoppable and wellnigh indestructible. Nowhere did I describe it as a four-legged beast on loan from Panto-Horses-Are-Us. Nor was the double death at the end mine. I had the base captain live and the Silurian die. Given the dilemma of the Silurians – beings pledged not to kill, but driven by necessity to wipe out humans, and manipulating events in a way that would honour the former and accomplish the latter – I felt that this situation had greater emotional impact.' Writer Johnny Byrne contributing to a 1995 Internet discussion on the story.

● 'I did have a male double-dealing scientist on board the seabase. But nowhere did I describe him as a drop-kicking Rhine-maiden. I was also very specific in my description of the base – rusting, leaking, virtually forgotten by all except those on board. The tension caused by neglect, decay and low morale was demonstrated in the very first scenes – when the guy plugged into the weapons systems computer completely bombs out. The onboard atmosphere and look, which I described in the script, was something like in *Alien* – with the Myrka essentially a lurking deadly presence waiting to reveal itself.' Writer Johnny Byrne contributing to a 1995 Internet discussion on the story.

● 'I liked the basic story, the concept behind it, and I was pleased to see the Sea Devils and Silurians again. Unfortunately, we had lighting problems – it was all too bright, so some of the potential atmosphere was lost.' Script editor Eric Saward interviewed by Richard Marson for *Doctor Who Magazine* Issue 94, published in November 1984.

COMMENT

DJH: Peter Davison seems to have had a run of bad luck with his season openers. After the poor Castrovalva *and* Arc of Infinity *comes another below-par story. In the case of* Warriors of the Deep, *the flaws are due to the fact that the production standards simply do not match the quality of the script. Here we have a Sea Base that is so brightly lit that it is surprising that the crew don't have to wear sunglasses the whole time. The Sea Devils and Silurians are dreadful recreations of the Pertwee-era originals, with little care taken in studio to ensure that masks are securely fastened under costumes. The Myrka is the biggest failure of all. A huge sea creature that could and should have been threatening and frightening is reduced to a pantomime spectacle due to over-lighting, overuse and over-exposure. Some of the characters are well acted (Vorshak, Bulic), some are bland (Preston, the Silurians,*

Maddox) and some are painful to watch (Nilson, Solow, Karina).
Overall, the story seems rushed and uninspired. (3/10)

SJW: Warriors of the Deep *is a classic case of good scripts being let down by inappropriate production. The basic premise of a future Earth where two superpowers are facing off against one another with their respective arsenals of nuclear weapons poised to fire is an intriguing one with a great deal of promise – and an added bonus is that writer Johnny Byrne, unlike Terrance Dicks in his later novelisation, astutely avoids identifying the two power blocs in conventional 20th-century terms. The plotting is also good, and the return of the Silurians and the Sea Devils in principle a welcome one. Unfortunately, much of this potential is simply thrown away. The spacious, floodlit sets of Sea Base 4 give the viewer no sense of its underwater location and engender none of the tension that would have been created had they been cramped and dark as Byrne had intended. The new, heavily designed costumes for the Silurians and the Sea Devils look very pretty but also fail to impress – particularly as they are not always properly fitted to the actors inside them. The realisation of the new monster, the Myrka, is simply terrible. Add to this some quite bizarre touches of direction from Pennant Roberts, such as in the scene in which he has Ingrid Pitt as Solow making an almost surreal kung-fu attack on the Myrka, and the final verdict can only be one of great disappointment. (3/10)*

The Awakening (6M)

EP	DATE	TIME	DURN	VIEWERS	CHART POS
1	19.01.84	18.41	25'18"	7.9	61
2	20.01.84	18.41	24'47"	6.6	84

Repeat (one-part omnibus edition)

1	20.07.84	18.50	25'18"	4.4	104

PRODUCTION DETAILS
Location Filming: 19.07.83–22.07.83
Studio Recording: 04.08.83–06.08.83 in TC6

In the village of Little Hodcombe in 1984, schoolteacher Jane
Hampden (Polly James) is being tormented by Colonel Ben
Woolsey (Glyn Houston), Captain Joseph Willow (Jack Galloway)
and their leader, Sir George Hutchinson (Denis Lill), who are on
horseback and dressed as roundheads. It is Sir George who has
organised a series of war games to celebrate the English Civil
War, which came to the village on 13 July 1643. Jane wants him
to stop the games but he refuses.

The TARDIS arrives in the crypt of a disused church after experiencing some time distortion and an energy field. The crypt is
full of broken masonry, and more falls as the Doctor and his companions watch on the scanner. The Doctor spots a fleeing figure
(John Kearns) and dashes out to help, but the figure has now
vanished. As the Doctor, Tegan and Turlough leave the church to
investigate, smoke starts to billow from a crack in the wall.

The three travellers are soon captured and taken to Sir George.
Tegan explains that they have come to this village to see her grandfather, Andrew Verney. She is informed that Verney is missing,
and runs off in disgust. The Doctor follows but loses her as she
has been trapped in a barn wherein she sees the ghost of an old
man.

Returning to the church, the Doctor meets Will Chandler (Keith
Jayne) who breaks through the wall. He has been hidden in a priest
hole and believes the year to be 1643. They are joined by Tegan
and Turlough, who has rescued her from the barn. The Doctor and
Will investigate the church. Tegan and Turlough meanwhile wait
in the TARDIS, where they see a sparkly projection on one of the
walls. They go to tell the Doctor but are re-captured. Turlough is
locked in an outbuilding with Verney (Frederick Hall) while Tegan
is forced to change into a May Queen costume by Willow.

The Doctor has found a secret passage back to Ben Woolsey's
living room under a slab marked with a picture of a creature that
Will identifies as the Malus. The Doctor and Will meet Jane

134

coming the other way through the passage – she was locked in the house by Willow and found the passage's other end by accident. They avoid Sir George, who has followed Jane down the passage, and the Doctor finds a small ball of metal with which the man has been playing. It is tinclavic, a metal mined by the Terileptils on the planet Raaga for the almost exclusive use of the people of Hakol, a planet in the star system Rifta, where psychic energy is a force to be harnessed.

Returning to the church, the Doctor and Jane are astonished when a massive alien face pushes its way through the crack on the wall, roaring and spewing smoke. They manage to escape from the psychic projection of a cavalier, and head back to the house via the tunnel. The Doctor realises that the Malus in the church was found by Verney and then exploited by Sir George. The psychic energy released by the war games will feed the Malus. The Doctor and Jane again try to persuade Sir George to stop the games, as the final battle will be for real. He refuses. Ben however joins forces with the Doctor.

Tegan, dressed as the Queen of the May, is taken in a horse-drawn cart towards the village green, where she is to be burned. When the cart arrives, however, a straw dummy has been put in her place by Ben. Sir George is furious, but Will causes a distraction which allows the Doctor, Jane, Ben, Tegan and Will himself to get back to the church, where they enter the TARDIS. The Doctor locks the signal conversion unit on the frequency of the psychic energy feeding the Malus, hoping to be able to direct it. Willow and a trooper (Christopher Saul) try in vain to break their way into the TARDIS, and Turlough and Verney knock them unconscious with lumps of masonry. The Doctor succeeds in blocking the energy, and the projection of the Malus in the TARDIS dies.

The Doctor and his friends all return to the main church, where they are confronted by three roundhead projections. The trooper in the crypt recovers but is beheaded by the roundheads when he enters the church. Sir George has been summoned by the Malus and now arrives, brandishing two pistols. Ben tries to reason with him but he will not listen. The Malus also summons Willow and, in the confusion, Will pushes Sir George into the Malus's face, killing him. The Malus goes wild. It is fulfilling its program and destroying the church in its death throes. To escape, Will, Willow, Jane, Ben, Tegan, Verney, the Doctor and Turlough all leave in the TARDIS.

The Doctor is persuaded to stay in Little Hodcombe for a while for a rest.

WHO FAX

- Novelised as *Doctor Who – The Awakening* by Eric Pringle in 1985.
- Working title: *War Game*.
- Locations: ford at Tarrant Monkton, nr Blandford Forum, Dorset; St Bartholomew's Church, Shapwick, nr Wimborne Minster, Dorset; village cross, opposite Anchor Inn, Shapwick; meadow near church, Shapwick, Dorset; Bishops Court Farm, Shapwick, Dorset; village of Martin, nr Fordingbridge, Hants; Martin Down, nr Martin, Hants; stable at rear of Damers Cottage, Martin, nr Fordingbridge, Hants.
- This story was commissioned and scripted as a four-part adventure, incorrectly rumoured to have featured the Daleks, and reworked into a two-part story at a later date.
- Two drummers were hired to appear on screen during the preparations for the May Queen ceremony in episode two. These were referred to in BBC documentation as Drummer Tuite and Drummer Cooney.
- The scene in which the trooper is beheaded was edited slightly for transmission as the recorded version was considered too horrific.
- The mentions of the Terileptils mining tinclavic on the planet Raaga were added by script editor Eric Saward as a reference back to his own Season 19 story *The Visitation*.
- The part of Sir John Hutchinson (later changed to Sir George) was originally offered to Clifford Rose on 4 July 1983, but he turned it down as he couldn't ride a horse. The role was subsequently offered to an actor named Charles Kay, whom director Michael Owen Morris knew from a programme called *Fall of Eagles*, and also to Anthony Valentine, but neither accepted.

- The part of Andrew Verney was originally offered to Maurice Denham.
- John Horton was originally scheduled to handle the visual effects for this story, but on 3 June 1983 producer John Nathan-Turner wrote to Michealjohn Harris, Head of Visual Effects, requesting that he be replaced as there had been a 'clash of personalities' between Horton and director Michael Owen Morris on a previous production unrelated to *Doctor Who*.
- This story was scripted to have included a scene in the TARDIS with Kamelion, but this was edited out of the final programme due to the episode overrunning.

QUOTES

- 'My inspiration stemmed partly from an interest in the English Civil War and a desire to set a *Doctor Who* story on Earth and to create a different kind of monster. I wanted to see what could be done by shifting time and, if possible, actually merge the two time periods. Obviously all this did not come off, but it was in my mind at some stage of preparing the story.

  'After the basic idea was sent I was asked to develop it into the equivalent of a short story. I then travelled down to London and had a long chat with Eric Saward, who told me of this character Turlough who hadn't been on television yet and so was completely unknown to me. I was then asked to develop that short story into a scene-by-scene breakdown, which was very difficult, and it was at this point that I realised that the plot might not have enough in it for four episodes. After another meeting I was asked to do a full script for the first episode, which was liked, and so I was commissioned to write a second episode. At this stage, I was asked to make the story into a two-parter; first compacting the two already written episodes, and then doing the same for the next two.' Writer Eric Pringle interviewed by Martin Day for *Doctor Who Magazine* Issue 172, published in April 1991.

- 'For the scenes outside the church I had to provide a little lichgate – which is probably the most well-remembered aspect of *The Awakening* due to the famous out-take where it was demolished by a horse and cart! I also had to supply a large gravestone for the cemetery and one or two other bits and pieces, such as the village maypole. Apart from that my main concern was to see the exteriors of the buildings for which I would have to create interiors in the studio. There were some nice scenes involving a barn, for instance, for which I knew I was going to have to match studio interior to location exterior so that viewers would believe the scenes were shot continuously on location.' Designer Barry Newbery interviewed by Stephen James Walker and David J. Howe for *The Frame* Issue 23/24, published in 1993.

COMMENT

DJH: Thankfully, following the painful experience of Warriors of the Deep, *there comes a little gem buried in this season. The Awakening is one of the best Davison adventures because it keeps it simple. The plot is elegant and the script moves along at a good pace. Historical settings work well in* Doctor Who *and here we have yet another twist, history being re-enacted. The cast are – with the sole exception of Jack Galloway as Willow, who is bland – excellent. Denis Lill is superbly maniacal as Sir George, and ex-Liver Bird Polly James is simply astonishing as Jane Hampden. Stealing the show, however, is Keith Jayne, who gives Will a believability and charm so often lacking in* Doctor Who. *I still wish that Will had continued to travel with the Doctor as he would have made an excellent companion. (9/10)*

SJW: The Awakening is a pleasant enough story, although it engenders a certain sense of deja vu *as it contains a number of elements – the country village cut off from the outside world; the alien menace in the church; the May Day celebrations; the climactic destruction of the church – that are highly reminiscent of the third Doctor story* The Dæmons, *in comparison with which it certainly pales. That said, the production is as polished and as glossy as one has come to expect by this stage of the fifth Doctor's era. There are some very good performances, including that of Keith Jayne as Will Chandler, and some rather less good, includ-*

ing that of Polly James as Jane Hampden. (5/10)

Frontios (6N)

EP	DATE	TIME	DURN	VIEWERS	CHART POS
1	26.01.84	18.41	24'39"	8.0	58
2	27.01.84	18.41	24'35"	5.8	115
3	02.02.84	18.40	24'30"	7.8	59
4	03.02.84	18.42	24'26"	5.6	112

PRODUCTION DETAILS
Studio Recording: 24.08.83–26.08.83 and 07.09.83–09.09.83 in
TC6

On the colony planet Frontios in the Veruna system, Captain
Revere (John Beardmore) is knocked unconscious when some sub-
sidence occurs in a mine. Security Chief Brazen (Peter Gilmore)
fetches help, but Revere's body has now vanished. Following this
incident, Brazen orders the research room closed – despite the
protestations of the scientist Range (William Lucas) and his daugh-
ter Norna (Lesley Dunlop), who feel that the investigations into
the meteorite bombardment that the planet is suffering should continue. Revere's son, Plantaganet (Jeff Rawle), takes over as leader.

The TARDIS is hovering above Frontios, upon which the last
surviving group of mankind is living following Earth's collision
with the Sun. The TARDIS is mysteriously affected by a meteorite storm and dragged down to the planet by gravity. The Doctor,
Tegan and Turlough emerge to investigate. The colonists injured
by the meteorite bombardment are being helped into the medical
area, and the travellers – despite the Doctor's earlier protestations
that he cannot get involved – all help out.

The Doctor needs better light in the medical facility. Tegan and
Turlough are sent to fetch a portable mu-field activator and five
argon discharge globes from the TARDIS but find that the ship's
inner door is stuck, preventing them from getting beyond the console room. Norna, Tegan and Turlough obtain an acid-battery from

the research room to power the lights. On their way back, however, they are forced to knock the Warnsman (Jim Dowdall) unconscious to avoid capture. Another bombardment occurs and, in the Warnsman's absence, catches the colony unawares. When the skies clear, the TARDIS has gone. Plantaganet wants the Doctor killed, but Turlough intercedes, using a surviving hat stand from the TARDIS as a weapon. Plantaganet tries to attack the Doctor with a crowbar but suffers a heart attack. The Time Lord manages to save his life using the battery, but Plantaganet is later dragged into the ground by some mysterious force.

Turlough discovers a passage under the research room and he and Norna explore, only for Norna to be captured by the creatures that live there. These are Tractators (George Campbell, Michael Malcolm, Stephen Speed, William Bowden, Hedi Khursandi). Turlough goes into shock at seeing them, as the experience dredges up a deep racial memory of the creatures invading his own planet. The Doctor and Range also find the tunnel, and then so does Tegan.

After many narrow escapes from the Tractators, the Doctor and Tegan find their way to the creatures' control centre. There, their leader the Gravis (John Gillett) explains that the Tractators have been on Frontios for 500 years. They brought the colony ship here 40 years ago, and have been causing the meteorite bombardments for the last 30 years. They need human minds and bodies to run their mining machines, and they plan to replace the current driver – Captain Revere, who is now dead – with Plantaganet. The Gravis knows of the Doctor and is very interested in his TARDIS.

Meanwhile Brazen, along with his deputy (Alison Skillbeck), has been holding an enquiry with Range, Norna and Turlough. Brazen and Range head back into the tunnels, followed by Turlough. In their absence, the research room is attacked by an orderly named Cockerill (Maurice O'Connell) and a group of retrograde colonists who feel that the present order is breaking down and want their independence.

When Turlough catches up with Brazen and Range, Range goes back to check on Norna's safety. Turlough rescues Tegan, who has been held in a gravity field by a Tractator, and they then move on to rescue the Doctor.

The Doctor tampers with the mining machine and causes the Gravis to suffer an electric shock. The creature falls unconscious and all the other Tractators then mill around in confusion. Plantaganet is rescued from the machine but, in a struggle, Brazen falls into the driver's seat and becomes hooked up instead. The machine goes wild and crashes into a wall.

The Doctor realises that the Tractators are building a gravity motor with which to pilot the planet out of orbit.

Plantaganet reveals that there are in fact two mining machines, and Turlough remembers an important fact about the creatures: if the Gravis is removed from the others, they all cease to be intelligent and return to a docile state.

Wandering in the tunnels, Tegan comes across bits of the TARDIS's inner walls. She is chased by some Tractators led by the Gravis, who has now regained consciousness, and comes upon one of the TARDIS's inner doors. Going through it, she finds herself in the TARDIS console room, which has bits of rock wall mixed in with its normal walls. The Doctor, Turlough and Plantaganet are already there. The Doctor ushers the Gravis in and then goads it into reassembling the TARDIS using its power over gravity. When the outer plasmic shell forms, the Gravis is effectively cut off from its fellow Tractators, which revert to a harmless state.

The Doctor and Tegan drop the Gravis off on the uninhabited planet of Kolkokron. Returning to Frontios, the Doctor gives Plantaganet the hat stand as a farewell token and asks that his own involvement in the affair not be mentioned to anyone.

Once the TARDIS has left Frontios, its engines start making a worrying noise. The Doctor can do nothing. The ship is being pulled towards the centre of the universe.

WHO FAX

● Novelised as *Doctor Who – Frontios* by Christopher H. Bidmead in 1984.

● The working titles *Frontious*, *Frotious* and *The Frontios* all appear on BBC documentation, but these are almost certainly misprints or misspellings of *Frontios*.

- Working title: *The Wanderers*.
- The transmission of the final episode was followed by a trailer of clips for the following story, *Resurrection of the Daleks*.
- The part of Range was originally to be played by actor Peter Arne, but he was murdered at his home prior to the start of recording.
- The helmets worn by Brazen's guards were originally used in *Blake's 7*.
- The actors playing the Tractators were all trained dancers as the script called for the creatures to curl around people like woodlice. The design of the costumes did not allow for this movement, however. Between takes, the actors also had to be fed oxygen via a tube under the base of their costumes, as very little air could get inside.
- The original designer on this story was Barrie Dobbins. He was replaced by David Buckingham around the start of July 1983.
- On 6 March 1984, script editor Eric Saward wrote to Christopher H. Bidmead to ask if he would be interested in writing another story featuring the Tractators and also the Master. His reply is unrecorded.

QUOTES

- 'Eric Saward phoned me up and asked me to do it. They wanted the monster element, which was a struggle because I always hated *Doctor Who* monsters – partly because they tended to look cheap and mainly because they were so limited on dialogue. Dialogue is so important in a low-budget show – it creates the whole effect.

  'Part of the complex ideas in *Frontios* involved the TARDIS. If you've got a story about gravity and things being sucked through the earth, then why not push the thing a bit further and actually break the TARDIS up? I wanted the Doctor to be no safer than these poor last vestiges of humanity. I wrote it around the time of the Beirut crisis and I was influenced by that. Without imposing any political angle, I always felt that *Doctor Who* could much better reflect the sort of things that were happening in the 1980s.

'The Tractators were based on woodlice – my old flat was infested with them and I used to watch them very closely. I was told we had no filming, which was an exciting constraint. As for characters, I found Turlough very interesting – Mark Strickson was an extraordinary actor – and Plantaganet I rationalised by saying that one of the things they were carrying over was their culture; Plantaganet as a name had echoes of history.' Writer Christopher H. Bidmead interviewed by Richard Marson for *Doctor Who Magazine* Issue 109, published in February 1986.

● 'It was an interesting idea. Chris is – and I mean this in the kindest possible way – a very idiosyncratic writer. His characters are always rather quirky and peculiar, in as much as we're all peculiar, along with all the failings and pomposity that we all have to varying degrees. Chris is brilliant at creating this, and he also has great skill at creating alien environments. In *Frontios*, he created for us another sort of culture that the audience could relate to – which is a very difficult achievement. You can't mention how they cultivate food, whether they have hot or cold water or whether the lavatories work – or even if they go to the lavatory. All the same, it has got to be in the back of your mind, and there has to be a lot of thinking through to get this believability. I did feel a little annoyed with Chris – who should after all appreciate my point of view – because *Frontios* boasted this huge ship with its vast chambers that he knew we couldn't do in his original requirements. He was, however, very receptive, and over the course of that story we had some wonderfully creative disagreements.' Script editor Eric Saward interviewed by Richard Marson for *Doctor Who Magazine* Issue 94, published in November 1984.

COMMENT

DJH: The season continues on a high note with this story of a colony in trouble. Frontios *is a simple idea, well presented. Its characterisation of the fifth Doctor is a little at odds with that seen in the other stories of the season, due to the fact that ex-script editor Christopher H. Bidmead wrote it with his own interpretation of the character in mind. However, the Doctor's new traits – he is unpredictable, flies off the handle easily and uses half-glasses when engaged in detailed work – all sit rather better with him than some of his usual ones. The villains of the piece are also pretty good. Obviously based on woodlice, the Tractators are original and nasty to look at. It's just a shame that the idea of them curling around victims couldn't be incorporated and that the voice of the Gravis is so obviously human. Mark Strickson has an interesting time here, and his acting of a panic attack and buried memories coming to the surface is pretty good. I think he does overdo it in some scenes, however. In detailed analysis the story has too much running about in corridors for it really to work in the latter stages. There are also some holes – what happened to Brazen in the mining machine, for example, and why did the TARDIS break up and become enmeshed in the structure of the planet? Otherwise, it's a good little tale. (8/10)*

SJW: *Frontios is a very well written story, a particularly notable feature of Christopher H. Bidmead's scripts being that they offer the three regulars some exceptionally strong material to work with. Davison, Strickson and Fielding all rise to the occasion, giving excellent performances. The guest cast are also highly impressive. The production is, as usual, very slick-looking, although certain aspects of it fail to convince – the Tractator costumes, for example, are rather too bulky and inflexible, and the planetary landscape rather too obviously studio-bound. The lighting, however, is outstanding, being very subtle and appropriate at a time in the series' history when something more akin to floodlighting was becoming the norm. (7/10)*

Resurrection of the Daleks (6P)

EP	DATE	TIME	DURN	VIEWERS	CHART POS
1	08.02.84	18.50	46'24"	7.3	73
2	15.02.84	18.52	46'52"	8.0	53

PRODUCTION DETAILS
Location Filming: 11.09.83–12.09.83
Studio Recording: 21.09.83–23.09.83 in TC1 and 05.10.83–07.10.83 in TC8

In London, 1984, a group of humanoids are gunned down by two policemen (Mike Braben, Michael Jeffries) using machine pistols. Two of the humanoids, Galloway (William Sleigh) and Quartermaster Sergeant Stien (Rodney Bewes), escape and return to a warehouse where a time corridor is situated. Galloway is killed, leaving the cowardly Stien alone.

Commander Lytton (Maurice Colbourne), who led the attack on Earth, transports back to his battle cruiser and prepares to attack a space station. On the station, the crew are demoralised and the equipment is malfunctioning. It is a prison station with just one prisoner.

The TARDIS is being dragged to Earth down a time corridor, but the Doctor manages to break free and materialise the ship on the banks of London's river Thames alongside some warehouses. Exploring, the Doctor, Tegan and Turlough come across Stien, who takes them to see the time corridor entrance in one of the warehouses. Turlough vanishes and the Doctor, Stien and Tegan are found by Colonel Archer (Del Henney), Sergeant Calder (Philip McGough) and Professor Laird (Chloe Ashcroft), who are with some troops in the warehouse to investigate some strange cylinders that defy analysis.

Lytton's battle cruiser docks with the space station after knocking out its defences. Doctor Styles (Rula Lenska), Mercer (Jim Findley) and some other troopers defend the station's airlock but it is blown in by a group of invading Daleks. The initial attack is repelled, but the Daleks then use a gas to wipe out resistance and their second assault is successful. Osborn (Sneh Gupta) tries to kill the station's prisoner, but the destruct button malfunctions. She and a crew member (John Adam Baker) then go to the cryogenic cell to carry out the task in person, but are both killed before they can do so. Lytton revives the prisoner from cryogenic sleep. It is Davros (Terry Molloy).

The Daleks (John Scott Martin, Cy Town, Tony Starr, Toby Byrne; voices: Brian Miller, Royce Mills) know that the Doctor is on Earth. A Dalek is sent through the time corridor to capture him, and Turlough, who has got on board the Dalek ship, sees it leave. When the Dalek arrives on Earth its casing is destroyed by Archer's men, but the mutant inside survives and Tegan is injured in the battle.

Styles suggests using the space station's self-destruct mechanism. She and a couple of other crew members make their way to the self-destruct chamber, where she manages to activate and set up the systems before she and her group are all killed by Lytton and his troops.

When Davros is revived it is explained to him that the Daleks lost their war against the Movellans. This was after the Movellans developed a virus which attacked only Daleks. The Daleks now need Davros to help them develop an antidote. Davros has his own ideas and initiates a technician, Kiston (Leslie Grantham), as his slave. Several troopers, a chemist (Nicholas Curry) and two Daleks are also recruited.

On Earth, the Doctor helps Archer's men defeat an attack by the Dalek mutant, but Archer himself runs into Lytton's two policemen while trying to summon help. The Doctor and Stien go to the Daleks' space craft in the TARDIS, but Stien turns out to be a traitor working for the invaders. The Doctor is captured and connected up to some equipment that will drain his memories. The Daleks plan to send duplicates of the Doctor, Tegan and Turlough to Gallifrey, where they will kill the members of the High Council of Time Lords. Stien – who is himself a duplicate – breaks down during the process and releases the Doctor.

Laird is killed by Archer and Calder, who have been duplicated, and Tegan is taken to the space station. There she meets up with Turlough and Mercer. They find the Doctor and Stien and all return to the TARDIS. The Doctor decides he must kill Davros, but when he confronts his enemy he find that he is unable to bring himself to do it.

Tegan and Turlough return to Earth in the TARDIS, which the Doctor had set to automatic. Mercer is killed by a Dalek trooper when Stien's conditioning reasserts itself, and Stien then heads for the self-destruct chamber. The Doctor meanwhile returns to Earth via the time corridor.

Davros and the Supreme Dalek send their respective groups of Daleks to Earth. The Supreme Dalek's force are accompanied by Lytton, but have orders to kill him. A battle ensues between the two groups of Daleks in the warehouse, with Lytton and Archer's duplicate troops getting involved as well. The Doctor releases a quantity of the Movellan virus, which destroys the Daleks. Lytton escapes with his two duplicate policemen.

Davros releases the Movellan virus on the space station but is himself overcome by it. However, there is a door to an escape pod nearby.

In the TARDIS, the Supreme Dalek appears on the monitor and informs the Doctor that duplicates have already been positioned on the Earth. The Doctor responds that they are unstable and will soon reveal themselves.

On the space station, Stien reaches the self-destruct chamber. Several Daleks arrive and exterminate him, but he falls on the activating lever and the station and Dalek ship are both destroyed.

As the Doctor prepares to leave Earth, Tegan suddenly says that she is not going with him. She is tired of all the death. She runs off, but returns just in time to see the TARDIS leave.

WHO FAX
- Working title: *The Return*.
- Story released by BBC Home Video in 1993 in a four-part version untransmitted in the UK.
- Locations: Butlers Wharf, Shad Thames, London.
- This story was written and made as a four-part adventure but re-edited into two approximately 45 minute episodes and shown on two consecutive Wednesday evenings (as opposed to the series' usual Thursday and Friday transmission days) as a result of rescheduling around the BBC's coverage of the Winter Olympics. The original four-episode edit was sold overseas by BBC Enterprises but some copies were without full sound effects and music. Episode two of that version had an additional

sequence and a different cliffhanger ending.

● Davros's laboratory assistant was played by Leslie Grantham who was later to find fame as 'Dirty Den' in the BBC's long running soap opera *EastEnders*.

● Davros's mask was sculpted by effects designer Stan Mitchell, who had also been responsible for the Silurian masks for *Warriors of the Deep*.

● During the Doctor's interrogation by the Daleks, clips of his past selves and various companions are seen. These are as follows: Turlough (*Terminus*); Tegan (*Logopolis*); Nyssa (*Black Orchid*); Adric (*Warriors' Gate*); Romana II (*Warriors' Gate*); Romana I (*The Ribos Operation*); K-9 (*Warriors' Gate*); Harry (*Terror of the Zygons*); fourth Doctor (*Pyramids of Mars*); Sarah (*Pyramids of Mars*); Jo (*The Mutants*); the Brigadier (*The Ambassadors of Death*); Liz Shaw (*Spearhead from Space*); third Doctor (*The Mutants*); Zoe (*The War Games*); Victoria (*The Enemy of the World*); Jamie (*The Enemy of the World*); the second Doctor (*The War Games*); Ben (*The Tenth Planet*); Polly (*The Tenth Planet*); Dodo (*The War Machines*); Sara (*The Daleks' Master Plan*); Katarina (publicity still); Steven (*The Time Meddler*); Vicki (*The Rescue*); Barbara (*The Daleks*); Ian (*The Daleks*); Susan (*The Daleks*); and the first Doctor (*The Daleks' Master Plan*). A clip of Leela was inadvertently omitted.

● This story had originally been planned to close the previous season (following directly on from *The King's Demons*) but had to be cancelled before production began due to disruption resulting from industrial action. The filming and studio dates for this original version were to have been as follows: film: 04.01.83–05.01.83; Studio: 16.01.83–18.01.83 and 30.01.83–01.02.83.

QUOTES

● 'The continuity can be an amazing limitation at times. There's lack of continuity over the years anyway – we're talking about 21 years of different writers, producers and script editors. The Daleks go back to story two, and there've been all sorts of inconsistencies. You try to bear consistency in mind, but it gets very confusing and hems you in. I think – and as the author I can say this – the story suffered because of that. I watched most of the Dalek stuff that still exists – and for those who are interested, it's over twenty-four hours, an awful lot of material. There are compensations, I hasten to add – one has to be objective. It's nice to have written a story about a creation that back in the sixties helped found the show's popularity. It was interesting for that.

'As a character, Davros is slightly over the top. He spends a lot of time ranting rather like his creations. You do try to underplay this tendency. The first story Davros appeared in, *Genesis of the Daleks*, is my personal favourite of all the Dalek stories. In that, he was extremely interesting – the story itself was good and excellently directed. In *Resurrection of the Daleks*, I found there was really too much to put in for four episodes – I could have done with another episode perhaps. My fault, as I chose the length, but as it turned out the plot swamped it.' Writer and script editor Eric Saward interviewed by Richard Marson for *Doctor Who Magazine* Issue 94, published in November 1984.

COMMENT

DJH: Only two seasons later and Eric Saward is re-making Earthshock *Dalek style. Like that earlier story,* Resurrection of the Daleks *is all gloss and very little substance. The plot unfortunately does not stand up to close inspection, although the direction is excellent and even in places inspired. Of the cast, Rodney Bewes is very good indeed, as are Del Henney and Philip McGough. Chloe Ashcroft's Professor Laird is wasted (literally) and Terry Molloy's Davros is forced. The crew of the prison ship are faceless as well as nameless – for some reason Saward doesn't give us their names when we first meet them and in some cases they are named, if at all, only in the second episode. The major credit must go to Maurice Colbourne's Lytton, who comes over as evil and believable. It is good that he survives at the end, as he is by far the most interesting character. The Daleks take a back seat*

*once more and the overall feeling is one of slight disappointment.
(7/10)*

SJW: Resurrection of the Daleks *is somewhat similar to the same
writer's earlier story* Earthshock, *in that it is a superficial yet un-
deniably entertaining action-adventure epic which cleverly exploits
the history and iconography of one of the series' most popular
monster races. It also ends with the dramatic exit of one of the
Doctor's trusty companions. The Daleks are at their most impressive for years – it is good, too, to see the Dalek Supreme making a
reappearance – and Davros, while not perhaps on a par with the
definitive interpretation in Season 12's* Genesis of the Daleks, *is
certainly much better than in Season 17's disappointing* Destiny
of the Daleks. *It all looks very nice, as usual, and the location
filming at Butlers Wharf is particularly effective. The downside is
that the plot is even more muddled than that of* Earthshock, *and
could certainly have done without the gratuitous complication of
the Daleks' plan to invade Gallifrey. (7/10)*

Planet of Fire (6Q)

EP	DATE	TIME	DURN	VIEWERS	CHART POS
1	23.02.84	18.41	24'26"	7.4	71
2	24.02.84	18.42	24'20"	6.1	102
3	01.03.84	18.41	23'57"	7.4	67
4	02.03.84	18.41	24'44"	7.0	74

PRODUCTION DETAILS
Location Filming: 14.10.83–19.10.83 (no filming was done on
the 16.10.83)
Studio Recording: 26.10.83–27.10.83 in TC1 and 09.11.83–
11.11.83 in TC6

The inhabitants of the planet Sarn are split into two factions: those,
led by the high priest Timanov (Peter Wyngard) and the 'Chosen
One', who worship the god Logar; and those, led by the 'Unbe-

lievers' Amyand (James Bate) and Sorasta (Barbara Shelley), who consider Logar to be a myth. The current 'Chosen One' is Malkon (Edward Highmore), found on the mountainside when he was a child, who has a strange overlapping triangle mark on his upper arm. Amyand and his friend Roskal (Jonathan Caplan) climb the fire mountain to see if it is true that, as Timanov preaches, Logar resides at the top. All they find is barren, steaming rock – there is no god.

On Earth, Professor Howard Foster (Dallas Adams), aided by a team of men led by Curt (Michael Bangerter), retrieves a number of ancient artefacts from the sea bed off Lanzarote. One of these has the overlapping triangle design on it.

In the TARDIS, a cry from Kamelion (voice: Gerald Flood) brings the Doctor and Turlough running to find the android connected to the ship's data banks. Turlough goes to the console to program an alpha rhythm to calm the creature. He notices that a distress signal is coming through and recognises it as being of Trion origin. He rips wires from under the console in order to disable it. The Doctor returns and notices that the co-ordinates have been reset – presumably by Kamelion. The TARDIS arrives on a beach in Lanzarote.

Howard's stepdaughter, Peri (Nicola Bryant), informs him that she intends to travel to Morocco with two English boys. He connives to strand her on his boat but, taking the strangely marked artefact which she hopes might be worth something, she tries to swim to shore.

The Doctor and Turlough meet up with Howard and Curt. The Doctor thinks that the intermittent distress signal may be coming from the wreck that the two men are scavenging. Turlough returns to the TARDIS to try to triangulate the signal.

Peri gets into trouble in the water and Turlough, seeing this on the TARDIS monitor, goes and rescues her. He puts her in one of the TARDIS's bedrooms to recover. The Doctor meanwhile hurries back to the TARDIS and finds the artefact, which Turlough has discovered in Peri's bag. Turlough also has one of the overlapping triangle marks on his upper arm.

When Peri dreams of her stepfather, Kamelion takes on his

form. The TARDIS then dematerialises of its own accord, and Kamelion-Howard and Peri reveal themselves to the Doctor and Turlough in the console room.

The TARDIS materialises on Sarn. Its arrival is witnessed by one of Timanov's lookouts (Simon Sutton), who reports to the high priest that 'the Outsider' has arrived. When Turlough and the Doctor leave the TARDIS to investigate, Kamelion changes his appearance to that of the Master (Anthony Ainley). Peri tries to escape, but Kamelion then becomes Howard once more and tells her to find the Doctor. He gives her a component – a comparitor – from the TARDIS. The Master reasserts his dominance over Kamelion and orders the android to release him from his TARDIS, which has just appeared outside. Kamelion and Peri go outside, but an earthquake knocks over the Master's ship – which is shaped like a column – and Peri is able to escape.

Turlough explains to the Doctor that the mark on his arm is the Misos Triangle – the symbol of his home planet, Trion. The two time travellers are met by Amyand and Roskal, who take them to their group's base in an underground control room. The Doctor and Turlough recognise the equipment, and Turlough confirms that it is from Trion. Amyand then takes them to see Timanov.

Kamelion-Master has meanwhile chased and cornered Peri, but been unable to obtain the TARDIS component from her. He meets Timanov, who assumes that he is a manifestation of Logar.

In the sanctum, Turlough recognises more components and also a symbol round Malkon's neck. He thinks that these have come from his own father's ship, which he and Malkon then rush off to find. Timanov and Kamelion-Master meanwhile arrive and order that the Doctor be burnt.

Turlough and Malkon find the ship out in the wilderness. Peri also makes her way there, and when she mentions the Master, they all rush back to help the Doctor. Turlough operates the machinery in the Unbelievers' cave to redirect the gas flow from the mountain and cut off the flames, thus saving the Doctor and the other Unbelievers from being burnt alive. Malkon is shot by one of Timanov's men but manages to relay to the Doctor that the Master is Kamelion. The Doctor confronts the android but the

Master manages to keep control and has the Doctor locked in the fire cave. Kamelion-Master and Peri then leave, and Turlough is able to release the Doctor. Turlough now thinks that Malkon is his brother.

With the assistance of Timanov and a group of Sarns, Kamelion-Master has the Master's TARDIS set upright. The android and Peri then enter the ship. The Doctor's intention to move his own TARDIS around the Master's is foiled as Kamelion has taken his temporal stabiliser. However, the navigational systems of the Doctor's TARDIS are locked onto the Master's ship. Kamelion-Master moves the Master's TARDIS to a seismic control room at the heart of the volcano, where he explains to a bemused Peri that numismaton gas is a rare catalytic reagent from inside the planet. Knocking Kamelion-Master over, Peri runs back into the Master's TARDIS, where she investigates a box which she assumes controls the android. Inside is a miniaturised Master and a control room.

The Doctor, realising that the fire-cave walls are coated with numismaton gas residue, re-diverts the gas there. When the flames burn blue, Malkon is taken into them and cured. The Doctor and Amyand go to the seismic control centre, while Turlough and Malkon place a distress call to Trion from the crashed spacecraft. Turlough reveals that the Misos Triangle denotes a prisoner – Sarn is where Trion prisoners are sent. He explains that there was civil war on his planet and his mother was killed. His father and brother were sent to Sarn, while he was sent to public school on Earth.

The Doctor and Amyand meet Peri in the hot, lava-runnelled wilderness and return with her to the cave. The Doctor takes the temporal stabiliser from the Master's TARDIS and sends Amyand to give it to Turlough. The Master reveals that his miniaturised state is due to an accident he suffered while building a more deadly version of his tissue compression eliminator. He revives Kamelion and, when the Doctor and Peri are distracted, the android moves the Master's TARDIS to the column of flame. Kamelion places the box containing the shrunken Master in front of his TARDIS. The Doctor and Peri disable Kamelion and, at the android's own request, the Doctor destroys it using the Master's eliminator weapon.

Amyand gives Turlough the component and he fits it into the TARDIS, which leaves of its own accord to follow the Master's ship.

The flame in the seismic control room turns blue and the Master grows to his normal size. However, the flame then turns back to orange and the Master vanishes in a puff of smoke, screaming in pain. As the control centre explodes, the Doctor and Peri leave in his newly-arrived TARDIS.

A Trion ship has arrived to ferry the survivors off the doomed planet. Turlough decides to go back to his home with the Trion Captain, Lomond (John Alkin), now that political prisoners are no longer persecuted. The Doctor bids him farewell.

Peri decides that she doesn't want to be returned home: she wants to travel and still has three months of her vacation left. The Doctor agrees that she can stay with him.

WHO FAX

- Novelised as *Doctor Who – Planet of Fire* by Peter Grimwade in 1984.

- Locations: all on the island of Lanzarote: Papagayo Beach and bay; Mirador del Rio (high observation point); quay and cafe at Orzola; Fire Mountain, Ridge, Asphalt Triangle, Cave of Doves, Valley of Tranquillity; Guides Cave, Steep Hill, high area near Camel Path, Volcano mouth, Yellow Area, Los Hornitos – all at Islote de Hilario, Montañas del Fuego.

- Working title: *Planet of Fear*.

- Part one features some stock music composed by J. Leach and 'From Other Lands No. 12' published by Music de Wolfe Ltd, and the track used is band seven, 'Zapateado', from side one, 'Spain'.

- Part three features a transparency of the Kouros Acropolis from the Sheridan Photo Library.

- Part four features stock footage of erupting volcanoes and lava from Movietone (33.5 seconds) and Visnews (5 seconds).

- Turlough's full name, rank and serial number are revealed as: Vizlor Turlough; Junior Ensign Commander; VTEC9/12/44.

- According to Peri's passport, she and Howard live on 45th Street, St Michelle, Pasadena, California. Her date of birth is 15 November, but the year is unreadable.
- The following beings were, according to Turlough, Trion agents keeping track of their prisoners: an agrarian commissioner on Vardon; a tax inspector on Derveg and – in Turlough's own case – an eccentric solicitor in Chancery Lane, London.

QUOTES

- 'Peter Grimwade was commissioned to write the story with a very heavy brief given to him first. He had to write out Turlough, introduce Peri, we wanted him to use the Master as villain and John Nathan-Turner wanted to use the Lanzarote location. For this we had long discussions on where we were going and where we thought we should go with the story. One thing we definitely aimed for was to tie up the loose ends of where Turlough had come from and where he was going. Peter had, of course, written Turlough's first story and it was fitting that he should write him out – albeit by a happy accident.' Script editor Eric Saward interviewed by Richard Marson for *Doctor Who Magazine* Issue 94, published in November 1984.

COMMENT

DJH: Another season and another overseas location, but this time the money is well spent. The use of the volcanic wastelands of Lanzarote as the desolate planet Sarn is inspired, and lends this story a believability missing from studio-bound adventures. As with other stories of this period, the brief presented to the writer was complex: Turlough and Kamelion must go, Peri must join and the story must have location work in Lanzarote. Peter Grimwade has done an admirable job of tying all these elements together although, once more, the major failing is the inclusion of the Master. Ainley is becoming decidedly trying and, as there is again no explanation as to how the character escaped after his previous encounter with the Doctor, the fact that he apparently burns to death at the end does not bother the viewer too much. Nicola Bryant is superb in her debut story, managing to present a companion with both independence and determination – something missing from the confident yet calm Turlough and the predictably sassy Tegan. An enjoyable yarn with a few faults. (7/10)

SJW: *As someone once observed,* Planet of Fire *is not so much a story as a series of explanations. Peri is introduced; the Master is brought back for a further return appearance; Kamelion is destroyed; Turlough's background is at last revealed; and finally Turlough is written out. Given all these prerequisites, however, and also that of the Lanzarote location, the end result achieved by writer Peter Grimwade is by no means as bad as it might have been. The plot involving the inhabitants of the volcanic planet Sarn is actually quite an interesting one even if, with all the other elements eating up screen time, it is rather less well developed than it might have been. The location filming in Lanzarote is also a lot more appropriate than was that in Amsterdam for* Arc of Infinity *– although it was perhaps a mistake to have it representing both Sarn and Lanzarote itself, as it is immediately obvious to the viewer that the sequences have all been shot in the same place. It is sad to see Turlough go, as he was definitely one of the best of the Doctor's companions, but Peri makes a very promising start. (6/10)*

The Caves of Androzani (6R)

EP	DATE	TIME	DURN	VIEWERS	CHART POS
1	08.03.84	18.41	24'33"	6.9	66
2	09.03.84	18.41	25'00"	6.6	75
3	15.03.84	18.42	24'36"	7.8	62
4	16.03.84	18.41	25'37"	7.8	62

Repeat (BBC2 – Chart Pos refers to BBC2 programmes only)

1	19.02.93	19.15	24'33"	2.1	27
2	26.02.93	19.15	25'00"	1.9	27
3	05.03.93	19.15	24'36"	1.8	outside top 30
4	12.03.93	19.15	25'37"	1.4	outside top 30

PRODUCTION DETAILS
Location Filming: 15.11.83–17.11.83
Studio Recording: 01.12.83–02.12.83 cancelled due to strike.
15.12.83–17.12.83. Remount on 11.01.84–12.01.84 in TC6

The TARDIS arrives on the planet Androzani Minor. Examining the ground, the Doctor finds traces of fused silica – evidence of a visiting spacecraft. He also points out to Peri a set of tracks leading to and from some nearby caves, which they then visit to investigate further.

Peri slips and falls into a strange sticky substance which makes her legs sting, and the Doctor helps her brush it off with his hands. Moving deeper into the caves, they find piles of weaponry belonging to gun runner Stotz (Maurice Roeves) and his hired hand Krelper (Roy Holder). They are captured by Captain Rones (unknown) who assumes they are gun runners and has them sent to General Chellak (Martin Cochrane).

The General uses a holographic communicator to report to Morgus (John Normington) back on Androzani Major. Morgus is the head of several conglomerate companies and is involved in funding the war against the gun runners. He seems concerned on learning that some gun runners have been caught, but when he sees the Doctor and Peri he orders that they be shot immediately, despite Chellak's feeling that they could be a source of useful information. Chellak has his aide Salateen (Robert Glenister) place the Doctor and Peri in detention.

Chellak's conversation with Morgus has been monitored by a black-garbed and masked figure who takes a fancy to Peri. He starts to assemble components in his laboratory and orders androids four and nine to join him.

Peri's legs and the Doctor's hands are coming out in blisters. The Doctor is suspicious of Morgus, and of Salateen. Someone enters their cell via a secret door.

Morgus receives the President (David Neal) in his office and gives him some spectrox – a drug that at least doubles the life span of humans. The war is holding up spectrox supplies and the President is considering offering an armistice to Sharaz Jek, the person responsible for it. Morgus is horrified.

On Androzani Minor, the Doctor and Peri are apparently executed by firing squad. However, they are revealed to be androids.

The real Doctor and Peri have been 'rescued' by the figure in black, Sharaz Jek (Christopher Gable). Although attentive to Peri, he is unstable and apparently insane with loathing for Morgus, whom he blames for all his problems. He declares he will stop the war only when he has Morgus's head delivered to him, and states that he has no intention of letting the Doctor and Peri go. Via his communication network, he knows everything that Chellak is planning and is confident that he can hold out for long enough against the army. The Doctor and Peri meet Salateen, who has been held captive for some time while one of Jek's androids takes his place at Chellak's side.

Salateen laughs when he realises that the Doctor and Peri have contracted spectrox toxæmia from touching raw spectrox – deposits from colonies of bats which live deep in the caves under Androzani Minor. The time travellers are experiencing cramp, which is the second stage of the illness. Salateen initially tells them that there is no cure but then admits that there is an antitoxin, discovered by Professor Jackij, which is found in the milk from a queen bat. Unfortunately all the bats have gone to the deep caves, which are devoid of oxygen and prowled by a vicious magma creature (Colin Taylor). Jek explains that he wears a mask because he was hideously burned when Morgus trapped him in a mud-burst; he was able to get to a baking chamber to escape the mud, but in the process was scalded nearly to death.

Jek goes to meet Stotz to argue over the amount of payment for the recent shipment of lost weapons. In his absence, the Doctor is able to disarm the guarding android as it is programmed to recognise humans and his anatomy is different. The Time Lord has decided to get the queen bat milk himself.

The Doctor is wounded when he, Salateen and Peri are attacked by an android while moving through the caves. Salateen hurries Peri off to General Chellak, and the Doctor then has a close encounter with the magma beast as it attacks Stotz's party, who have been trying to find Jek's private store of spectrox.

The Doctor is recaptured by Jek who uses his androids to torture him until he discloses where Peri is. Stotz wants to take the Doctor back with him to Androzani Major and Jek agrees. Meanwhile Chellak and Salateen are planing to feed Jek disinformation through the android Salateen and through broadcasts to Morgus regarding an attack on a fake location for Jek's base. In this way they hope to catch Jek unawares when they mount an attack on him in his true location.

Returning to his spacecraft, Stotz reports to his boss back on Androzani Major. It is Morgus. Morgus sees the Doctor on the ship and regards this as proof that the President must suspect him. He therefore kills the President by pushing him down a lift shaft and makes plans to travel to Androzani Minor to negotiate with Jek in person.

Stotz's ship takes off, but the Doctor manages to free himself and pilot it back to Androzani Minor.

Jek recaptures Peri who is by now very weak indeed. He raves about everything being Morgus's fault.

As the Doctor races across the surface of Androzani Minor, chased by Krelper and his men, Chellak and Salateen make their way towards Jek's base. Jek has not been fooled at all, however, and the troops are ambushed by his androids. Salateen is killed along with some of the troopers, but Chellak pushes on. Eruptions on the surface herald the start of a mud-burst and Krelper returns to the spaceship to find Stotz and Morgus in conversation. Krelper is sent away and Morgus offers Stotz a share of the spectrox. He intends to take Jek's private store of the drug and live on another planet in the Sirius system.

Jek's androids are being overrun by Chellak's men. Jek goes to see if any of them can be repaired, but he too runs into the troops. Chellak chases Jek back to his lab where the two men struggle. Jek's mask is pulled off and Chellak recoils in terror. The distraction allows Jek to push him outside into the path of a mud-burst, where he is killed.

Morgus calls his office and discovers to his horror that his secretary Timmin (Barbara Kinghorn) has taken control of his business – she is now Chairman and Chief Director of Sirius

Conglomerates and has given evidence against him. His empire is finished and all his funds have been sequestered. With Morgus no longer in a position of power, Krelper rebels. He wants to return to Androzani Major with the spectrox they already have. Stotz guns him down, along with the remaining gunrunner (Gerry O'Brien). He and Morgus then go to the cave system to try to find Jek's spectrox store.

Jek is mourning Peri, who is almost unconscious when the Doctor arrives. The Time Lord borrows an oxygen cylinder from Jek and tells him to keep Peri cool while he gets the bat's milk. While the Doctor is gone, Stotz and Morgus find Jek's lab. Jek throws himself at Morgus and forces his head into the path of a laser beam, killing him. Stotz shoots Jek but the android Salateen arrives and kills Stotz. As fire breaks out in the lab, Jek dies in the arms of the android Salateen. The Doctor returns with the milk in time to carry Peri out.

As the planet erupts around him, the Doctor gets back to the TARDIS and gives Peri the milk. She recovers quickly but there is none of the antidote left for the Doctor, who regenerates in order to save his own life.

WHO FAX
● Novelised as *Doctor Who – The Caves of Androzani* by Terrance Dicks in 1984.
● Working title: *Chain Reaction*.
● Story released on BBC Home Video in 1992.
● Locations: Masters Pit, Stokeford Heath, Gallows Hill, Wareham, Dorset.
● The closing title sequence for episode four features the face of the sixth Doctor.
● The regenerating Doctor sees and hears five companions – Tegan (Janet Fielding), Nyssa (Sarah Sutton), Adric (Matthew Waterhouse), Turlough (Mark Strickson) and Kamelion (Gerald Flood) – and also the Master (Anthony Ainley). These were specially recorded sequences rather than clips from previous episodes.
● When the Doctor is in the control room of Stotz's ship, he

apparently has a premonition of his coming regeneration when he sees the same patterns as those at the story's conclusion.

● 'John Peyre' is credited for 'design effects' on part four. This is a misspelling of the name of Jean Peyre, a Frenchman who created the matte paintings for the shots where the Doctor travels down to obtain the bat's milk.

QUOTES

● 'The regeneration idea emerged out of general discussion. Originally *The Caves of Androzani* was mainly about the two gunrunning elements of the plot, but as we went on the use of spectrox toxaemia to cause the regeneration seemed a good idea, and so it was used. I think Bob Holmes's story was excellent – I get along with him as a person tremendously well, his writing is so good and we have a lot in common.' Script editor Eric Saward interviewed by Richard Marson for *Doctor Who Magazine* Issue 94, published in November 1984.

● 'As the writer, of course, there were one or two little things that I missed that were in the script and that had been cut in the post-editing, presumably in order to bring the programmes in at the right length. I think the only one of these that mattered was a scene in the last episode where Sharaz Jek, attempting a last-ditch stand, called on any surviving androids to join him at the base. And the android Salateen (who had been sent out, you may remember, on a purposeless patrol) picked up this call in a distant cave and turned to answer his master's voice. . . Without this bit of preparation, I thought Salateen's sudden arrival at the base – where he bumped off Stotz – seemed rather providential. However, this is only a minor quibble and as I've had no complaints about it perhaps no one else noticed!' Writer Robert Holmes in a letter to David J. Howe, dated 25 March 1984.

COMMENT

DJH: It is a shame that this should be Peter Davison's last story as the Doctor, as it is also the best story of his era and one of the best Doctor Who *stories ever made. There is really nothing to criticise as the whole thing hangs together so well. The counter-pointing of John Normington's coldly evil Morgus with Christopher Gable's breathtaking performance as the unstable Sharaz Jek is a joy to behold. All the minor characters are believable and well cast, and the direction by newcomer Graeme Harper is inspired and dynamic. This is a true classic, a story that unfolds with human drama and tragedy, suspense and horror, and the best teaming of the Doctor and his companion ever seen.* Doctor Who *at its finest. (10/10)*

SJW: Robert Holmes has acquired a reputation as Doctor Who's *best writer, and with stories as strong as this one it is easy to see why.* The Caves of Androzani *is excellent drama, pure and simple, and is extremely well complemented by Graeme Harper's imaginative and stylish direction. The production is hard to fault, the only really negative aspect being the rather poorly realised magma monster. There are some excellent performances too, particularly from Christopher Gable as Sharaz Jek, and Peter Davison deserves a special mention for his best ever work as the Doctor. It is perhaps a little ironic that the fifth Doctor's era ends just as it really hits its peak. (9/10)*

STORIES: APPENDIX

The fifth Doctor has also appeared in one other production which, while not forming a part of the established *Doctor Who* canon, is detailed here.

Dimensions in Time

EP	DATE	TIME	DURN	VIEWERS	CHART POS
1	26.11.93	20.08	7'34"	13.8	15 *
2	27.11.93	19.23	5'27"	13.6	10 **

* = Shown as a part of the 1993 Children in Need appeal.
** = Shown as a part of *Noel's House Party*.

In both cases the Viewers figure is for the fifteen-minute segment of the programme containing the *Doctor Who* 'episode'. The Chart Pos is for the whole programme.

PRODUCTION DETAILS
Studio Recording: 21.09.93 at Fountain TV studios, New Malden, Surrey
Location/OB: 22.09.93–24.09.93

The Doctor (Jon Pertwee, Tom Baker, Peter Davison, Colin Baker, Sylvester McCoy) foils a dastardly scheme by renegade Time Lord chemist the Rani (Kate O'Mara), and in doing so frees his first two incarnations from her clutches.

WHO FAX
- This was a two-part skit produced for the BBC's annual *Children in Need* telethon.
- The story was made to be watched through special polarised filter glasses to achieve a 3-D effect.

COMMENT
Peter Davison is outstanding in his only return appearance as the fifth Doctor. However, despite its admittedly worthy charitable aims and the highly commendable efforts of the many contributors who gave their services free of charge, this remains a dreadful travesty of a Doctor Who *story. Fortunately, it is not generally regarded as part of the genuine* Doctor Who *canon. (0/10)*

4: Rewriting the Myth

Every era of *Doctor Who* brings new elements to the series' developing mythology. Story after story, new facts are invented by the scriptwriters and added to what is already known of the Doctor's universe. Some new pieces of this ever-growing jigsaw puzzle interlock neatly with what has gone before, while some fit so poorly that the viewer is forced to start rebuilding the picture from scratch. Many hard-core *Doctor Who* fans expend great amounts of time and energy trying to find an order that gives all the seemingly contradictory facts and stories some kind of logical continuity.

Plot continuity has always been a bug-bear of long-running television programmes. It could be argued that good continuity is essential in a popular soap opera for the sake of believability, but is it really so vital in a series such as *Doctor Who*? None of the three script editors who worked on the fifth Doctor's era regarded it as being of overriding importance, particularly where they felt that it would get in the way of telling a good, entertaining story. There was, however, a conscious effort made by the production team to avoid committing any really major errors; and indeed the series' mythology was drawn upon more heavily than ever before as a source of inspiration for new plot ideas and elements (see Chapter 6), giving rise to many continuity developments.

A number of new facts about the Doctor become apparent right from the outset. In *Castrovalva*, the transformation of his physical appearance leaves him suffering after-effects far more traumatic than any experienced by his three predecessors, leading him at one point to think that the regeneration is actually failing (no reason for this is ever given, but one explanation might lie in the severity of the injuries he sustained in the fall that triggered the process).

As with the regeneration of the first Doctor into the second, the mysterious process has affected not only the Doctor's body but also his clothes – his boots have metamorphosed into shoes, and his scarf is starting to unravel. He quickly decides to discard his old outfit altogether in favour of some period cricketing gear found near a pavilion-like room within the TARDIS. Later in the story he dons a pair of glasses to read; and in the following one, *Four to Doomsday*, he reveals that he is short-sighted in his right eye and carries a magnifying glass in his pocket.

Also in *Four to Doomsday*, the Time Lord is seen to be able to survive for several minutes in the freezing vacuum of space without the benefit of a pressure suit. It is, however, possible that the helmet-like apparatus that he is wearing to enable him to breathe is also generating some sort of a protective force field around him. Certainly the cricket ball that he throws during the course of his space walk behaves in a manner that would not normally be expected in the absence of any other forces.

The Doctor's improvised use of a cricket ball reinforces the impression given by his clothing that he has something of an affinity for the sport. This is confirmed a little later on, in *Black Orchid*, when he actually takes part in a match in 1920s England and gives a good all-round performance. As the fourth Doctor was also familiar with cricket (evidenced in stories such as *The Ark in Space* and *The Hand of Fear*) but the first was completely unaware of it (established in *The Daleks' Master Plan*), it might perhaps be logical to assume that the third was introduced to it during his period of exile on 20th-century Earth.

In the Buddhist-influenced *Kinda*, the Doctor appears unaffected by the Box of Jhana, a representation of the power of meditation, suggesting that he is already in touch with his inner self. In its sequel *Snakedance*, however, he is unable to find the 'still point' at the centre of his consciousness without the psychic aid of the elderly shaman Dojjen.

The Visitation sees the destruction by the Terileptil leader of the sonic screwdriver, a multipurpose tool introduced during the second Doctor's era in the story *Fury from the Deep*, moving the Time Lord to comment that he feels as if he has lost an old friend.

In *The Five Doctors*, the Doctor is taken ill and then starts to fade away altogether as his previous incarnations are taken out of time and space by the Time Lord President Borusa, causing him to reflect that, 'A man is the sum of his memories, you know – a Time Lord even more so.'

An ability to swim is revealed by the Doctor in *Warriors of the Deep*, when he is knocked into a water tank and forced to make his escape through a hatch beneath the surface. *The Caves of Androzani*, on the other hand, sees two weaknesses disclosed. First, the Doctor confides to his companion Peri that he is allergic to certain gases 'in the praxis range of the spectrum' – hence his habit of wearing a stick of celery on his lapel, as this will turn purple if exposed to the gases in question and so warn him of their presence, following which he will eat the celery. Secondly, he is seen to succumb to spectrox toxæmia after touching some strands of raw spectrox, a substance apparently peculiar to the planet Androzani Minor. It is this that ultimately causes him to regenerate once again, after he selflessly uses the last of the antidote to cure Peri of her similar affliction.

The Doctor's ship, the TARDIS, also gives up a few more of its secrets during this period of the series' history. *Castrovalva* involves the Doctor and his companions venturing into some previously unseen areas of its interior, including the pink-hued zero room – a tranquil environment shielded from all external influences (or supposedly so, at any rate, as an image of the Doctor's young male companion Adric is at one point projected inside). This room is part of the random 25 per cent of the ship's interior that the Doctor subsequently jettisons when he adjusts the architectural configuration circuits to provide the extra energy needed to pull the TARDIS clear of imminent destruction at Event One, the primordial hydrogen inrush towards which it has been directed by Adric under the Master's evil influence.

It is another of the Doctor's companions, Tegan, who discovers during the course of *Castrovalva* that the TARDIS has a computerised information system, accessible from the main control console. Although she is later disabused of the notion that she has succeeded in piloting the ship to *Castrovalva* by following instructions from this source, she does manage to initiate a short trip in the following story, *Four to Doomsday*, and proves quite proficient at operating the craft later on, most notably in *The King's Demons*.

In Season 20, *Mawdryn Undead* sees the TARDIS making an emergency landing inside a giant spacecraft after colliding with its warp ellipse field. The same story then brings a reminder of the series' past when the Doctor produces a TARDIS homing device first seen, although in a different form, in *The Chase* during the era of his first incarnation and also used by Adric in the fourth Doctor story *Full Circle*.

Terminus presents further problems for the Doctor when his young companion Turlough, coerced into sabotaging the TARDIS, operates some switches behind one of the wall roundels and then partially pulls out a piece of equipment called the space-time element from beneath the control console. The time rotor starts to jam, leaving the Doctor no option but to operate the cut-out. He then refocuses the scanner screen to show images of the ship's interior – another capability not previously displayed – and discovers that a wall of shimmering light is encroaching on its dimensions.

The TARDIS has, in fact, melded itself to a ship headed for the space station Terminus, and an interface soon appears in the form of a doorway in the TARDIS's laboratory area.

The Doctor completely refurbishes the TARDIS console at the start of *The Five Doctors*, but fails to cure it of its temperamental behaviour. In *Warriors of the Deep*, the ship is revealed to be susceptible to attack by energy weapons fired from a satellite orbiting the Earth around the year 2084, and the Doctor is forced to perform a materialisation flip-flop in order to remove it from the area of danger. Then, in *Frontios*, the possibility arises that the ship may actually have been destroyed by the power of a creature called the Gravis and his Tractator drones. In truth, however, it has become fragmented and interspersed with the rock of the eponymous planet's surface, and the Doctor is able to trick the Gravis into reassembling it. No sooner has this crisis been averted than, in *Resurrection of the Daleks*, the ship gets caught in a time corridor operated by his oldest adversaries. Finally, in *Planet of Fire*, the Doctor's short-lived android companion Kamelion resets the ship's destination co-ordinates by plugging himself into the data banks via one of the wall roundels, and Turlough performs some further minor sabotage by pulling out a number of wires from beneath the control console in order to cut off an incoming distress call.

Amongst a host of familiar characters returning to the series during the fifth Doctor's era is Brigadier Alistair Gordon Lethbridge-Stewart. He is first seen in *Mawdryn Undead*, working as a mathematics teacher at Brendon, a boys' public school, after his retirement in 1976 from service in the United Nations Intelligence Taskforce (UNIT). He suffers a nervous breakdown and loses his memory in 1977 as a result of the events of the story, but saves the day after the TARDIS takes him forward in time to 1983 where he meets his future self and, in so doing, inadvertently triggers a release of energy – the Blinovitch Limitation Effect (described in rather different terms in the third Doctor story *Day of the Daleks*) – that enables the Doctor to avoid the threatened loss of his remaining regenerations.

It is also mentioned at one point during *Mawdryn Undead* that the Brigadier's former subordinate Sergeant Benton left UNIT in 1979 and is now working as a used car salesman, and that the Doctor's one-time companion Harry Sullivan has been seconded to NATO and is now doing 'hush-hush' things at Porton Down. However, as the dates given in this story are completely at odds with those given during the fourth Doctor's era, from which it was clear that the Brigadier, Benton and Harry were all still serving in UNIT in the early 1980s, it may be that *Mawdryn Undead* takes place in a parallel universe (as did certain of the events of the third Doctor story *Inferno*). An alternative explanation would be that, for reasons unknown, a significant change has since occurred in the course of Earth's history.

The Brigadier's other appearance during the fifth Doctor's era comes in *The Five Doctors*. Here, he is attending a reunion at UNIT's British HQ, now under the command of his successor Colonel Crichton, when he encounters the second Doctor – who has for once been able to steer the TARDIS correctly, albeit at the expense of bending the Laws of Time – and is whisked off with him to the Time Lords' home planet Gallifrey. At the end of the story, the pair depart in what appears to be an offshoot of the fifth Doctor's TARDIS, presumably on their way to further, undisclosed adventures in time and space.

The Five Doctors sees also the return of the Doctor's other previous incarnations, along with his former companions Susan, Sarah Jane Smith, K-9 and the second Romana – not to mention phantom appearances by Jamie, Zoe, Liz Shaw and Captain Mike Yates of UNIT. The first Doctor and Susan and the third Doctor and Sarah also depart in their own respective offshoots of the fifth Doctor's TARDIS once the crisis is over, again heading for destinations unknown.

It is never stated from what points in their respective lives the Doctor's previous incarnations have been taken by the timescoop device used to transport them to Gallifrey. The fourth could easily have been abducted during the course of an untransmitted adventure from his own era. (In fact, the footage was culled from the abandoned Season 17 story *Shada*, although opinions differ as to whether or not this should be regarded as part of the true *Doctor Who* canon.) Where the first, second and third are concerned, however, this explanation would appear to be ruled out both by their appearance – they all look somewhat older than they did at the end of their own respective eras – and by their circumstances – they are all initially without companions, for instance, and at least two of the three appear to be aware of events that occurred at or after the point when they regenerated into their successors. Another apparent anomaly with regard to the second, third, fourth and fifth Doctors is that none of them has any recollection of having already experienced the events of the story in their previous lives.

Similar continuity problems arose in relation to the Season 10 story *The Three Doctors* (and would arise again in relation to the

Season 22 story *The Two Doctors*) and, although various different theories have been advanced by fans as possible solutions to them, it is perhaps safest to say simply that they remain unresolved within the fiction of the series itself.

A further point of note about *The Five Doctors* is that no energy release or other apparent adverse reaction occurs when the different incarnations of the Doctor meet up with one another. Although in line with the events of *The Three Doctors*, this appears on the face of it to be inconsistent with what happened when the Brigadier encountered his future self in *Mawdryn Undead*. It may be, however, that Time Lords are less affected by such temporal displacements than mere human beings (just as they are less affected by temporal disturbances, judging by events in the third Doctor stories *The Time Monster* and *Invasion of the Dinosaurs*).

The Five Doctors is just one of a number of stories in which the fifth Doctor encounters members of his own race. The Master, having recently taken over the body of Consul Tremas of the planet Traken, makes several return appearances, attempting to ensnare the Doctor in the sophisticated trap of Castrovalva (*Castrovalva*); to gain control of the awesome power of the alien Xeraphin (*Time-Flight*); to prevent the signing of the Magna Carta (*The King's Demons*); and to reverse the effects of an accident that has left him stranded in a miniaturised state on the planet Sarn (*Planet of Fire*). In *The Five Doctors* itself, the Master actually attempts to aid the Doctor – at the behest of the Time Lord High Council, who have promised him a whole new regeneration cycle in return – but is thwarted when his old opponent refuses to trust him.

Even more so than in the incarnation encountered by the third Doctor, the Master demonstrates a remarkable ability to disguise his normal saturnine features, taking on various false identities during the course of these stories. He also makes greater use than ever before of his trademark weapon, now referred to as a tissue compression eliminator, which reduces its victims to miniaturised corpses (as previously seen in the third Doctor story *Terror of the Autons* and in the fourth Doctor story *The Deadly Assassin*). One ability of which he makes rather less use than in the past, however, is that of hypnosis.

Arc of Infinity sees the return of another of the Doctor's old adversaries. This is Omega, the legendary stellar engineer whose work provided the Time Lords with the initial power that they needed to enable them to travel through space and time. In his introductory story, *The Three Doctors*, he was shown to be trapped in a universe of antimatter beyond a black hole, his physical body utterly destroyed and his existence preserved only by his enormous force of will. In *Arc of Infinity*, he makes a further attempt to escape back to his home universe, and again looks to the Doctor to act as the unwilling provider of the means for him to do so. Enlisting the aid of an Ergon servant (an energy creature presumably similar in nature to the Gelguards featured in *The Three Doctors*) and Councillor Hedin, a traitorous member of the Time Lord High Council who is apparently responsible for providing him with a TARDIS, he conspires to create a new corporeal form for himself by bonding with the Doctor's. The scheme fails, however, and Omega is apparently destroyed when the Doctor fires a matter converter at him.

The Doctor's old Time Lord teacher Borusa, first seen holding the rank of Cardinal in *The Deadly Assassin* and then that of Chancellor in *The Invasion of Time*, has gone one better and become President by the time *Arc of Infinity* takes place – all three stories featuring different incarnations of the character. Other Time Lords encountered during the course of this latest Gallifreyan sojourn include: Damon (an old friend of the Doctor's, although not previously seen in the series); Chancellor Thalia; the Castellan (either a different incarnation of the Time Lord who held that post in *The Invasion of Time* or a different Time Lord altogether); and the Chancellery Guard Commander Maxil (whose physical appearance is subsequently adopted by the Doctor when he regenerates into his sixth form in *The Caves of Androzani*).

Arc of Infinity also involves the Doctor visiting once more the virtual reality of the Matrix – the repository of all Time Lord knowledge – as previously featured in both *The Deadly Assassin* and *The Invasion of Time*. This occurs when, despite capital punishment having been long abandoned on Gallifrey, the Time Lord High Council make an unsuccessful attempt to have the Doctor vaporised in order to prevent Omega from succeeding in his plan.

President Borusa features again in *The Five Doctors* – again in a different incarnation – and it becomes clear as the story unfolds that he has now gone insane. It is he who is responsible for bringing all the Doctors and their companions together on Gallifrey, in an area known as the Death Zone. The grim history of this desolate place and of the Game that was played there is explained by the second Doctor as follows:

'In the days before Rassilon, my ancestors had tremendous powers – which they misused terribly. They set up this place, the Death Zone, and walled it around with an impenetrable force field. And then they kidnapped other beings and set them down here.'

At the centre of the Death Zone lies the Dark Tower – the tomb of Rassilon, 'the greatest single figure in Time Lord history'. Official Time Lord lore maintains that Rassilon was a good man, but the second Doctor recalls many rumours and legends to the contrary:

'Some say his fellow Time Lords rebelled against his cruelty and locked him in the Tower in eternal sleep.'

Later, it is revealed that Rassilon's consciousness does indeed live on within the Tower, although his body lies immobile on a bier, apparently in suspended animation. It transpires, however, that, in keeping with the official history, he is not a cruel tyrant but a wise and benevolent figure. He set up the Game of Rassilon as a trap for those, such as the deranged Borusa, who would seek immortality. These power-crazed individuals are given what they desire, but not in the way that they expect: they are turned into living statues along the side of Rassilon's bier.

The Castellan puts in a further appearance in *The Five Doctors*, but is killed after being falsely accused of treachery. The Chancellor is now a woman named Flavia, who at the end of the story invites the Doctor to return to the Capitol (which, like the planet itself, appears to be called Gallifrey) as President of the Time Lords. The Doctor, however, beats a hasty retreat in the TARDIS.

The Black Guardian and the White Guardian, introduced in the fourth Doctor's era as awesomely powerful opposing forces superior even to the Time Lords, are featured again in a trilogy of stories comprising *Mawdryn Undead*, *Terminus* and *Enlightenment*. The Black Guardian is determined to avenge himself against the Doctor after their earlier encounter and, unable to intervene directly in the affairs of the universe, co-opts Turlough as a reluctant pawn to bring about his destruction. Ultimately, however, when faced with the choice of handing over either the Doctor or a huge, glowing diamond that he has been offered by the Guardians, Turlough opts for the latter. The Black Guardian is apparently consumed in flames, but the White Guardian warns the Doctor to remain vigilant: 'As long as I exist, he exists also, until we are no longer needed.'

The fifth Doctor's era also sees the return of a number of monstrous alien races introduced in earlier periods of the series' history.

In *Earthshock*, a force of Cybermen under the command of a Cyber Leader is attempting to destroy an interstellar peace conference on Earth in the year 2526. As on a number of previous occasions, the creatures' appearance has quite significantly altered since they last crossed paths with the Doctor. This story also contains the first hint that they may now have acquired a limited time-travel capability. Not only do they have visual records of events that took place around the 29th century in the fourth Doctor story *Revenge of the Cybermen* (as well as of incidents in the first Doctor story *The Tenth Planet* and in the second Doctor story *The Wheel in Space*), but one of their devices causes a spaceship to travel back in time after it is tampered with by the Doctor's companion Adric. Another innovation is their use of two deadly androids to guard a powerful bomb that they have concealed on Earth. The Doctor eventually thwarts the Cybermen's plans, in part by exploiting the fact that, as established in *Revenge of the Cybermen*, gold dust is lethal to them when forced into their chest unit breathing apparatus.

The Doctor's oldest foes, the Daleks, are back in action in *Resurrection of the Daleks*, attempting to free Davros from imprisonment on board a military space station orbiting the Earth. They have lost their long war against the android Movellans – as seen in the fourth Doctor story *Destiny of the Daleks* – and hope that their creator will be able to find a cure for the deadly virus created by their enemies that is wiping them out. They also aim to usurp the power of the Time Lords by infiltrating Gallifrey with android duplicates of the Doctor and his companions. Davros, however, has plans of his own, and begins to inject the Daleks with a substance that makes them subservient to his will. This second faction of Daleks then comes into conflict with the one still loyal to the Dalek Supreme (making its first appearance in the series since the third Doctor story *Planet of the Daleks*), although in the end, both groups are wiped out when the Doctor releases some of the Movellan virus. Davros, although himself affected by the virus, apparently reaches the safety of an escape pod.

The Five Doctors features a Dalek, a force of Cybermen and also, from the second Doctor's era, a Yeti (which, judging from its appearance, is a real creature from Tibet, as seen at the end of *The Abominable Snowmen*, rather than one of the Great Intelligence's controlled robots). These creatures have all been transported to the Death Zone on Gallifrey as part of Borusa's scheme, but little new information is revealed about any of them on this occasion.

The Silurians and a force of Sea Devil warriors – survivors of the reptilian species that ruled the Earth before the rise of humankind – attempt to take over an underwater nuclear weapons facility around the year 2084 in *Warriors of the Deep*. Unlike in *Doctor Who and the Silurians* and *The Sea Devils* – the third Doctor stories that gave them their respective debuts – the creatures are this time identified by individual names: the Silurians are led by Icthar, Scibus and Tarpok, while the Sea Devils are commanded by Sauvix. Icthar is described as being the last surviving member of the Silurian Triad and is already known to the Doctor, indicating that there must have been an earlier, untelevised encounter between them. Like the Cybermen in *Earthshock*, both the Silurians and the Sea Devils have undergone a number of changes since their races last appeared in the series. The Silurians' third eyes – which previously acted as weapons and tools – now flash in synchronisation with their voices when they speak, and their voices are themselves completely unlike those heard in *Doctor Who and the Silurians*. In the Sea Devils' case, however, the changes are confined to their clothing: they now wear Samurai-style armour instead of the blue mesh garments seen in *The Sea Devils*. Other new developments in *Warriors of the Deep* include the Silurians' use of a huge amphibious cyborg, the Myrka, to attack the humans' base, and the revelation that exposure to hexachromite gas is lethal to all reptiles.

Many new characters and monsters are introduced during the fifth Doctor's era, but few go on to make return visits. The Terileptils, for instance, appear only in *The Visitation* (although they do subsequently receive one further mention, in *The Awakening*, when the Doctor explains that – as indicated in the earlier story – they mine a substance called tinclavic on the planet Raaga, and also a cameo in *Time-Flight*). One exception to the rule is Lytton, an alien mercenary seen assisting the Daleks in *Resurrection of the Daleks*, who turns up again in a sixth Doctor story, *Attack of the Cybermen*. Another is the Mara, which also features in two stories: *Kinda* and *Snakedance*. As explained in *Snakedance*, this evil intelligence, which manifests itself in the form of a snake, originated on the planet Manussa. The Manussan scientists had used molecular engineering to produce a Great Crystal attuned to the wavelength of the human mind and able to absorb its energy; only the evil aspects were absorbed, however, and when amplified and reflected by the Crystal these brought into being the entity that became known as the Mara.

Significant though the many continuity developments were during the era of the fifth Doctor, they would be equalled and indeed surpassed during that of his successor, when the series would come to rely ever more heavily on the rich heritage of its own mythology.

PART THREE – FACT

5: Script Editing

It was in early 1963 that the BBC's then Head of Drama Sydney Newman – one of the creators of *Doctor Who* – set up within the Drama Group a system of production teams, each of which would be responsible for making a particular series, serial or strand of plays. Following the precedent already established in many of the ITV companies, these teams would consist of two permanent staff members, namely a producer and a story editor, along with secretarial support. The producer would be given overall artistic, administrative and financial control of the production, overseeing the work of the different directors who would be brought in to handle individual episodes or programmes, while the relatively junior story editor would have the task of finding and working with freelance writers to come up with the required scripts – a function previously performed by the now-defunct Script Department.

The story editor's role was described in more detail by Drama Group Organiser Ayton Whitaker in a loose-leaf Editors' Guide produced in October 1968 for internal use within the BBC:

> The primary function of the editor is to find, encourage and commission new writers. He should concern himself with the details of television scripts so that his producer's horizon can be kept clear. The editor is the writer's representative in the Television Service and is responsible for looking after the writer's interests right through to the time of production. While encouraging writers to practise their art with as much freedom

as possible, it is yet the editor's job to guide them on matters of television grammar and the necessary disciplines of the Service, e.g. timing, number of sets, size of cast, amount of film which can reasonably be used...

The Guide also set out and codified other aspects of the editor's duties, including the need to follow policy guidance on questions of sex, violence and bad language. It went on:

The principles underlying editorial control are based deeply on the assumption that the finding and encouraging of all those creative and wayward and surprising talents that go into making television programmes is a major part of the Corporation's responsibility to the public. But, as every truly professional writer will be aware, it is from the disciplining of creative talent, not from its reckless indulgence, that true art emerges.

Other matters covered in the Guide were: checking names in scripts (e.g. to ensure that they could not be misconstrued as referring to real-life people); preparing scripts for typing; keeping track of amendments; and using the services of the Drama Script Unit (the vestigial successor to the old Script Department) in areas such as copyright, briefing procedures, contractual agreements and staff contributions. Also included were a number of articles written by current story editors, explaining how they saw their own jobs in practical terms.

By the early 1980s, most editors were freelancers working on fixed-term contracts rather than permanent members of the BBC's staff. Little else had changed, however. The Guide was still in use – albeit revised and updated, taking into account, amongst other things, the switch of formal job title from story editor to script editor that had been instituted in June 1968 – and the basic functions of the job were still essentially the same as they had been back in 1963.

Three different script editors had an influence over the stories of the fifth Doctor. The first was Christopher Hamilton Bidmead, who worked on Tom Baker's last season – Season 18 – and played a major part in setting up Peter Davison's first – Season 19. Having initially studied acting at the Royal Academy of Dramatic Art, Bidmead had since earned his living as a radio and television writer and as a journalist specialising in scientific and technical articles. He had been offered the *Doctor Who* post after being recommended by one of the series' former writers, Robert Banks Stewart, and had decided to accept it after being assured by producer John Nathan-Turner and executive producer Barry Letts that they disliked as much as he did the humorous, fantasy-orientated style that had been favoured by the previous production team.

'So often in the past,' noted Bidmead in an interview with Richard Marson for a 1986 edition of *Doctor Who Magazine*, 'it had been a case of the Doctor effectively waving a magic wand, which amounted to teaching children that the scientific way of looking at things was nonsense. It was a sort of infusion of late sixties hippie ideas that derived from Third World cultures, which had sort of filtered its way down into *Doctor Who*. Now, John liked the idea that it was going to be as different from the previous era as possible. In other words, I got the job on the premise that we would go back to basics.'

Bidmead enjoyed the challenge of taking the series in a new direction but found the job a very gruelling one, and it was this that ultimately resulted in him spending only a year on the production team.

'About 70 per cent of Season 18 was written by me, in two senses. One was quite legitimate: as script editor I would have brainstorming sessions with each of the writers, and there I would contribute at least half the ideas. The slightly less rewarding side of the job was that far too often writers would come back and, for a variety of reasons, they would fail to achieve what was required and I would end up working far into the night writing stuff myself. Part of the reason for this was my own failure to communicate to them what was needed; part was that they went away in such a frenzy of enthusiasm that ideas would expand beyond our original strictures. It was also partly through lack of experience. I had to attempt to get writers to hammer the stories back into shape, but we needed to feed the juggernaut of the production schedule, so more often than not I'd have to do it myself.

'I think the script editor has an impossible job, which is indirectly why I left: I mean, I wanted to stay on, but I also wanted the BBC to pay me the sort of money that recognised the kind of effort I was putting into the show. The BBC didn't feel able to do that, so I left. I think you get what you pay for, and subsequent script editors quite rightly didn't have the time to devote to scripts that fans often rightly criticise.'

Before his departure, Bidmead was heavily involved in discussions with Nathan-Turner about the characterisation of the fifth Doctor and about other aspects of the nineteenth season, for which he commissioned a number of stories. He had by this point prepared a revised format document headed '*Doctor Who*: Notes for New Writers', which was sent out to all prospective writers. The document was updated from time to time to reflect new developments, but its basic contents remained unchanged. The version dated 14 November 1980 began with the following general summary of the series' requirements:

THE NATURE OF THE SHOW

What we're looking for from new writers are not complete scripts or even involved scenarios, but fresh and readably presented (i.e. brief) storylines.

We're interested in plots that rise convincingly out of characterisation and well-thought-out situations; in particular, storylines should indicate how the idea fits into the four episode shape in which we (usually) serialise our stories. An example, not intended to be definitive, might be: 1. Exposition, 2. Complication Leading to Crisis, 3. The Real Situation Exposed, Revealing the Awful Truth, 4. The DOCTOR Battles Against the Odds But Finally Wins Through.

This kind of thinking gives rise and fall to the narrative, and should throw up strong cliffhangers in which characters are forced to deal with changing situations, as opposed to the *ad hoc* 'in one bound our hero is free' variety.

There is no *DOCTOR WHO* formula, but experience shows

that the format allows for three main kinds of story:

a. Space Fiction

Recently the programme has been developing a more solid science-fiction basis, and while we feel this is probably a welcome change we're anxious to avoid importing wholesale the familiar clichés of the genre. Of course it's impossible to avoid the sci-fi icons – exploding supernovae, menacing robots and so forth – but they need to be as far as possible rethought into our unique context.

b. Earth-Bound

The appeal of an Earth-bound story is that it gives both the team and the viewers an opportunity to get out on location for a breath of fresh air. But filming is very expensive, and night filming, immensely appealing though it is as a device to wind up the tension, is almost completely outside the scope of our budget. Writers should try to keep all filming to no more than fifteen minutes in a 100-minute story.

c. Historical

These are probably the most difficult to handle, and new writers are recommended to avoid the genre unless they are particularly sure of their ground. Many new writers seem drawn to Kitsch-History themes (Doctor Who meets Machiavelli), but the result is usually an unhappy pot-pourri of fact and fantasy.

It's a well-understood convention that a Time-Travelling Hero does not change history; additionally we tend to shy away from the sort of story that 'reveals' that the truth about a particular historical event is different from what we always thought it to be. Thus, unless very carefully handled, a story based on the idea that the First World War was actually triggered off by refugees from a *coup d'etat* on the planet Zorrella, is not going to appeal to us.

Having said this, we are in the business of transmitting 'Science Fiction Adventure Stories', and this element mustn't be overlooked.

The adventures of a time-travelling renegade Time Lord are of course built on a premise of wildest fantasy. But without inhibiting creative ideas, we'd prefer writers to work within this concept in a way that acknowledges the appropriate disciplines. Charged Particle Physics (to pick a topic at random) is mapped territory accessible to many of our viewers (there are *Doctor Who* Appreciation Societies in universities all over the world); and writers who want to bring the topic into the story should at least glance at the relevant pages of the encyclopedia. History of course deserves similar treatment. Imaginative extrapolation of 'the facts' should be preferred to pure gobbledegook.

I should add that having the DOCTOR go back in time to do a fix that solves the problem by not allowing it to arise is a favourite storyline idea we've had to outlaw. If recursive solutions are allowable, our audience will ask why the DOCTOR doesn't always do this, and there'll never be any adventure.

A WORD ON PRESENTATION

Putting characters' names in CAPITALS makes it considerably easier for the reader to track back on plot. Double spacing with proper margins also improves readability. Four pages should be adequate to put across the essence of the idea you want to sell us. I've already suggested that storylines should show clearly how the material fits into the four-part format; but it's sometimes helpful to lead off with a short preface that sets out the premise on which the story is based.

FINALLY

Notes on the DOCTOR, his current companions and the TARDIS follow.

I'm appending a copy of the Introduction to the US edition of a recent *Doctor Who* novel. While it doesn't necessarily represent our official line in all respects, it does give a good overview of what the show is all about.

I'm also enclosing extracts from 'Guide to *Doctor Who* Storylines', written by Douglas Adams when he was script editor of this programme. I think he makes some good points.

Storylines you send in will be warmly welcomed and read. It's always helpful if the writer can include some brief details about his writing history and aspirations. Obviously previous television writing experience is a valuable asset, but we have in the past produced a number of scripts written by newcomers to the medium. A useful book to put you in the picture is *Writing for Television* by Malcolm Hulke (another former *Doctor Who* script editor [sic]), published by A. & C. Black.

We'll acknowledge all submissions as soon as we can – though experience shows that due to our heavy production schedule our replies are often far from instantaneous. How we proceed from there will obviously depend on the quality and suitability of the ideas submitted.

The US-derived attachment mentioned by Bidmead had in fact appeared as the introduction to all the editions of the Target *Doctor Who* novelisations issued in that country by Pinnacle Books. Written by well-known science fiction author Harlan Ellison, it explained why he considered *Doctor Who* to be the greatest science fiction series of all time.

The appended extract from Douglas Adams's earlier document, headed 'The Script Editor's Guide to *Doctor Who* Storylines', read as follows:

* Brevity is the soul of storylines.

We don't want to plough through 20 pages of closely-typed prose trying to work out what the story is about. At the initial stage of story ideas, we just want to know what the idea is, how it resolves, and whether it promises sufficient areas of conflict to sustain a hundred minutes of tension and drama. If that takes more than two or three pages then the idea hasn't been thought out well enough. There is absolutely no point in working out all the complicated details of the plot mechanics – who is running after whom at what time and with which monkey wrench – until the basic plot concepts have been properly hammered out.

A script writer is basically in the business of selling his ideas. Imagine the reaction of a harassed script editor faced on the one hand with a very lengthy and detailed exposition of a complicated plotline that he can't fully understand on one reading, and on the other hand with a short, pithy idea that is irresistibly concise.

* Daleks

Don't bother to submit stories involving Daleks. Terry Nation invented the beasts, he owns the copyright, and quite properly reserves the right to write Dalek stories himself. In fact the copyright in all monsters and characters is owned by the writer who invented them. It's far better to invent your own.

* Whose Story?

This point seems almost too obvious to mention, but it's surprising how often we get storylines which are quite clearly based on previous *Doctor Who* stories, or at least elements of them.

Obviously it's terribly difficult to be thoroughly original after a hundred stories, but no one ever said that writing *Doctor Who* isn't terribly difficult.

I'm writing these notes on the assumption that most people who submit storylines are seriously interested in tackling the very tough professional job of writing for the programme.

It was not a new writer but Bidmead himself who became responsible for writing the fifth Doctor's introductory adventure when the story originally planned for that slot – *Project Zeta-Sigma* by John Flanagan and Andrew McCulloch – fell through at a late stage.

'With *Castrovalva*,' he noted in his *Doctor Who Magazine*

interview, 'it was super to start off a new Doctor. It was written at short notice, because another script had fallen through and it was quite a slow burn. They weren't quite sure how Davison was going to work out, and I was asked to write the script accordingly.'

Following his departure from *Doctor Who*, Bidmead resumed his career as a freelance writer. His successor on the series' production team was Antony Root. Root, unlike Bidmead, was not himself a writer.

'I don't write,' he told Philip Newman in an interview for a 1992 issue of *The Frame*. 'I never write scripts. I suppose I'm one of those old-fashioned script editors who believes that script editors are sometimes better when they don't write, because what they're actually doing is, like a publishing editor, trying to get the best work out of other people; helping them achieve what they want to do. I know *Doctor Who* has a tradition of writer/script editors, but I was not one of those people.

'After I left university, I worked in live theatre for five years, initially as a theatre manager and then as a publicist.

'Then, at age 25, I decided that I didn't want to stay in live theatre any longer and got a holiday relief job for three months as an assistant floor manager with the BBC. I suppose that must have been in the summer of 1979 – and, funnily enough, the show I did was a four-part *Doctor Who* directed by Ken Grieve [*Destiny of the Daleks*]. At the end of that holiday relief period, they advertised some permanent positions. I applied, and became a fully-fledged assistant floor manager, a job I did for about 18 months to two years I guess. After that, I started an internal training course as a script editor and subsequently went on to do programmes.

'What happened was that I went to Graeme McDonald, the person who was then Head of Series and Serials, and asked him what the opportunities were. He gave me some advice which led me to approach the TV Drama Script Unit, where I got what was called a "training attachment" as a script editor. This involved a period of time – about three months, I think – at the Script Unit followed by a spell back in the Drama Series and Serials Department as a trainee.

'At the end of my time at the Script Unit, Chris Bidmead

decided to leave *Doctor Who* and they needed someone to plug the script editor job for a limited period while they found a replacement. I arrived back with perfect timing and was asked if I would do it – which, of course, I did.'

'Root was only meant to be temporary,' explained Bidmead. 'I was getting increasingly bogged down with unsolicited scripts and he was working at the Drama Script Unit, where I used to send stuff. He knocked me out by coming back with a beautifully argued, well condensed report on one of the scripts. That was how he came to my attention.'

'Oh yes,' agreed Root. 'It was always going to be temporary. I don't think I commissioned any new work; I inherited a lot of it. I think I was around for about two stories with John Nathan-Turner.'

Root had followed *Doctor Who* since childhood, and remembered hiding behind the sofa to watch stories of the first Doctor's era. It was partly because of the series' long history that he ultimately found the process of working on it a somewhat trying one.

'It was one of the worst jobs I could imagine a script editor having to do, because the weight of history was so great that it was actually totally stultifying. I was used to working to a fairly broad brief about what one might do in a script and I was very excited about the possibilities of doing almost any story one could envisage and shaping it within the mould of *Doctor Who*. But then, within 24 hours of arriving there, I was introduced to the *Doctor Who* mail, which would often come to the script editor to advise on what the reply should be. You know, you would look at 50 letters which said something like, "Sprodget No 5 in the TARDIS cannot be pressed to do the function that you think it can!" It seemed to me that the weight of history wasn't working to the show's benefit. So I approached it with great hopes but found it an extremely difficult thing to engage with.

'John Nathan-Turner had seen out Tom Baker and was seeing in Peter Davison, whom he knew extremely well from having been production associate on *All Creatures Great and Small*. I think that any difficulties were to do not with the casting but with the usual thing in TV series, like, "The production starts shooting in three weeks' time – which script are we going to do?" But Barry

Letts was executive producer at that time, so he was always there to turn to.

'I remember I spent a lot of time with Eric Saward on his Great Fire of London story [*The Visitation*], though I don't know that I made any real contribution to it. The other story I remember, with great affection, was written by somebody called Christopher Bailey and entitled *Kinda*. I thought that was really a very interesting script indeed, because it had shades of Buddhist philosophies as well as being quite entertaining on the surface. I have vague memories of the first one we did [*Four to Doomsday*], by Terence Dudley, and another about a cricket match set in the 1920s [*Black Orchid*], but that one was done mostly after I'd gone.

'My job at the time was basically to firefight and to make sure that there were scripts ready to achieve the production schedule that was set. It was a very, very intense time of sleepless nights – I do remember that. I felt like I'd been thrown in right at the deep end. But, as always with script editing, it was about delivering up to directors and production crews, on the day they were meant to start, material they could use that fitted the brief. And obviously I wasn't working solo, but with John Nathan-Turner on that.

'My attachment expired at the end of the *Doctor Who* period and I was told that I would have to go back to being an AFM because, after all, that was technically what I was, as far as the staffing of the BBC was concerned. I said that I didn't want to do that and that I would be leaving the BBC if that had to be – although I understood the reasons why, if it did. A couple of days went by and then they called me in and asked if I'd like to work on *Juliet Bravo*. So I went and worked on that for a season under Joan Clark, who was the doyenne of series script editors. I then went on with the same producer, Terry Williams, to do the second series of *The Chinese Detective*. Following that I worked for a couple of years on various things as script editor to a former *Doctor Who* producer, Philip Hinchcliffe. I finally left the BBC in 1984 to go to Euston Films, where I'd been offered a job as their script editor.'

At Euston, Root worked as script editor and script executive on a number of programmes, including a five-part gangster series called *Fear* which he also co-produced. A few years later he moved to a company called Working Title, where he continued to serve as a producer on such projects as *Newshounds* (a co-production with the BBC), *Lorna Doone* (a co-production with Thames) and the acclaimed Derek Jarman film *Edward II*. Today he continues to pursue a career in film and television production, having always seen script editing as simply a means to that end.

Root's successor on *Doctor Who* was Eric Saward, the writer commissioned by Bidmead to script the pseudo-historical story *The Visitation*. Born in December 1944, Saward had attended grammar school until the age of 18 and then some time afterwards moved to Holland, where he had lived for three years and been briefly married. On his return to England, he had trained and worked for a short time as an English teacher.

'I had started writing by that stage,' he recalled in a 1993 interview, 'and I decided that I didn't like teaching – in fact, the only reason I had gone into it was that there were long holidays and I could spend my time writing, which was what I really wanted to do. I had just started to sell scripts to radio on a fairly regular basis – always drama – and as I had no family commitments I decided to have a go at being a full-time freelance writer. I had nothing to lose.

'I was about 30 then, and I always managed to stay afloat through one thing or another. I picked up the odd job. I worked in the theatre briefly as a self-taught electrician, including on *Hair* and *The Canterbury Tales* at the Phoenix in Shaftesbury Avenue. I bobbed along like that for a while, and then became involved with *Doctor Who*. Chris Bidmead approached the senior drama script editor at BBC radio and asked – quite boldly – if he could recommend anybody to write for the series. I was doing very well in radio and so, along with a few others, I was recommended.

'Chris rang me up and asked if I would be interested, and I said "Why not?". I hadn't watched *Doctor Who* in years, so I really didn't know what I was letting myself in for.

'I wrote a storyline, *The Visitation*, which John Nathan-Turner disliked as one of the characters was an actor – John had a thing about not showing actors on television. That was around the March of 1980, I think, and my reaction was, "Well, that's it, I'll just get on with my life." Then, around the September, Chris rang up and said, "Do you remember that storyline you wrote, that John didn't like? Would you like to do us a scene breakdown?" I was initially inclined to refuse, but Chris said that they would pay me a fee, which I think was about £400, and as I needed the money I agreed to do it. He liked what I came up with, and I think that by that stage they really had to go with it as they needed to fill a slot in the production schedule. I delivered the full scripts about eight weeks later, in January 1981, and that's how I got started in television.'

It was shortly after this that Saward was invited to join the *Doctor Who* production team.

'I went there originally for three months. Antony Root had been working on the series, but unfortunately knew very little about putting scripts together. That's not deriding him; he was just inexperienced. Even after he had done three months on *Doctor Who*, the powers-that-be still wanted him to do something else before they would offer him a staff script editor post – this was how the BBC viewed *Doctor Who*, which in my own view was the most difficult assignment anyone could be given. So Antony went to work on *Juliet Bravo* and then on *The Chinese Detective*, where I gather that he had a really horrible time as it was written by the very distinguished Ian Kennedy Martin and the producer, Terry Williams, didn't want his star writer to be criticised at all.

'Anyway, there was a lot of humming and hawing, and they kept extending my contract by a month at a time as they didn't know if Antony was going to be coming back to *Doctor Who* or what was going to be happening. We had this messing around for about three months, which was really very aggravating. In the meantime I had written *Earthshock*, which went more or less immediately into production. Eventually they decided that I would be staying, and I was then given a nine-month contract.'

Like Root, Saward sometimes found himself at odds with the series' fans.

'I remember that when we killed Adric in *Earthshock*, we had just a short scene at the beginning of the next story, *Time-Flight*, where the Doctor was sort of in mourning. This brought a tremendous outcry from the fans. People were saying: "Oh God, he should have been in mourning throughout the whole story, and the next one as well." Well no, sorry, it doesn't work like that! *Doctor Who* is about the Doctor going off and having adventures. The dramatic impact of Adric dying had been had at the end of *Earthshock*, and that was it. As in life, you move on.'

On questions of continuity, too, Saward felt that many fans were often overly pedantic, devoting their time to picking up small contradictions in the scripts rather than simply enjoying them as entertaining stories.

'You've got an audience with the fans, you see, who know infinitely more about the series than any person working on it can or perhaps even wants to. That accumulation of knowledge can get in the way of telling a good story; you're so busy trying to get the continuity right that the story goes down the tubes.'

Saward was, however, keen to avoid making any really major continuity errors, and so he – like Nathan-Turner – occasionally sought advice on these matters from prominent fans such as Ian Levine.

'Ian Levine did a hell of a lot of work during that time, all uncredited. I mean, all the clips that were needed for flashback sequences, he sorted them out all in his own time and without payment. He was very, very useful when it came to continuity. I turned to him lots of times, especially when we were using established things like Daleks and Cybermen. We still made loads of mistakes – for which I don't apologise, as there was never any strict continuity on the series – but we tried not to counter massively what had been previously established. So we didn't suddenly have Cybermen who could fly, for example.'

Another aspect of the script editor's job is to check and approve any changes that cast members or directors want to make to scripts during the course of production.

'You don't sit in your office like some demon king, saying: "You can't do this," or "You can't do that," to directors. On the other hand, the script editor is obliged to safeguard the rights of the writers – it's in the agreement that the BBC has with the Writers' Guild. Also, he's an independent person in the sense that he's outside the production of the particular story – he's not at rehearsals all the time. Changes will come out of enthusiasm as much as anything else. I was always very strict about any changes that affected the plot, because if it hadn't made sense when it was all cut together then I was the one who was going to be hounded down the corridors by people demanding to know why I had agreed to changes that had ended up ruining it.

'A director is hired to interpret a story, not to rewrite it. In the same way, actors are booked to appear in it, not to rearrange it. If someone comes up with a brilliant line, though, then obviously it's not going to be refused. Lines will also get dropped, because action takes over or because an actor needs only an expression to convey something to the audience.'

Although vigilant about changes being made to scripts after they had been finalised and agreed with the writer, Saward found that – like Bidmead before him – he was often having to carry out a considerable amount of rewriting himself before that stage was actually reached.

'Script editors are a blessing and a curse. I worked for a long time in radio – I still do – and the fact is that, in that medium, what you write is what goes out. I mean, the director will talk to you, if he or she is a little concerned about something, but it's like in the theatre where the writer is viewed as being a little more important than in television series. I think that's a mistaken attitude on the part of television. If you've got lousy writers you've got lousy shows; that's always been so and always will be so. On shows where there is a well known writer – someone like Andrew Davies, for example – I assume that the script editor just makes the tea, because you ain't gonna be playing with his scripts without an awful lot of discussion and an awful lot of reasons why you want to change things. To my mind that's absolutely right, and most writers will respond to that sort of treatment. I mean, if they know the thing is all right, why the hell should they change it? On a lot of shows, that works. You don't have script editors rewriting or wanting to change the scripts.

'My attitude towards script editing was that what the writer wrote ought to be, wherever possible, what was produced. But

Doctor Who is one of those old-fashioned shows which is very difficult to write. It requires strong characterisation, strong stories, action, humour, adventure, thrills; the whole gamut. Other shows like *Casualty*, for example, simply aren't that demanding. I'm not knocking *Casualty*, but it's got a stock setting, stock characters and stock situations. The writers just have to weld on their own idea: a road accident, a schizophrenic on the run with a meat axe, or whatever. Half the work is done for them, because they are using the established elements. In *Doctor Who*, the only ongoing characters are the Doctor and the companion. The rest, the writers have to invent for themselves.

'The problem is that modern television writing makes writers very lazy. Up-and-coming writers are used on soaps like *EastEnders*, which have stock characters, and on shows like *Casualty*, which require, to my mind, a limited amount of characterisation and plotting. My experience – and I tried many, many different writers – was that a lot of them just couldn't characterise to the standard that was wanted. Their imagination wasn't developed sufficiently. I mean, imagination is not a gift one is given at birth; it's something that can be developed. The more one works at it, the stronger it becomes. And a lot of writers never have that opportunity. The reason so much rewriting went on by me and by my predecessors was that it was very hard to find people who could do it well.

'Another problem was getting writers to work within the constraints of what could be achieved on our budget. The first hour of my discussion with any writer would always be about the technical limitations: what could be done, what couldn't be done, the number of sets we could have, the number of talking parts. I mean, we would always try to do whatever the writer wanted, but I would have to say things like, "Never give a creature tentacles, because we can't manage that." There were certain things we just couldn't do, because we didn't have the money or the time. The writers had to be realistic about what could be achieved. I assume that Terrance Dicks, Douglas Adams, Christopher Bidmead and all the other script editors down the decades must have said very similar things to their writers, because it's pointless sending a writer away to write something and then finding out that it can't be done.

'I still carry the *Doctor Who* burden, because whenever I write something I'm always careful about the number of sets I have. I'm always thinking: "Am I justifying the use of this set?" It's good training from that point of view, because one can easily go into fantasy land and have a set for this, a set for that and so on, and it'll never happen because television just doesn't work like that.'

Saward would generally have three different types of writer in mind when planning each new season: those who had already established a good track record on the series; those who were successful in other fields but had not previously worked on *Doctor Who*; and those who were complete or relative newcomers to television.

'I never drew lines about choosing scripts – there was no prescribed mix between established writers and new ones. I would always use new talent if I could – it was a BBC policy – but at the same time I obviously wanted to go back to writers who had done good work for me in the past. Most of the time it was a case of writers coming to us with original ideas. Occasionally they would come with a thought rather than a fully worked out idea, and then it would be a matter for discussion. And as with any discussion, the original concept would often change drastically.'

A notable feature of the fifth Doctor's era was that more ultimately unused material was commissioned than during any other equivalent period of the series' history. This included the following:

Title	Writer	Commission	Date
Mark of Lumos*	Keith Miles	Storyline	14/03/80
Mouth of Grath*	Malcolm Edwards and Leroy Kettle	Breakdown	18/03/80
Farer Nohan*	Andrew Stephenson	Breakdown	18/03/80
The Dogs of Darkness*	Jack Gardner	Breakdown	29/03/80
		Scripts	11/08/80
Soldar and the Plastoids	John Bennett	Breakdown	10/04/80

Psychrons	Terence Greer	Breakdown	13/06/80
Project '4G' (aka Project Zeta-Sigma)	John Flanagan and Andrew McCulloch	Breakdown Scripts	15/08/80 07/10/80
The Torsan Triumvirate	Andrew Smith	Breakdown	25/11/80
Hebos	Rod Beacham	Breakdown	05/12/80
The Enemy Within	Christopher Priest	Breakdown Scripts	05/12/80 06/02/81
Title unknown	Tanith Lee	Scripts	06/02/81
Way Down Yonder	Lesley Elizabeth Thomas	Breakdown	23/04/81
Space-Whale (aka Song of the Space Whale)	Patrick Mills and John Wagner Scripts	Breakdown 02/12/81	07/09/81
Parasites (aka The Parasites)	Bill Lyons	Breakdown Scripts	22/09/81 16/02/82 23/04/82
Domain**	Philip Martin	Breakdown Scripts (1) Scripts (2–4)	13/04/82 14/10/82 27/01/83
Poison	Rod Beacham	Breakdown Scripts	27/04/82 27/05/82
The Place Where All Times Meet	Colin Davis	Breakdown	10/06/82
The House That Ur-Cjak Built	Andrew Stephenson	Breakdown	10/06/82
The Six Doctors***	Robert Holmes	Breakdown	04/08/82
May Time (aka Man Watch)	Christopher Bailey	Breakdown Scripts	24/08/82 16/09/82
Ghost Planet****	Robin Squire	Breakdown Scripts	05/01/83 20/05/83

*   May have been initially envisaged for the fourth Doctor's last season.

**   Ultimately reworked as *Vengeance on Varos* for Season 22.

*** See Chapter 7.

**** May have been envisaged for the sixth Doctor's first season.

Other writers who had discussions with the production team during 1980 but who (judging from surviving BBC documentation) were not subsequently commissioned during the fifth Doctor's era included John Gribbin, Richard Sparks, Ian Marter (who as an actor had earlier played the Doctor's companion Harry Sullivan), James Follett, David Tebbet and Geoff Lowe (who submitted an outline entitled *Romanoids*).

'I was always looking for new writers,' notes Saward. 'The first problem was finding people who were actually prepared to do it, because – in spite of what the fans think – it wasn't considered a great privilege to work on the show. *Doctor Who* was viewed within the Department as something that just sort of happened rather than as a prestigious show worth looking at. Our budgets were awful – we always had problems with that – and, as I've said before, new writers found it very difficult to come up with the strong characters and plots that we wanted. Really what I needed was six Charles Dickenses. That would have been brilliant. But I never found them. I had Bob Holmes and I had Philip Martin, but it took me several years to get that far.'

Although he enjoyed his first year as script editor, finding it a new and exciting challenge, Saward became increasingly disaffected with the job as time went by. This was due not only to the gruelling nature of the work, but also to a widening divergence of opinion between himself and Nathan-Turner as to the direction in which the series should be moving and the manner in which it should be produced. This eventually resulted in his acrimonious and controversial departure from the production team during the era of Peter Davison's successor, Colin Baker. Since then, he has continued to pursue a career as a freelance writer, including for German radio (his scripts being translated into German for production). Of his involvement with *Doctor Who*, he is now left with distinctly mixed feelings.

'There were script editors in the building who used to come in at 10 o'clock in the morning and be gone by 12, and there was I working weekends, working evenings... My life was just not my own. And I did five years of it. Bob Holmes had done three and a half years back in the seventies, and he said that he didn't know how I'd managed to get to the fifth year. He was absolutely right. I was knackered. The only reason I hung on was that it was quite well paid. I mean, I enjoyed talking to the writers, I enjoyed getting things going, I enjoyed seeing the programme being made, but it was really too much for one person, in the end, with all the problems and all John's messing around. It all piled on in an unnecessary way.

'Most of the stories had massive input from me. Not out of choice, I might add, but because I had to pull the thing round. I mean, if you've got a director sitting across the hall and the scripts are still in a thousand pieces you can't say, "Excuse me, we're waiting for the muse to strike." He's got only a few weeks to prepare for production, and he wants the scripts. You have to come up with something. I didn't enjoy doing it a lot of the time. I always feel that if you rewrite something you don't necessarily make it better, you just make it different, you make it you, or more you. And I can't be brilliant every day of the week. No one can, alas.

'During the years that I worked on *Doctor Who*, I could have gone up as co-author on almost every story.'

6: Production Development

The production of a TV drama series relies heavily on teamwork, with many different people – script editor, writers, directors, designers and actors among them – all influencing the form and content of the finished product. Probably the most influential contributor of all, however, is the producer, who has overall responsibility for the making of the series.

During the 1980s, *Doctor Who* had only one producer, John Nathan-Turner, who consequently oversaw the whole of Peter Davison's era as the Doctor. He was initially aided by one of his predecessors, Barry Letts, who had been appointed as executive producer to the series for the fourth Doctor's last season, Season 18, after acting as such on an informal basis during the previous year. However, Letts's involvement was essentially supervisory in nature – commenting on scripts, giving advice and approving major production decisions at a time when the BBC's Drama Group was undergoing a major reorganisation and the new Head of Series and Serials, David Reid, had yet to settle into his job – which lasted until only August 1981, by which time the reorganisation was complete and it was clear that Nathan-Turner had fully grasped the reins of the series.

One of Nathan-Turner's chief concerns in planning the fifth Doctor's debut season was to retain the loyalty of *Doctor Who*'s regular audience. Davison's predecessor, Tom Baker, had remained with the series for an unprecedented seven years and built up an enormous following amongst the general viewing public, many of whom were no doubt unaware that there had ever been any other actors playing the Doctor. To recast the lead role in a long-running and popular series is always a high-risk endeavour, and Nathan-Turner felt that Baker's successor would be bound to have an uphill struggle to win the acceptance of *Doctor Who*'s many avid followers.

One way in which the producer aimed to smooth the transition from the fourth Doctor to the fifth was to arrange, in addition to the usual summer reruns (which this year comprised *Full Circle* and *The Keeper of Traken*), a season of repeats from earlier eras of the series' history, thus reminding viewers that there had indeed been actors other than Baker in the lead role. Despite the trouble and expense involved in re-negotiating rights on 'out of time' repeat material – that is, material more than three years old – the powers-that-be acceded to Nathan-Turner's request, and a season of five stories – *100,000 BC*, *The Krotons*, *Carnival of Monsters*, *The Three Doctors* and *Logopolis* – was transmitted in an early-evening BBC2 slot in November and December 1981 under the banner title *The Five Faces of Doctor Who*.

Another strategy developed by Nathan-Turner with a view to maintaining regular audience loyalty was to make Season 18's last two stories – *The Keeper of Traken* by Johnny Byrne and *Logopolis* by Christopher H. Bidmead – and Season 19's first – *Project Zeta-Sigma* by John Flanagan and Andrew McCulloch – a loosely linked trilogy of adventures, in which the Doctor's old arch enemy the Master would be reintroduced in a new physical form. Even after the abandonment of *Project Zeta-Sigma* (in which the Master was to have adopted the guise of an alien scientist named Sergo), this plan was followed through with the commissioning of a replacement Master story in the form of Christopher H. Bidmead's *Castrovalva*.

To provide still greater incentive for regular viewers to keep faith with the series, Nathan-Turner decided upon the introduction at the end of Season 18 of two new regulars to join the Doctor and his established companion Adric on their journeys – the theory being that these characters would quickly gain their own respective groups of fans who would want to follow their adventures and see how they coped with the new Doctor.

The first of the newcomers, Nyssa, had originally been created by Johnny Byrne as a one-off character for *The Keeper of Traken*, but Nathan-Turner had quickly decided to keep her on for a further three stories. (Even before rehearsals for *The Keeper of Traken* had begun, actress Sarah Sutton had signed a contract for an additional 12 episodes, with an option on the BBC's part for her to appear in a further 16 of the following 20 – later reduced to 16 out of 18 after Season 19 was allocated a total of 26 episodes instead of the 28 originally planned for.)

The second new regular was Tegan, who made her debut in *Logopolis*. Created by Nathan-Turner and Bidmead to be a more long-term companion, she was characterised as an argumentative air hostess from Australia – a country of origin chosen by the producer partly in order to break the precedent of exclusively British human companions and partly with a view to increasing the chances of gaining a co-production deal for the location filming of a story in Australia.

One consideration that Nathan-Turner had very much in mind in choosing this mix of regular characters was that it ought to give the series a very broad-based appeal. This he felt was ultimately borne out, as he told journalist David Hirsch in a 1982 interview for *Starlog:*

'The younger viewers have Adric and Nyssa to identify with. Tegan, judging by the fan mail, is very popular with some of the older boys and the dads. Peter Davison is very popular all around, but he has a huge female following. Consequently we have a line-up of people who provide something for everyone.'

There were other reasons, too, why Nathan-Turner was keen to experiment with a three-companion set-up, as he explained to Hirsch: 'I brought in three companions because I liked the original line-up of the first Doctor with the two teachers and the grand-daughter. I thought it worked very well. With four people on board the TARDIS, you can have two storylines going and you can have plenty of dialogue. Or you can have four storylines, with the regulars speaking only to non regulars. It's a very useful device but, like everything, after a time it begins to bore. Keeping four characters on the air throughout the story can be a difficult responsibility.'

It was partly due to his concerns over the difficulty of ensuring that all three companions were given sufficient to do that Nathan-Turner originally intended to have Nyssa written out in Season 19's second story, Terence Dudley's *Four to Doomsday*. He changed his mind, however, when Davison raised strong objections to this plan. The actor, although sympathising with the producer's desire to dispense with one of the companions and thus make the TARDIS a little less crowded, was keen that the one to go should not be Nyssa, whose pleasant, refined character he considered made her the most suited of the three to accompany his Doctor. Nathan-Turner therefore decided to have Adric written out instead – an arrangement with which Davison was content – and this was achieved in the later Season 19 story *Earthshock*, written by the series' new script editor Eric Saward. Saward himself was similarly pleased to see the number of regulars reduced, as he explained in a 1982 interview with Jeremy Bentham for *Doctor Who Monthly*: 'I didn't like the set-up at all of writing for the Doctor and three companions, particularly when they're all together in the TARDIS; it's like doing a crowd scene! All the dialogue seems totally artificial when you consider it's mostly the Doctor who has to come up with all the information and the ideas. The companions are forced more and more to become ciphers – something I totally disapprove of – and I'm pleased that we have in fact now lost one of them. Ideally I think it could come down to just one companion, so we could then take that character and develop a full personality to him or her and not just a stereotype.'

One issue over which Davison and the production team continued to disagree was the relative merits of Nyssa and Tegan. Nathan-Turner's view, as he told *Starlog*, was that Tegan was the stronger of the two characters:

'I think Tegan's one of the most interesting companions that there's ever been. She isn't a typical *Doctor Who* girl. In the old days, they used to say that the two basic requirements of being a *Doctor Who* companion were to be able to run down corridors and to say: "So what do we do next, Doctor?" with conviction. Now, here's this bossy lady who stumbled into the TARDIS, who gets irritated by the Doctor, and the Doctor gets irritated by her because she speaks her mind. Tegan, being the outsider, is representing the average viewer's point of view.'

Saward also considered Tegan to be a stronger companion than Nyssa, although he did not always see eye to eye with Nathan-Turner as regards the way her character was used, as he explained in a 1993 interview:

'Of all the companions I was involved with, I thought Tegan was the best, because she was ballsy, she had an energy. There was always a struggle with John, though, because whenever a writer gave her something strong to do he would say, "No, she's a stupid, dumb Australian." Well, the actress is neither stupid nor dumb, the character she was playing was a strong, independent woman, and I thought it was pointless wasting her as we did. We could have developed her. She could have acquired skills under the tutelage of the Doctor. I mean, we could have taken her wherever we'd wanted.'

Having said this, Saward conceded that there had to be a balance struck between the regulars: 'With Peter Davison we had a Doctor who was a softer, younger, more vulnerable person, so if we'd built up Tegan to be a much stronger, tougher companion, that would have overwhelmed.'

Nathan-Turner explained in the introduction to his 1986 book *Doctor Who – The Companions* why he was wary of making the Doctor's companion too strong a character: 'One of the problems I discovered with companions of my own devising was that the more rounded the character, the more it required development. And development of character takes air-time and this reduces the amount of dramatisation air-time and before you know where you are, a science-fiction adventure series is taking on a soap-opera flavour. So, slowly but surely, writers and script editors and producers decide to play down the character development of the companion (in any case, after 23 years we know comparatively little about the Doctor) and concentrate on the drama of the story'.

Despite Davison's affection for Nyssa, the production team eventually decided to have her written out in the Season 20 story *Terminus*. They also decided to have introduced – in *Mawdryn*

Undead, the story immediately prior to her departure – a replacement character: a young male companion named Turlough. Interviewed by Richard Marson for a 1984 edition of *Doctor Who Magazine*, Saward explained how the creation of a new companion was approached: 'If someone wants to leave or the producer decides it's time for a change, we'll discuss a new companion. Based to a degree on the conversation I've had with John, I'll write an audition piece reflecting the character we want to end up with. Then it's up to the actor in the audition to make it his or her own.

'Turlough in his situation piece was a rather shifty, unreliable young man who at the same time was confused. He was self-centred but he had reason to be scared. Here he was, stuck on Earth, an alien, and suddenly this hideous creature [the Black Guardian] comes out of nowhere and orders him to kill somebody [the Doctor] in order to return to his own planet. It's going to disorientate the toughest of individuals, and we wanted to explore that through Turlough.

'That said, we knew he would have to settle down and become enough of a companion – friendly with the Doctor – for it to be credible, otherwise we'd have had a situation whereby Turlough spends umpteen episodes lurking about the TARDIS sharpening his knives and polishing his stun gun. The Doctor has got to buy Turlough for what he is – a rather selfish, uncertain individual who has only thrown his lot in with the Doctor to some extent. Turlough too has to accept the Doctor ultimately for what he represents.

'A lot was left to the actor, Mark Strickson, who always maintained a slight edge. Whatever he was doing and however much he had to do, he always had an air of menace. The viewer could never be quite certain. I thought he was an excellent companion.'

A return to the three-companion set-up came with the introduction of the shape-shifting android Kamelion in Season 20's final story, *The King's Demons*. This proved less than successful, however, as near-insurmountable problems arose with the robot prop that had first attracted Nathan-Turner to the idea of accommodating the character. Kamelion would thus appear in only one

Season 21 story, *Planet of Fire*, and at the end of that would be written out.

It was decided that Tegan and Turlough should also make their respective departures during Season 21, and that the Doctor should then go back to having just a single female companion – an arrangement that Nathan-Turner recalled having worked particularly successfully during the third Doctor's era.

Davison still felt that Nyssa was the companion best suited to his Doctor, and attempted to persuade the producer to bring her back into the series.

'I thought Nyssa worked best with the Doctor's character,' affirmed the actor in an interview with Graeme Wood, Mark Wyman and Gary Russell for a 1991 edition of *TV Zone*. 'I did tire of the abrasiveness of arguing with Tegan, getting annoyed with Adric. But Nyssa always seemed down-to-earth and sympathetic, fulfilling those things an assistant has to. It may be demeaning, but the companion is there to help the Doctor, to be "in this thing together" as friends. I did suggest that John consider bringing Nyssa back miraculously from the lazars' planet, but he didn't buy it.'

It was shortly after this that Davison decided to leave the series once his contract expired.

The new companion devised by Nathan-Turner, Saward and writer Peter Grimwade was Peri, an American botany student who was introduced in Grimwade's *Planet of Fire* – Davison's penultimate story.

'With Peri,' recalled Saward in his 1984 interview for *Doctor Who Magazine*, 'John decided we should have an American girl to break away from the stereotype of the English girls. We talked about her background and what she should be like and, as with Turlough, I wrote an audition piece. Nicola Bryant read for us, made the part come alive and turned out to be the most suitable... Peri is quite a strong girl. She doesn't like to be pushed around, but at the same time she's a gentler character than Tegan.'

Davison had disliked having an Australian on board the TARDIS, feeling that this was simply a misguided attempt on Nathan-Turner's part to increase the series' appeal to Australian viewers, and his initial reaction on learning that her successor was to be an American was one of great disappointment.

'There was the American girl coming in,' he recalled in a 1986 interview with Ian Atkins for *Wholook*, 'which I didn't think was an awfully good idea. I mean, the American aspect; Nicola Bryant was very good, but I didn't feel that the American aspect was a very good idea. Apart from anything else, the Americans like *Doctor Who* because it is English, not because it has American elements. I would like to have done more stories with Nicola. I think that if I had made the choice later, then I might well have stayed on, but as it was I went straight into another series.'

One notable aspect of the fifth Doctor's companions that distinguished them from their predecessors was that – like the Doctor himself – the costumes they were given to wear were essentially uniforms: distinctive, highly stylised outfits that generally remained unchanged from one story to the next. This development was motivated in part by a wish to save money on the series' costume budget. A far more significant factor, however, was Nathan-Turner's desire to help keep the series in the public eye by ensuring that the regulars had recognisable, unvarying images for marketing purposes. This strategy was successful, in that these images – the Doctor in his cricketing gear, Nyssa in her aristocratic Traken garb, Tegan in her air-hostess uniform, Adric in his Outler's tunic, and so on – became very familiar to the general viewing audience and often adorned the packaging and contents of spin-off merchandise produced during this period of the series' history. When Tegan and Nyssa did finally have a complete change of costume, in the Season 20 stories *Arc of Infinity* and *Snakedance* respectively, this was actually thought significant enough to be made the subject of a press photocall, and gained considerable publicity.

The same philosophy extended also to other aspects of the series. The Master, for instance, generally adopted a disguise in the early stages of each story in which he appeared, whether or not there was any reason for him to do so in plot terms, as this was perceived by the production team to be an established and popular aspect of his character. To many fan critics, however, this new focus on identifiable images had the downside of damaging the series' credibility.

Viewers, they argued, found it difficult to suspend their disbelief in characters who never changed their clothes; and the series also took on aspects of the fantastical superhero genre, which had been spawned in American comic books and had since entered popular culture more widely, with its easily recognisable, uniform-wearing characters such as Superman and Batman.

This development went hand in hand with *Doctor Who*'s recent adoption by Marvel Comics in their regular   publication devoted to the series, which during the fifth Doctor's era was known variously as *Doctor Who – A Marvel Monthly*, *Doctor Who Monthly* and *The Official Doctor Who Magazine*. Although *Doctor Who* strip stories had been running for many years in titles such as *TV Comic* and *Countdown*, these earlier ventures had been very much a part of the long tradition of British children's comics. Marvel's strips, on the other hand, were principally influenced by the American, superhero-dominated comics genre.

There were other respects, too, in which the Davison-era stories came to resemble aspects of American comic book fare. One of these was their increasing preoccupation with the series' own internal continuity, which manifested itself in numerous continuity references; in frequent return appearances by old monsters and other characters; in 'team up' adventures like *The Five Doctors*; and in plots, such as that of *Planet of Fire*, largely devoted to writing out established regulars and introducing new ones.

This growing reliance on the reuse of popular elements from the series' history was initially discernible in the trilogy of Master stories that saw out the fourth Doctor and introduced the fifth. It was taken to a higher level, however, in *Earthshock*. The Cybermen's return appearance in this story, their first in eight years, was one of the most talked about and popular aspects of Season 19, and generated considerable publicity – although, in order to preserve the surprise, Nathan-Turner made sure that the Cybermen's involvement was kept under wraps prior to the transmission of the first episode, even to the extent of turning down the offer of a *Radio Times* front cover photograph and article.

The success of *Earthshock* encouraged Nathan-Turner to

continue the trend by reviving other popular characters in the following season. Saward would later express the view that the producer was motivated in this regard solely by a desire to appeal to the series' fans. In fact, however, the large amount of press coverage and positive comment generated by *Earthshock* had led Nathan-Turner to suspect that such an approach would be welcomed not only by the fans but also by the general viewing public; and in order to test this hypothesis he had gained agreement to the transmission of a further season of largely 'out of time' repeats under the banner heading *Doctor Who and the Monsters* (amended slightly from *Doctor Who Meets the Monsters* in his original proposal). The good ratings and positive feedback generated by these repeats – edited compilation versions of *The Curse of Peladon*, *Genesis of the Daleks* and *Earthshock*, transmitted on BBC1 rather than on BBC2 as *The Five Faces of Doctor Who* had been – had convinced the producer that he was on the right track.

The revival of old monsters was initially welcomed by the series' leading man, too. '*Earthshock* was my favourite story from my first season,' noted Davison in a 1983 interview with Stephen Collins for *Zerinza*, 'and one of the reasons for this was that it featured the first old enemy I'd faced, apart from the Master. I think old enemies are good.

'I think that possibly in my second season there weren't quite enough really, but that was not the fault of anybody except the people behind the standard BBC strike which seems to come once a year, usually at Christmas time for some reason. Anyway, we were four episodes short, and they would have featured old enemies. I think it's nice to have old enemies back.'

The strike-hit four-parter to which Davison referred was Saward's *The Return*, featuring the Daleks, which was to have been transmitted after *The King's Demons* as the closing story of Season 20. Despite its temporary loss (it would eventually appear in slightly revised form as *Resurrection of the Daleks* in Season 21), Season 20 still drew much more heavily on established *Doctor Who* continuity than had Season 19, making Davison's expression of disappointment seem somewhat surprising. Indeed, there was at least one element from the Doctor's past in every story – a fact that, after it was pointed out to him by fan Ian Levine, Nathan-Turner used as part of his promotion of the series in its 20th anniversary year. The special anniversary story, *The Five Doctors*, itself afforded still further evidence of the series' increasing reliance on its own mythos to provide the inspiration and substance for new stories.

'We drew on the series' past far too much,' reflected Saward in 1993. 'Again it was a case of John wanting to appeal to the fans. I think *Doctor Who* works best when the production team are going for it and inventing their own things.

'To my mind, the best period of the series' history was in the mid-seventies when Philip Hinchcliffe and Bob Holmes were in charge. Bob Holmes was the best writer the series ever had, and when he was script editor he – like many others before him and after him – rewrote a lot of the stories. He made them very Bob Holmes, and because he was very confident and very strong, the scripts were very confident and very strong and very inventive. He had in Philip Hinchcliffe a producer who was new to the job and who would go for it; he would be down in the visual effects workshop, for example, trying to get them to do the best they possibly could. He was doing the producer's job, which is to support the script. He had in Tom Baker an excellent Doctor, and he had in Lis Sladen and Louise Jameson two interesting companions, in their very different ways.

'Hinchcliffe and Holmes still used old monsters like the Cybermen and the Daleks, but they also brought a lot of new things to the series themselves. We didn't do that when I was script editor, and I always felt that was a tremendous drawback. We weren't adding to it, we were just living off it. It's always better to invent your own things. That's not just an ego trip; you often do better when you invent your own instead of using somebody else's. Writers shouldn't be told, "I want you to do this, this, this, this and this." They'll say, "No, I'm not interested." They should be given as much freedom as possible. What Peter Grimwade got lumbered with on that awful story *Planet of Fire*, for instance, was utterly lunatic. I mean, I felt embarrassed. Turlough leaving, Peri joining, the Master, Kamelion, the Lanzarote location – it was ridiculous.'

Davison, although more restrained in his comments than Saward, has also in later interviews expressed the view that the series came to rely rather too heavily on its past successes. Despite any doubts that there might have been from these quarters, however, Season 21 saw a continuation of the policy of bringing back old monsters – in particular in *Warriors of the Deep*, which featured both the Silurians and the Sea Devils, and in *Resurrection of the Daleks*, the Dalek story postponed from Season 20.

Notwithstanding Saward's contention that little of substance was added to the series' mythos during his tenure as script editor, the frequent reuse of old characters and concepts in fact gave rise to many new continuity developments (see Chapter 4). In addition, most of the returning monsters – including the Cybermen, the Silurians and the Sea Devils – appeared in redesigned form. Although many fan critics would later express the view that the new designs were generally somewhat less effective than the originals, these changes were initiated by Nathan-Turner as part of a conscious policy of giving the series a more glossy, expensive and up-to-date look. The phenomenally popular cinema film *Star Wars* had dramatically increased the public's expectations of science fiction in the media, and the producer was keen to counter the commonly-held perception of *Doctor Who* as a cheap series with relatively low production values and substandard visual effects. (The aforementioned reduction of Season 19 from 28 episodes to 26 was made at his request as he considered that the budget allocated to it was insufficient to support the extra two episodes without sacrificing production quality.)

'Looking back to the time I worked on the series,' commented Saward's predecessor Antony Root in an interview with Philip Newman for a 1992 issue of *The Frame*, 'there was then – and frankly it's still to be resolved – a crisis about what you could actually do with television science fiction post-*Star Wars*. On *Doctor Who*, you used to be able to get away with an exploding wall and a weird monster, but once you'd had the cinema, with its massive special-effects pictures, showing people what could be achieved, you had to find something else for the show to do, some other way in.'

Nathan-Turner was expert in budgetary matters – he had been production unit manager, responsible for managing *Doctor Who*'s resources, prior to his appointment as producer – and made it a top priority to ensure that the limited money available to the series was spent in ways that would be readily apparent on screen. This was a policy on which he expounded in his 1982 interview for *Starlog*:

'I removed a lot of the location work, which is very expensive. In a way, it's very restricting because we try to do it within 25 miles of London, which nearly always looks like it's within 25 miles of London! For *Time-Flight*, we had a studio landscape created, which looked absolutely marvellous. Totally alien. Had we more money, I guess we would have gone on location. When you remove the location work, it does put a bit more money at your disposal for things that count. Actors count, designs, costumes, make-up and visual effects. My motto is: "Spend the money where it shows." If it doesn't show, let's stop spending it.'

As one aspect of this policy, Nathan-Turner decided that any major location shoots done for the series should generally be in countries other than Britain, which would automatically tend to give the finished product a more expensive look. Thus trips were made to Amsterdam for *Arc of Infinity* and to Lanzarote for *Planet of Fire*; and both stories featured extensive sequences showing off their respective locations, to guarantee that full value was gained from the money spent.

Another manifestation of the producer's policy was the frequent casting of popular television celebrities in guest-star roles, ensuring that the budget allocated to hiring actors had maximum on-screen impact. Amongst the many examples here were Stratford Johns (best known for his work in *Z Cars*) in *Four to Doomsday*; Nerys Hughes (*The Liver Birds*) in *Kinda*; Michael Robbins (*On the Buses*) in *The Visitation*; Beryl Reid (distinguished actress and comedienne) in *Earthshock*; Liza Goddard (*Take Three Girls*) in *Terminus*; and Rodney Bewes (*The Likely Lads*), Rula Lenska (*Rock Follies*) and Chloe Ashcroft (*Play School*) in *Resurrection of the Daleks*.

Nathan-Turner's hopes were certainly borne out as far as press coverage was concerned, as both the overseas location shoots and the celebrity guest stars gained considerable publicity for *Doctor Who*. Again, however, many fan commentators had reservations, feeling that the use of overseas locations was unwarranted by the plots of the stories in question, which consequently had to be adjusted to fit around them, and that the inclusion of familiar television personalities made it even more difficult for viewers to achieve the all-important suspension of disbelief.

Nathan-Turner, in response to the latter criticism, pointed out that the celebrity guest stars, although admittedly best known in many cases for their comedy or light entertainment work, were in fact jobbing actors who had previously played a wide variety of different roles, not only on television but also in radio, theatre and – in some cases – film. He likened *Doctor Who* to *The Morecambe and Wise Show*, in the sense that many distinguished performers were delighted to be asked to appear in it, and prided himself on taking a bold approach to this aspect of his job rather than resorting to type-casting as was more commonly the case in British television. The critics, however, remained concerned that a higher priority was being placed on achieving a slick, expensive-looking production than on telling well-plotted, convincing stories, and that content was thus being sacrificed in favour of style.

Nathan-Turner was in fact unusual amongst *Doctor Who*'s producers in that he had never been an editor or a writer of scripts and had few aspirations in that direction – a recognition, as he candidly admitted in interviews, of his own limitations. He consequently played rather less emphatic a part than had some of his predecessors in defining the overall dramatic style of the series in story as opposed to production terms, and was more reliant on his script editors to take the initiative in this regard. He did, on the other hand, have strong views about certain aspects of the series' scripting. One example of this was his determination to ensure that humour was used only very sparingly; a point on which (as noted in Chapter 2) he was somewhat at odds with Davison.

'I wanted more humour,' affirmed the actor in an interview with Terry and Andy Kerr for a 1985 edition of *Skonnos*. 'John cut the humour for my first two seasons. You see, prior to that we'd had quite a lot of humour in Tom Baker's time, and I don't think John quite liked it. Occasionally I'd find the early drafts of scripts, which had a bit more humour in them, and I'd say to John, "I quite like this," and show it to him at the producer's run. Sometimes we'd keep those bits, and sometimes we wouldn't. More often, though, I wouldn't see those earlier drafts.

'I remember watching one of Tom's stories, where the Doctor was about to be executed, and he was laughing and joking and offering everyone jelly babies. I think Tom, Douglas Adams and Graham Williams got together to create this image. I don't think Tom and John saw eye-to-eye about humour.'

When Davison decided to leave the series after his third season in the role, Nathan-Turner again became concerned with the question of retaining audience loyalty over the change of Doctors. The series had done well in the twice-weekly weekday evening slot that it had occupied for the past three years, winning very respectable ratings (although more so for Season 19 than for Seasons 20 and 21), and he was keen to ensure that these viewers – many of whom he suspected were fans of Davison from his years in *All Creatures Great and Small* – were given every possible encouragement to 'stay tuned' (a favourite expression of his) for the sixth Doctor's era.

One way in which the producer approached this problem was to introduce, just before the change of Doctors, a new companion character, Peri, who he hoped would help to bridge the gap between the two eras – repeating the tactic he had adopted on the previous occasion with the introduction of Nyssa and Tegan. This time, however, he decided to go one stage further by bringing in the new Doctor himself for the final story of Season 21, thus giving viewers a chance to get acquainted with the newcomer before the series went off the air for its between-seasons break. Thus, in a departure from recent precedent, Davison would make his exit in the penultimate story of the season rather than in the last.

'That was John's idea,' confirmed Saward in 1993. 'He always felt that he wanted to leave the audience with a taste of what was to come. I thought he was worrying unnecessarily, to be honest, because *Doctor Who* is engraved in everyone's minds, and who's playing the lead won't be the reason why people will tune in; they'll tune in because they enjoy *Doctor Who*, or they have memories of it, or they're getting their kids to watch it or something.'

Davison's last story, *The Caves of Androzani*, marked the return to *Doctor Who* of Robert Holmes, Nathan-Turner having been persuaded by Saward to make a rare exception to his long-established policy of using writers and directors new to the series rather than bringing back those who had worked on it during earlier eras of its history. The result was a story considered by many to be the finest of all those in which Davison appeared. The high production values pursued by Nathan-Turner and the strong scripting sought by Saward came together and complemented each other perhaps more successfully than at any other time during the previous three years, ensuring that the fifth Doctor bowed out in considerable style.

7: From Script to Screen –

The Five Doctors

Introduction

To try to analyse comprehensively the development of a *Doctor Who* adventure is not an easy matter. A television production is the result of many months' work by a large number of people, and what is ultimately seen on screen may have been affected and influenced in greater or lesser degrees by all of them.

Unless one is afforded a fly's eye view of every meeting and every aspect of the creative process, then any attempt to try to dissect the production is limited by the memories and personalities of those people to whom one speaks.

Bearing all this in mind, this chapter presents an in-depth look at just one of the fifth Doctor's stories. In doing so it reveals the process of making *Doctor Who* at this point in the series' history and – a factor common to every story – some of the behind-the-scenes discussions and thought that go into a production.

The production chosen for this case study is *The Five Doctors*, a story made to celebrate *Doctor Who*'s 20th-anniversary in 1983.

In many ways, *The Five Doctors* was a typical story of the era, involving location filming as well as studio recording and a large number of complex visual-effects sequences to realise. In other ways it was atypical as, being a celebration of 20 years, it had constraints and requirements that other stories did not.

For our fly's eye view of the production we have turned primarily to director Peter Moffatt and to visual-effects designer John Brace who recall, scene by scene, the work that went into it. We have also incorporated comments from other participants: the producer, John Nathan-Turner; the writer, Terrance Dicks; the designer, Malcolm Thornton; the costume designer, Colin Lavers; the composer, Peter Howell; the sound-effects designer, Dick Mills; and also some of the cast. The primary source for much of this supporting interview material is a publication edited and published by David J. Howe for the *Doctor Who* Appreciation Society in 1984, which looked in detail at the making of this story. We are grateful to Jan Vincent-Rudzki, who conducted the original interviews with Malcolm Thornton and Colin Lavers, for allowing us to reproduce his work here. Thanks also to Patricia Holmes, wife of the late Robert Holmes, for allowing us to reproduce her husband's original synopses for the story.

The Scripts

Every *Doctor Who* adventure that appears on screen starts life as an idea. This idea may be in the mind of a writer; it may come from the producer or the script editor; or, as is more often the case, it may develop out of a discussion between two or more of these people. Once the initial contact has been made, a story outline or synopsis will generally be commissioned from the writer. Assuming that all is well when that is delivered, one or more of the actual scripts themselves will then be commissioned. Depending on the status of the writer, these stages may be compacted or expanded accordingly.

In the case of *The Five Doctors*, the idea of celebrating the anniversary originated with *Doctor Who*'s producer, John Nathan-Turner. He started thinking about this as early as July 1981, and on 3 August that year sent to David Reid, the Head of Series and Serials, the following memo:

Further to our conversation of the other week, I should like to request that next year's *Doctor Who* season transmits in the

Autumn of 1982.

We must get back to an Autumn transmission in readiness for the 20th anniversary programme in November 1983. (The 10th anniversary programme in 1973 starred all the actors who had played the Doctor up until then (William Hartnell, Patrick Troughton, Jon Pertwee), and if I am still producing the show in 1983, I would like to do something really spectacular!!)

As I have had to release Peter Davison for eight weeks during the current season's production period, it became impossible to transmit this season till Week 1 1982. (In any case Controller of BBC1 did not want *Doctor Who* and *Sink or Swim* to transmit at the same time.) The result of the above is that currently *Doctor Who* is off the air for nine months as opposed to the usual six months. As you know, interest has been retained in the programme, as we have a new Doctor, in August of this year there are two four-parter repeats on BBC1 and in November of this year a season of repeats – *The Five Faces of Doctor Who* (five four-parters) on BBC2.

I would suggest we capitalise quickly on the anticipated popularity of Peter Davison's Doctor, and have only a six-month break between seasons next time.

I am sure I can transmit next year's season from Week 36 1982, even if the programme remains bi-weekly – provided I do not release Peter Davison for *Sink or Swim* during *Doctor Who*'s production period. *Sink or Swim* could then go into production after my final recording and still transmit in Week 1, if required.

To simplify, I suggest next year *Doctor Who* transmits in the Autumn, and *Sink or Swim*, if required, in the Winter. I do hope this can be achieved, as it would be most beneficial to the programme and its future.

Nathan-Turner's idea was that a celebratory story could be transmitted on the anniversary and within the planned structure of the regular season (something that would happen in 1988 with *Silver Nemesis* for the 25th anniversary).

After discussions with Alan Hart, David Reid replied on 25

August as follows:

> Controller of BBC1 is not prepared to change *Doctor Who* trans-
> mission to the Autumn of 1982. He will think again about 1983
> but is not prepared to put undue pressure on Comedy for the
> release of Peter Davison. He is concerned that *Sink or Swim*
> might finish up being off the air for too long.
>
> Alan has, however, suggested that he would be interested
> in, perhaps, a 90-minute special to coincide with the anniver-
> sary in November 1983 to trail the series in the Winter. This is
> not a silly thought and perhaps we might discuss it.

As plans for the special developed, Nathan-Turner and script editor Eric Saward decided that they wanted a production that would
feature all five of the television Doctors to date as well as numerous companions and monsters.

One early problem was how best to get around the problem of
the first Doctor, in view of the fact that William Hartnell, the actor
who played him, had died in 1975. It was felt that the best option
was to cast another actor to play the part. In July 1982, a check
was made on the last BBC fee paid to actor Geoffrey Bayldon,
who had appeared in the 1979 *Doctor Who* story *The Creature
from the Pit* and who was considered by many fans and profes-
sionals to be an ideal choice for a new Doctor.

To write the anniversary story Saward and Nathan-Turner had
little hesitation in approaching writer Robert Holmes.

Holmes had script edited *Doctor Who* for three and a half years
during the Tom Baker era, and had seen several of his own scripts
for the series reach fruition, the first being *The Krotons* back in
1968.

Holmes was approached, and, despite many misgivings, agreed
to have a think and see what he could come up with. In an undated
letter to the production office, he outlined three possible scenarios,
one in great detail and the other two only sketchily. The entire
content of his five-page note was as follows:

The main problem we face is to find a satisfactory and plausible explanation for all the Doctors, plus companions, appearing at the same point in the space-time continuum. I feel that this – dramatically – is what our audience will expect. However, the clash of mighty egos has been mentioned and it is possible for them to appear in the same story without appearing together.

The purpose of this discussion document is to survey the various options open to us.

1) The planet Maladoom. Doctor Will and companion striding across a misty landscape. They've obviously just arrived as he is pointing out various botanical features and making deductions about the nature of the planet.

We pull back to see that the Doctor is being watched on video. Voices of unseen watchers comment admiringly – 'Really remarkably lifelike,' etc. (Eventually, about an hour from now, we shall learn that Doctor Will and Carol Ann are cyborgs, created by cyber-technology. This will explain why the Doctor is not quite as we remember Hartnell.)

Tardis. The Doctor helpless at the controls. Tells Tegan the machine is being drawn into a time vortex. It could mean destruction. Maybe we do some clever mirror-work and show more than one police box whirling down this sudden fissure in the ordered universe.

Maladoom. The Doctor and Tegan arrive. He is now very angry. Some irresponsible idiot must be interfering with the delicately balanced polarity of time and matter. Incredibly dangerous lunacy that could create chaos. Must put a stop to it.

Now, one by one, the other Doctors arrive with their companions. All have approximately the same reactions – although Doctor Tom may speculate that some other race has discovered the power previously known only to Time Lords. But, anyway, all go off to put a stop to it.

The Doctor and Tegan are heading across rough terrain towards a pulsing light that seems to be coming from inside a distant, craggy hill. In the shadow of a low cliff they see, apparently inset into the rockface, a rectangular panel of some shiny black substance. As they examine this curiously, concealed jets puff out vapour. They collapse unconscious. Then the panel begins to open.

One by one the other Doctors are inveigled into other automated traps.

Cryogenic chamber. The Doctors and companions lie unconscious. The Master comes in for a gloat. At last he has all the time entities that comprise the total Doctor at his mercy. If he turns the freezer down a few more degrees he will achieve final triumph over his oldest adversary. So why doesn't he? Probably because he daren't, at this stage, upset his allies, the Cybermen.

Doctor Pat is carried off to the operating theatre. The Cybermen prepare for surgery. An injection revives the patient for preliminary tests. The Cybermen intend to find the organic mechanism that separates Time Lords from other species. When they find it they will separate it and implant it into their familiar cybernetic machinery, thus turning themselves into Cyberlords.

This aspect of the plot is brought out in conversation between the Master, Doctor Pat and the top Cyberman.

As the operation begins the Doctor goes into terminal collapse. Resuscitation procedures fail. The patient is pronounced extinct. The Cybermen aren't too concerned; they expect to lose a few Doctors before discovering the vital organ. That is why, with the Master's help, they have drawn all the manifestations of the Doctor's form from their various time loops.

Doctor Pat is returned to the cryogenic chamber where he recovers from his self-willed cataleptic state.

Fighting against the numbing cold, he disconnects the freezer panels. As the temperature rises the Doctors slowly begin to stir.

In the operating theatre the Cybermen are reviewing their techniques before investing in another patient.

In the cryogenic chamber total bafflement at finding themselves all together. An impossible situation which they resolve by deciding they are trapped in a temporal paradox created by the Master.

The Cybermen come to collect Doctor Jon. Docs and companions take them by surprise and effect an escape.

Film. Trial by ordeal. Cybermen hunting Doctors who are all intent now on their original objective – restoring the time-space continuum to its natural order before permanent damage is done to the universe. And to this end they are heading for the shining hill.

Doctor Will – the fake cyborg – tries to lead them into an ambush. But at the last moment he is spotted as a phoney. He bounces down a cliff and all his springs fall out. Carol Ann, too, is shown to be a cyborg. This is tough on Frazer because he was getting to like her.

They struggle on and finally reach the shining hill. Its core is a mass of technology linked to the Master's Tardis, the effect of which is to raise its power a thousandfold. Projected through the space-time continuum this enormous force has created a time vacuum into which all Time Travellers (principally our Doctors) were inevitably drawn.

The trouble is that it is now feeding upon itself, like a nuclear reactor running out of control, and in a very short while the whole of this part of the universe will implode into a black hole. Unless they can slow the whirligig down and stabilise matters.

We've all been through this one before. The Master will, of course, turn up to provide some last-moment impediment. But, in the end, the Doctors get the machinery into phase before it goes critical. As it slows they, together with appropriate companions, disappear back into their own sectors of time – the relative dimensions effect.

The Doctor and Tegan are alone at the end.

The sharp-eyed reader will ask what happened to the Cybermen. Well, we won't have that many to start with. Some will be blown up when the Doctors escape because, before departing, they sabotage the operating theatre. Others will be disposed of variously – buried under rock falls, sunk in swamps, pushed off cliffs and so on – during the film chase.

2) The other option. Much the same general shape of story but we open with the present Doctor and stay with him until the operating-theatre scene.

The effect of the Cybermen tampering with his metabolism, however, is that he starts to regress through his various phases – i.e. turns first into Doctor Tom, then into Doctor Jon and so on.

While doing this, of course, he is also escaping, combating the Cybermen and trying to reach the shining hill. When he reaches his Doctor Will incarnation he knows he is on his last legs. If he doesn't make it before his time runs out, he will be finally dead.

(This, too, offers a possible explanation as to why he doesn't exactly resemble the real Hartnell.)

The attraction of this shape is that it would allow us to have all the Doctors in the story without having them meet up. Its difficulty is in finding a convincing reason for Tegan also to slip back through various companion incarnations. Maybe mental projection? In each of his forms he would see the companion he had at that time?

3) We might use the Tardis as a kind of tuning fork. We postulate that within its structure lie the echoes or 'vibes' of all who have ever been aboard. Given the right technology, therefore, it is possible to recreate any of all of the former Doctors and hold them in corporeal form as long as the energy supply lasts.

The present Doctor – perhaps finding himself out of action – might be compelled to activate this 'memory function' in order to seek help from his predecessors.

This could be a battle of wits between the Doctors and the exhausted old computer at the heart of a starship that has been drifting for 20 million years. But I see no Cybermen in it.

The substance of these ideas is of interest as, although Holmes was ultimately not to use them for the anniversary story, the idea of an alien race trying to find the organic basis for the Time Lords' power was later revived by him in his 1985 sixth Doctor story *The*

Two Doctors.

On 4 August 1982, Holmes was formally commissioned to provide a scene breakdown for the 90-minute special now with the working title *The Six Doctors*, reflecting the idea that the version of the first Doctor in the storyline was a fake.

Because Holmes was very unsure as to whether he would be able to come up with a workable scene breakdown by the delivery date of 23 August, Saward and Nathan-Turner decided to ask another writer to 'stand by' in the event of Holmes being unable to resolve the logistic problems presented by the story. This was Terrance Dicks, another ex-*Doctor Who* script editor with numerous stories to his name.

On 24 August, Saward wrote to Holmes thanking him for keeping the office advised of progress on the breakdown, and requesting that he provide the document a day before their forthcoming meeting on 1 September to give himself and Nathan-Turner a change to digest the work so far. On the same day, Saward wrote to Dicks apologising for the delay, and stating that they would be making a final decision on the story once they had seen Holmes' work.

Following the meeting with Holmes, Saward wrote to Dicks on 2 September saying that Holmes had decided to try and write the first 20 minutes of the script, despite the fact that he had huge reservations about whether he could make it work.

Ultimately Holmes delivered his scene breakdown on 13 October, and on 18 October Terrance Dicks was commissioned to provide a scene breakdown as well. Holmes' version was subsequently dropped. Following delivery of Dicks' breakdown on 1 November, at which point the story had been renamed *The Five Doctors*, Dicks was commissioned on 16 November to write the script which was formally delivered on 20 December and accepted on 27 January 1983.

'I knew from the beginning that the job was going to be appallingly difficult and complicated and full of the most enormous hassles, as indeed it was,' said Dicks. 'Since I was prepared for that, nothing actually threw me. I knew it was going to be like jumping into a combine harvester from the very beginning.'

Dicks was presented with the same set of guidelines that Holmes had been working to. 'My standing joke about it was that it was like that game where you make up a story about objects that come out of a box. This particular box had an awful lot of objects in it!

'First of all, you knew it had to be all the Doctors – they had already come up with the idea of having Richard Hurndall as the look-alike first Doctor – and some of the monsters – they already knew that they wanted the Cybermen as the lead monster and, as well as the Cybermen, there had to be other villains and other monsters. It wasn't all one way – obviously they wanted my ideas as well. At first they weren't too keen on having Daleks in but I told them that they'd got to have Daleks, even if it's only one Dalek. They weren't too happy about having K-9 either, but eventually they agreed and said he could put his head around the door.

'There was the problem of the companions – who was going to be in it and who wasn't. Some they were sure of, like the Brigadier, Susan and Sarah, others kept changing. One of the things that kept happening was that they would ring up and say, "Have you written so-and-so in?" I'd say that I had and they would reply, "Well, write him out again, he can't do it. You can have such-and-such." There was a lot of toing and froing with the companions. In fact it wasn't absolutely set who were going to be the "cameo companions" until almost the last moment. Those bits where they pop up in the corridors on the way to the tomb were almost the last things to be put in the script. They had to be done very simply because by that time the budget had nearly been used up. The brief was complicated enough, and I still needed a story.

'The problem was to put all these elements together to make some kind of sense. They didn't want a pantomime, they wanted a story that would stand on its own even if it wasn't the 20th-anniversary special. The main problem was coming up with a plot to pull all these elements together. It all began to come together for me when I came up with the idea of the game. Almost before anything else, I had this picture in my mind of a black-gloved hand picking up this little figure and putting it on a board. Thinking of it as a kind of chess game gave it a basic shape. But this game was against the people on the board. The Player just sat and watched what they did. Then there was the question, who was the Player? The first thought I had was that it was the Master but, quite rightly, Eric Saward said that was too obvious; it would be an anticlimax. You have, however, got to come up with some type of surprise villain as the sting in the tail. If you are going to do that, then it's got to be someone significant, it can't be the third Time Lord on the left. The only candidate was Borusa.

'This happens very often in story writing, things just fall into place. Of course it's got to be Borusa, who else can it be? The thing about Borusa turning into a villain was that you didn't have a saintly character who suddenly went all bad. Borusa had always been a politician and an autocrat, someone who was prepared to be ruthless. I felt that you could believe that he could take that one stage further and say: "Well I'm the one who knows what's good for everybody; it would therefore be much better for Gallifrey if I were in charge forever!" So you just have to take the existing characteristics and push them a bit further over the edge into madness. It's very difficult stuff to play. I think Philip Latham did extraordinarily well.

'So that was the structure: it was Borusa manipulating the five Doctors in some way, kidnapping them out of time. That became the overall idea, which is the hardest bit. After that it's just a question of working it all out.'

In the final draft of the rehearsal script, dated 25 January 1983, Dicks included a scene involving the third Doctor and Sarah encountering several Auton mannequins in a ruined high street. The copyright clearance for this was checked by the BBC on 14 December 1982, but ultimately the Autons were dropped and on 11 February 1983 a sequence already in the script where the second Doctor and the Brigadier were attacked by an underground monster in the caves was altered to change the attacking creature into a Yeti.

'There just wasn't time to do it,' explained Dicks about the Auton sequence. 'What all that came down to was Sarah going over the cliff, which was a lot simpler.'

There were other aspects of the script and action which were refined as the director mapped out the various practicalities, and these are mentioned in the scene-by-scene of the televised story later in this chapter.

One of the most distinctive and memorable images from the production is the central tower to which all the Doctors are trying to get. Dicks included it specifically as a symbol of evil. 'This is the central citadel of evil; like in *The Lord of the Rings* where Frodo's going with the ring to the tower where the Dark Lord lives. There's also a poem by Browning, called *Childe Roland to the Dark Tower Came*. It's like a little fragment of a non-existent narrative poem. It describes the knight riding up to the old dark castle. There's a horn hanging outside it and he raises it to his lips and blows. That's all that happens and I think it was in my mind as an image.

'After that I worked Rassilon into it. Again, it had to be Rassilon who was going to resolve it. There was a time when I wasn't sure whether it was going to be a good Rassilon or a bad Rassilon; I trailed that maybe Rassilon had been a monster of evil and that the Time Lords had covered it all up which was quite fun, as that seemed to be a very Time Lord thing to do – a Bob Holmes type Time Lord thing to do. I quite liked the idea that the Time Lords had some very shabby episodes in their own history that they were ashamed of and hushed up.'

Casting

Whereas normally the casting of a *Doctor Who* story would be carried out by the director in collaboration with the producer, in this instance, many of the cast were returning characters from *Doctor Who*'s history and therefore the question wasn't so much who could play the part, as was the required actor available.

The first problem tackled by the production team was someone to play the first Doctor. This was resolved when John Nathan-Turner remembered an actor called Richard Hurndall. 'I was asked to play the first Doctor,' recalled Hurndall in 1983, 'because John Nathan-Turner saw me as Nebrox in *Blake's 7* and thought I looked very like William Hartnell.

'I remembered William's approach to the part very well and

decided it would be stupid to try and "mimic" him, so I hope I split the difference between his performance – his personality – and mine.'

'He was marvellous,' confirmed Nathan-Turner. 'I did offer him tapes of Bill Hartnell to look at but as he did remember Bill, he decided that rather than view the tapes and try to do a "Mike Yarwood" on it, it would be better if he just went for his instinct.'

Director Peter Moffatt asked Hurndall to suggest Hartnell's portrayal of the first Doctor with some of his mannerisms, such as holding his lapels and using his vocal 'Hm? hm?' and then gradually moulding this to his own interpretation.

'I really believe he gave us a beautiful performance, and one accepted him on his own merits,' said Peter. 'I know he was very nervous of the undertaking as the other Doctors had only to drop back into their old performances whereas he, as a newcomer, had to create his, and then not in his own mould but in that created by a very celebrated and much loved actor who had made an enormous impression on the public 20 years earlier. However, he really did a wonderful job and succeeded in conveying a vivid impression of Bill and making the part his own at the same time.'

Hurndall agreed to play the first Doctor on 6 October 1982. William Hartnell's original costume had been hired from theatrical costumier's Bermans and Nathans and so was not held by the BBC. In designing Richard Hurndall's costume, Colin Lavers went by photographs in a magazine published in 1973 by the *Radio Times* to celebrate *Doctor Who*'s tenth anniversary. The original outfit featured a morning coat and that was fairly easy to keep to, but the original waistcoat had been an authentic Victorian one so a look-alike was made. The script emphasised the age of the first Doctor and so Lavers used mittens to make him appear older and slightly feeble. The mittens also hid the fact that he wasn't wearing the first Doctor's blue ring, as it was felt that the colour would be too noticeable. There was also a photograph in the magazine of William Hartnell in a hat and scarf but Lavers considered that the scarf was by this point associated firmly with the fourth Doctor and the hat with the fifth, so those two items were not re-introduced.

Because Nathan-Turner wanted to have something of the original first Doctor in the story somewhere, he decided to use a clip from *Flashpoint*, the final episode of *The Dalek Invasion of Earth*, as a pre-title sequence trailer.

Patrick Troughton, playing the second Doctor, presented Nathan-Turner with a problem of scheduling. Troughton was working on *Foxy Lady* for Granada television during the original proposed location filming dates for the story in April, and so Nathan-Turner, recognising that the inclusion of the Doctors, and for them to be played by the original actors, was essential to the production, moved the dates forward to March to ensure that Troughton would be available to appear.

Most of Troughton's scenes in the draft script were on location and Colin Lavers was keen to develop a costume that would keep the actor warm. The fur coat used in *The Abominable Snowmen* was suggested, but the original could not be used as it was made of real fur and to have had two of them would have been very expensive, so two close substitutes were used.

The trousers worn by the second Doctor originally featured a large, inch-square check pattern. The BBC was in the early eighties trying to establish a new picture clarity for Direct Broadcast Satellites and some striped and checked materials had become unsuitable for use. Bearing this in mind, Lavers opted for a light plaid pattern for the trousers.

Jon Pertwee's third Doctor was less of a problem as the actor was available on the required dates and happy to reprise his role. His costume was a variation on that worn by the actor for a photocall to publicise *The Three Doctors* back in 1973.

Tom Baker, playing the fourth Doctor, presented by far the greatest challenge to the production team.

'I think I first approached Tom in April 1982,' recalled John Nathan-Turner. 'Initially he said that he was interested but would like to see a script. Then our first writer fell through, so we had hoped to have a script within three months but we didn't and the time was going on. Eventually in the December we were filming *The King's Demons* somewhere down south, and I knew that Tom was appearing at the Theatre Royal in Brighton and so I sent him the first 70 pages of the script, which was all we had. I met him after one of his shows to talk about it and at that time he had agreed to do it. We were then able to contact Terrance and tell him that Tom was to be included. Within about ten days or so, he pulled out and changed his mind.

'That was an extremely big hurdle to overcome, because we were saying up front that it's *The Five Doctors*, and really it was four and a bit, and one of those was a re-cast, so suddenly it started to look as though it was falling round my ears.'

In order to ensure that the fourth Doctor was represented in the show, Nathan-Turner had the idea of incorporating into the narrative some scenes from the *Doctor Who* story *Shada*, which had been partially completed in 1979 before industrial action at the BBC forced it to be cancelled. To this end on 10 January 1983 he wrote to both Tom Baker and Lalla Ward, who played his assistant Romana in the story, requesting permission to use clips from the cancelled story. Both artistes agreed.

'I knew this sort of thing was going to happen, but I don't think that even I was prepared for that!' exclaimed Terrance Dicks. 'At the start I asked Eric if they were sure that they'd got all the Doctors, and he said they were. But apparently there was some kind of confusion between Tom and Tom's agent and the BBC. Tom believed that he hadn't committed himself and the BBC genuinely felt that he had, and it was passed on to me that Tom was definitely going to be in it. I had in fact just completed my first draft, with Tom playing a major role, and the phone rang – this was happening every day, it was like a hotline to the *Doctor Who* office. It was Eric again. He asked how I was getting on and I told him proudly that I'd just finished the first draft and it was all ready to go to the typists. He said, "Oh my God," not the reaction I'd been expecting. I asked him what had happened now. He said, "You know what we said about Tom …" He explained about this confusion and was very apologetic. I had no choice but to go back to square one again.

'Tom in fact was going to steal the Master's transportation device and go back to Gallifrey, Davison was going to go to the Tower and work his way in through the front entrance and Hurndall was probably going to stay in the TARDIS with Turlough and Susan – all three would arrive with the TARDIS. There was also a sub-plot so you might feel that Tom was the villain or maybe he was going to ally himself with the villain. I felt that the Tom Baker Doctor was the one that you could believe would go bad: he has a darker side to him. Eric told me about the footage from *Shada*, the sequence in the punt, and so I came up with the idea that we could see Tom kidnapped. But that was all we could do with him – we couldn't have him in the story. Once again it all fell into place. The obvious thing was to have his kidnap bungled. The equipment was ancient and Borusa wasn't all that good at it anyway. So, we had the fourth Doctor trapped in a time warp. This gave me another menace, with the Baker Doctor being like a hole in the dyke.

'There was a danger that the Davison Doctor, followed by all the other Doctors, would be sucked in, giving a sense of urgency. If the Doctors didn't solve the problem by a given time, they would disappear together.

'My feeling is that it all worked better the way it ended up. Five Doctors were just too many to handle but four worked very neatly, and you do at least see Tom. The other thing that I found quite amazing was how well the scenes from *Shada* fitted in. I'll swear that if you didn't know, you would think it was written for the special.'

With all the Doctors covered, the remaining problem was the companions. Nathan-Turner was keen to include one companion per Doctor, and the original idea was to team Susan with the first Doctor, Victoria with the second Doctor, Jo with the third Doctor and Sarah with the fourth Doctor. However, despite agreeing to take part quite late in the day, Deborah Watling then had to drop out from playing Victoria as the location filming dates clashed with another project she was involved in, *The Dave Allen Show*, which was subsequently hit by a strike and never made. Katy Manning could not travel from Australia to play Jo and so Sarah was paired with the third Doctor instead and the Brigadier was put with the second Doctor.

Nicholas Courtney was actually asked whether he would appear in the special while he was recording *Mawdryn Undead* during August and September 1982. 'When I heard that all my old friends were going to be in it, Terrance Dicks was writing it and he had been involved with so many of the ones I had been in; I was going to be with Pat, I thought I had to be in it. Having been around with the programme for so long, I couldn't miss being in the special.'

As Dicks mentioned, the 'guest star' companions were confirmed at a very late stage, and among the casualties was John Levene who was approached to reprise his role as Sergeant Benton but who was unable to make the dates.

With regards to casting the other roles in the production, Charles Grey was considered for the part of Rassilon and Denis Quilley was felt suitable to play Borusa. Richard Bonehill was originally going to play a Cyberman in the studio, but he dropped out to be replaced by Mark Bassenger.

The costume and make-up fittings for the cast took place between 27 January and 28 March, with actor Richard Mathews, playing Rassilon, having a face cast made on 24 February. This was to allow an unknown actor to play Rassilon's body lying on top of the tomb.

'I cast Richard Mathews because he's a splendid actor,' explained Peter Moffat. 'I worked with him years ago in repertory when I was an actor and had always been impressed by his presence and his voice, rasping and deep and full of authority. He played a judge for me in an episode of *Lady Killers* for Granada TV and when I first read the script of *The Five Doctors* he immediately sprang to my mind. He had a difficult scene to play as he was, so to speak, disembodied. We did have his effigy lying on the top of his tomb and maybe he could have sat up out of this, but I felt in the end that he would have more impact by suddenly appearing in space above Borusa's head. After all, he had no longer any connection with that tomb, he was an all-pervading spirit.'

Pre-production

Unlike other *Doctor Who* productions, *The Five Doctors* was being produced in addition to the scheduled season and therefore the money with which to finance it had to be obtained from outside the standard allocation of funds to the programme. Realising that the show had a very great potential to be aired outside the UK, the BBC approached the Australian Broadcasting Commission with a view to obtaining co-funding. After numerous discussions, an agreement was signed on 7 April 1983 by the BBC and on 16 May 1983 by the ABC which brought in 60,000 Australian dollars towards the production budget, although the agreement stated that no credit to the co-producer would appear. The agreement meant that *The Five Doctors* was effectively pre-sold to the ABC in Australia.

With work on the script underway, there were several areas of concern in getting this particular programme off the ground, and another early requirement was the appointment of a director. John Nathan-Turner's original thought was to return to the very start of *Doctor Who* and to see if the services of the first director to work on the show could be secured. Waris Hussein was therefore approached about directing *The Five Doctors*, but on 20 December 1982 he declined to take part. The directorial duties were therefore taken up by Peter Moffatt, a freelance director who had already worked on the *Doctor Who* stories *State of Decay*, *The Visitation* and *Mawdryn Undead*.

Peter recalled being temporarily confused by the script when he first read it. 'Well to be quite honest, I didn't really understand why the Doctors were lifted one by one in the time scoop and then prevented from doing what was required of them by so many obstacles being set in their paths – they were enticed and then repelled. But as I began to work on the script I understood more and more. It was a game set for the satisfaction of Borusa with the Doctors being reacted upon like pawns in a game of chess, and the more times I read the script, the more I appreciated the basic theme. This is nothing unusual for me; I may be slightly blank about the content of the script on first reading and then as I begin to visualise it all happening on the screen the whole concept catches fire, my adrenaline begins to flow, my enthusiasm mounts and the whole script becomes an intrinsic part of me and for better or worse we march together, as one, towards the final realisation.'

On Location

For *The Five Doctors* Peter Moffatt was permitted to travel further afield than might normally have been considered for a *Doctor Who* production. He had initially thought that Scotland might offer the various bleak landscapes as described in Dicks' script but on further consideration he felt that this was perhaps too far from London and would eat into the allocation of filming days with travelling to and from the location. Instead he opted for Wales.

Jeremy Silberston, the production manager, managed to find all the required settings around the Ffestiniog area in North Wales – caves, mountainsides and bleak flat areas. When Moffatt visited the area with Silberston for a technical recce from 21 to 23 February 1983, everything was covered with deep snow; however, when they came to work there, the snow had melted and in its place were freezing winds, rain and mists which caused specific problems of their own. Also present on the recce were John Baker (film cameraman), John Gatland (sound recordist), Archie Dawson (lighting), June Collins (production associate), Malcolm Thornton (designer), John Brace (visual effects designer), Pauline Seager (assistant floor manager), Jean Peyre (design effects) and Gavin Birkett (television safety officer). A recce of the London locations took place on 24 February.

Following the recce, Gavin Birkett submitted a report to Jeremy Silberston dated 28 February, in which he listed several points to be borne in mind while at the Manod Quarry, one of the Welsh locations. These included the provision of safety harnesses for the Raston robot sequence, care when the Cyberman's hand pokes through a hole in a wall and the double checking of a loose slab of stone above one of the caves. The remainder of the report noted that safety helmets should be provided for everyone; there should be emergency lighting and hand-torches available; that unused areas should be cordoned off; and also that a landline telephone system be employed to communicate with the outside in case the walkie-talkie system failed. Finally, no gas appliances of any kind were to be taken in the caves, and everyone was to be warned of the dangers of exploring the various sites.

Prior to the location filming itself, there was a read-through of the script for the full cast on Friday 25 February in a conference room at BBC Television Centre, followed by location rehearsals at the BBC's Acton rehearsal rooms between 28 February and 3 March. Then the unit – comprising some twenty-nine cast and crew – set off for North Wales on Friday 4 March 1983, arriving just after midday, so that everything would be prepared and ready for the first section of filming on the following day.

The first location was Plasbrondanw at Llanfrothen which was to be used for the scenes set at the Eye of Orion and also for the sequence when the first Doctor was picked up by the spinning obelisk from his garden. The scenes with the fifth Doctor, Tegan and Turlough were filmed first, followed by the first Doctor being snatched from his garden.

Filming at Carreg Y Foel Gron, a desolate area just off the B4407, started on Monday 7 March. This was to become a waste-land area and the first scenes filmed were of the first Doctor and Susan traversing a rock-strewn area just prior to their discovery of the TARDIS. For this scene, the Doctor had to rest on a rock and, despite the fact that the valley was littered with them, there was not one single piece in the right position for Richard Hurndall to sink upon in an exhausted fashion. Therefore, amongst all the lumps of real rock were two pieces of fake rock supplied by the Visual Effects Department.

The next scene to be filmed was where the fifth Doctor, together with Susan and Tegan, discover the Master and are ambushed by the Cybermen. This sequence was continued the following day, with the Master joining forces with the Cybermen, and finally the scenes where the Cybermen prepare to detonate the bombs they have placed around the TARDIS were filmed. Also on 8 March, a special photographic session for the *Radio Times* took place.

The final scenes to be filmed at this location were on Wednesday 9 March. The crew had planned to start the day with some glass shots of the tower seen through the mountains, but the bad weather meant that these had to be scrapped. The shots were subsequently created electronically in the studio. The first scenes filmed this day, therefore, were shots of the Doctor and the Brigadier looking at the tower as the Doctor realises they are on the Death Zone in Gallifrey. A later scene featuring the Doctor and the Brigadier was also filmed. In the sequence when Patrick Troughton and Nicholas Courtney approached a cave beneath the tower, Peter Moffatt recalled seeing a wonderful vertiginous view of a mighty cliff face above a rocky path which the two actors had to cross to reach the cave mouth.

'As the cameras turned over to shoot the scene, down came a thick barrier of mist, blotting all else out of sight. Through the various takes necessary to shoot the scene, there were a brief few minutes when the mist vanished and all was dramatically revealed. Unfortunately the assistant cameraman had been obliged to go back to the car to get a new magazine of film and though I kept saying to myself, "Come back, come back!" by the time he did (and he could not really have been quicker), the mist swirled down again and the cliff face was obliterated. However, it looked all right in the end – bleak, isolated and unwelcoming. But I did miss that rocky precipice!'

The crew then moved to the third location, Manod Quarry, wherein a ruined building would be used for the sequence in which a hidden Cyberman grabs the Brigadier's arm through a hole in a wall. The quarry was also used on the following day to film a sequence set in the caves, where the second Doctor and the Brigadier are attacked by a Yeti but frighten it off with a firework.

By prior agreement, and in order to get all the material they needed to be filmed complete, while Peter Moffatt was supervising the filming of the sequence in the caves, so John Nathan-Turner was directing a series of visual effects close-ups to be edited into the battle between the Cybermen and the Raston Warrior robot elsewhere in the Manod quarry. 'Peter asked me to direct it before we went on location,' said Nathan-Turner. 'It was always scheduled as one day where we had a second unit. Originally Peter had asked me for another day on location but unfortunately we couldn't run to it so instead he asked for a second unit and asked me to direct it. I had the most marvellous day, blowing up the Cybermen.

'The night before, Peter and I had sat down with a map and

worked out where Jon and Lis would be and which ways all the shots should be and so on. The only real problem with the sequence was that Visual Effects put some substance on one Cyberman's mask to make it smoke but the smoke blew inside the mask and we had to rip, and I mean rip, the helmet off as the actor was nearly suffocating. It was almost a very nasty accident.'

The next day, Friday 11 March, Peter continued with the wide-angle shots of the Cybermen coming over the cliff edge, the robot materialising and vanishing and then later the moments when Jon Pertwee and Lis Sladen entered the scene and reacted to all that was going on. When edited together it all worked as required but it had been a toss-up as one day was misty and the next day was not and there was a fear that it might be difficult to join everything up together seemingly continuously. All this unending care over a long period of shooting resulted in about three minutes of final edited footage.

On the same day some further sequences were filmed with the second Doctor and the Brigadier.

After a day off, the crew returned to the quarry and, on Sunday 13 March, filmed the scenes where the third Doctor and Sarah are nearly caught by the Cybermen and become trapped between them and the Raston robot. The following day, and still at the quarry, the scene where the third Doctor and Sarah swing across to the tower was filmed as well as the short sequence where the third Doctor meets Sarah in the Death Zone for the first time.

The lake Cwm Bychan in Llanbedr was the final Welsh location. Film was shot here on Tuesday 15 March for when the Master first appears in the Death Zone as well as the meeting between the third Doctor, Sarah and the Master.

The shooting in Wales had many problems, not least of which was the weather. The location filming took place in March and at 1,500 feet up it was so cold that, as costume designer Colin Lavers commented, 'teeth hurt and faces turned blue'. Often the team were in the clouds and there was a cutting wind from the sea. As much thermal underwear as possible was worn, and because of the damp any costumes and props that could get wet had to be duplicated.

Obtaining two of nearly every costume caused its own problems. Because of the deepening economic recession, shops were not inclined to stock two items of the same size, and so this dictated in part what could be used. For instance Colin Lavers found what he wanted for Sarah's costume in John Lewis in Brent Cross but the shop had to obtain duplicates from branches in Oxford Street and Swiss Cottage.

The amount of water present on the location, both on the ground and in the air, was a constant problem. The Cybermen had to be glued together after they had been blown up with explosive charges. Lavers discovered that no glue would work well in the wet conditions and eventually one aerosol adhesive was found that just about worked. A large amount of silver paint was used on the Cybermen. The explosive charges would be put on, followed by a quick wipe with the hand, and then the paint spray. By the time they had finished they had used four dozen cans!

On Wednesday 16 March, having completed all the filming in Wales, the crew returned to London.

On Thursday 17 March, filming took place at Tilehouse Lane in Upper Denham, Buckinghamshire for the sequences where the third Doctor was snatched by the time scoop. From there the unit moved to a Ministry of Defence/YMCA Hostel in Hayling Lane which was to become the exterior of UNIT HQ, from where the second Doctor and the Brigadier were snatched. This location was the same as that used for the exterior of UNIT HQ in *The Three Doctors*.

It was while the crew was at this location that a final photo-call took place, this time for the press. Because of the absence of Tom Baker from the line-up, John Nathan-Turner had arranged for a waxwork effigy of him to be brought from Madame Tussaud's in London, and the other four Doctors dutifully posed with the dummy of the fourth Doctor.

This was something of a stroke of inspiration as it almost ensured good newspaper coverage on the following day with the papers variously asking readers to spot 'Who' was not 'Who'.

The crew finally moved to outside a house at 2 West Common Road in Uxbridge, Middlesex, where the scenes of Sarah bidding farewell to K-9 and being snatched as she waited for a bus were filmed.

The final day's filming on Friday 18 March took place at the Television Film Studios in Ealing, where sets had been erected for the interior of UNIT HQ and for the top of the tower which the third Doctor and Sarah slide down a wire to. Once all these scenes had been completed, preparation started for the studio recordings which were, by now, only eleven days away.

In Studio

As soon as they returned from the location work, the cast were straight into rehearsals for the studio sessions. These took place at the BBC's rehearsal rooms in Acton up until the 28 March. On the 26 March, a technical run-through took place where any final questions or problems with the technicalities of the studio recording were ironed out and resolved.

Much of designer Malcolm Thornton's planning time before recording was spent in trying to balance only three days of recording with the number of studio settings. There were ten sets to shoot and turn around over the three days – almost as many sets as for a normal four-part story which would be spread over two studio sessions, one of three days' duration and one of two days'. The initial studio requirements were: the metal corridors, the Brigadier's office, interior of the Tower (three levels), the ante-room with the chequered floor, Rassilon's tomb, the TARDIS interior and the roof of the Tower. The amount of setting and striking overnight dictated how much could be recorded in the time available and this was why it had been decided to film at Ealing Television Film Studios in addition to recording at BBC Television Centre.

Another planning problem for Thornton and Moffatt was working out the order of studio recording. All the most important scenes had to be shot so that if anything went wrong there was time to correct it. A lot of the scenes in the TARDIS control room with Tegan, Turlough and the Davison Doctor were left to the end just in case the studio recording did overrun. It would have been much easier, and less expensive, to recall these actors than most of the rest of the cast.

Thornton decided to use post-production techniques for various wide shots using mattes, such as the roof of the Tower and the ceiling of Rassilon's tomb. This technique had been successfully used in *The Hitch-Hiker's Guide to the Galaxy*, and is a method by which one can pre-record, or pre-film, sequences of action and then electronically reduce that action and expand the surrounding background using painted images and the Quantel electronic image processor, to create a composite picture. Another example in *The Five Doctors* was the front door that the first Doctor and Tegan entered by. (The door opening was achieved by moving a piece of flat scenery behind an electronic wipe!)

This technique also replaced the planned glass shots and model shots on location. Here the crew were very much working against time with wet and windy weather conditions that were not at all good enough for glass shots. Model shots were impossible in the unexpectedly high winds and at one point the team were instantly making decisions to scrap model shots and to drop in matte shots later.

For the design of the sets and costumes for the various rooms on Gallifrey, the overall style had already been established in previous stories, most notably *The Deadly Assassin* and *Arc of Infinity*, so Thornton and Lavers had to consider what had been seen before.

The hieroglyphics used on the obelisk in Rassilon's tomb were based on some Time Lord symbols originated in Piccolo Books' *The Making of Doctor Who* published in 1972. Through John Nathan-Turner, Thornton got hold of a copy. This is why the symbols which, in the book, denote the Doctor's name appear on the obelisk – it was not an intentional reference to the Doctor.

Thornton also devised a lightning symbol which he used on the obelisk and all over the interior of the tomb. He and John Brace were talking about the model of the Tower and they remembered the scene where the Master nearly gets zapped by lightning bolts in the wastelands and thought it a good theme to use as a decorative logo. So they used the inverted lightning flash as a device throughout.

The metal corridors in which the first Doctor and Susan encounter a Dalek were described in the script as 'highly polished'. Originally it had been thought that these sequences might be filmed somewhere on location but it was later realised that it would have cost too much to dress as required, so it was decided to do it in the studio. In the end Thornton decided to make the whole thing look as confusing as possible, rather than being regularly linear, with right angles and square panels. He felt it would be much more effective if any recognisable surfaces were destroyed, so stock flattage was used, dressed up using silver-brushed aluminium, polished mirrors and plastics that reflected into each other. The idea was that when the Dalek appeared it had three images when it passed. Thornton worked out carefully which surfaces would play onto others, the reflections that would be achieved and where they would appear. But, scenery being the way it is, by the time it had been moved around and finally put up in the studio during the first night (in place of the Tower corridors set) the optical perfection had been lost. However, once it had been lit and patched up it did exactly what had been wanted. Instead of optically pure images there were extraneous and distorted reflections which made the whole thing look sinister and even more confusing.

The problem with the Tower corridors was that a single set, for economic reasons, was available to represent the upper, middle and lower levels of the Tower. Thornton designed it so that it would look different when shot from three different positions, to give the effect of coming up from below, coming down from above and passing through on ground level. He had a few of the lightning symbols put on or taken off, and subtly changed the lighting and dressing.

Overnight on the second day of the studio recording the Gallifrey composite (corridors, game control and conference room) was taken down and Rassilon's tomb was put up. It had been decided to use a post-production matte to create a high-vaulted roof, so when the scenes were recorded the studio lights could be seen above the set walls. The final set had the tomb in the middle, a series of architectural elements around to define the space, the transmat at one end and the entrance to the tomb at the other. Because this was a long sequence with a lot of action, the production ended up using the whole width of the studio. After the tomb scenes had been recorded the central raised tomb was then removed to reveal a painted chequer-board and the architectural elements re-arranged to create the ante-room where the Cybermen were to be destroyed. While Rassilon's tomb was being changed into the ante-chamber the scene with the first Doctor and Tegan entering the Tower was being rehearsed and recorded in another part of the studio.

John Nathan-Turner had commissioned Visual Effects to build a new TARDIS control console and in one of the first rewrites had insured there was inserted a scene with the Doctor fiddling with the new console. Therefore Thornton felt that there was some justification in re-vamping the console room interior as well. This was an additional design requirement to the original script but it was something that would be seen in many programmes to come. John Nathan-Turner wanted to keep the roundels, and knowing the form that the new console would take, Thornton thought they could subtly make the set more angular. So they made the TARDIS walls symmetrical, making the set easier to erect in studio.

The new design meant that the console could go in only one position in relation to the walls and each facet of the console related to a facet of the walls. Thornton's aim, which he felt he had achieved, was to get more relief interest in the walls. He used fewer roundels and also restyled the main doors slightly. When both doors were open on the new set the outside could not be seen from a normal cross-shooting camera position.

To indicate some of the considerations involved in making a *Doctor Who* story during the Peter Davison era, what follows is a scene-by-scene summary of *The Five Doctors*, with comments from some of those involved in the production. Additional information about the production is given in square brackets. The story was made and originally transmitted over ten years ago as a single approximately 90-minute production. It was split into four approximately 25-minute episodes primarily for overseas sales, although the four-part version was also shown in the UK in 1984. The episode endings for the four-part version are indicated at the points that they occurred.

The Five Doctors

In the TARDIS console room, the Doctor (Peter Davison) is flicking and polishing the controls with a duster.

Peter Moffatt: This was a new console room and that's why Peter is polishing it off, so that we can all see how beautiful it is.

John Brace: The new console was designed and built by a team headed by designer Mike Kelt who was brought in specifically to handle that task.

Tegan (Janet Fielding) enters, concerned that the TARDIS will now work properly.

PM: I had no say in the short skirted costumes for the ladies. John kept saying, 'Something for the fathers …'

The Doctor chides her and tries to open the doors. They don't operate and he bangs the console to make them open.
The TARDIS is at the Eye of Orion, a tranquil stopover point. Turlough (Mark Strickson) is outside, sketching.

PM: This was a lovely location with this wonderful view. I think the building was a ruined abbey.

Meanwhile, in a hidden control room an unseen, black-gloved person is operating the forbidden controls of a time scoop and is homing in on the Doctor's previous selves: the first Doctor (Richard Hurndall) is picked up by a black spinning obelisk in a garden.

PM: That garden was designed and built by Sir Clough Williams-Ellis, the same chap who designed and built Portmerion. Williams-

Ellis's widow, Lady Annabel, who owned the house, asked John and me to tea and it was a real old-fashioned affair with cake stands and little scones and everything just so. She was a lovely lady. Her house was Elizabethan, not an Italianate mixture as in Portmerion.

JB: The control consoles were all made from black perspex for the game control room set.

When the Doctor has been snatched, a small model of him appears in a box in the time scoop control room. It is picked up and placed on one of five segments on a games board.

JB: The bulk of the games board was made from vacuum-formed plastic, but we had to create the shape of the Tower in the middle. It was quite a large model and it was tricky to tie in all the elements. I think Tony Auger was involved in constructing the model. You always tried to apportion out single items of work to the design assistants and leave them to get on with it once you had talked with them about the initial ideas and what the prop had to do. This then allowed you to get on with the rest of the work. The game was always seen to be a key element in explaining what was going on and so we were able to spend a little bit more of the budget on it than on other elements which were perhaps not so key.

JB: All the miniatures had to be hand crafted and had to be proper caricatures. I remember talking to Julie Jones of BBC Marketing about the models to see if they could be exploited after the show.

The fifth Doctor suddenly clutches his chest in pain. A twinge of cosmic angst, as if he has lost something.
    The second Doctor (Patrick Troughton) and the Brigadier (Nicholas Courtney) are snatched from the grounds of UNIT HQ, where the Brigadier was to be guest of honour at a UNIT reunion with Colonel Crichton (David Savile), his replacement.

[In the rehearsal script, it is the Brigadier's last day in office before he retires. The Brigadier is handing over command to his replacement, Brigadier Charles Crichton.

The costume for the Brigadier was fairly easy as he was an ex-Army type, but Colin Lavers had to keep in mind that he had to be as warm as possible as he was on location as much as Patrick Troughton.]

PM: The spinning obelisk was put on in post-production. I wish it hadn't been a black triangle. It looks all right once the pictures get in it, but before it's just a bit blank.

The fifth Doctor again winces in pain and collapses. Two more figurines are placed on the board.

The third Doctor (Jon Pertwee) is driving in Bessie, his car, when he encounters the scoop. He thinks he has eluded it but he is snatched.

[Because Bessie needed an overhaul before it could be used in the production, John Nathan-Turner gained agreement that the production would pay the first £250 of the refurbishment costs, with the remainder to be covered by BBC Exhibitions who would be able to use the car thereafter.]

Sarah Jane Smith (Elisabeth Sladen) says farewell to K-9 (Voice: John Leeson) at her front gate despite the robot's warnings of danger.

[For Sarah Jane's costume, Lavers recalls that he chose something which would suit the actress's personality but which would not clash with the outfit worn by the third Doctor. Actress Elisabeth Sladen, however recalls that it was she who chose the costume.]

PM: I liked the area of water in front of the house because it adds interest to the location which would otherwise have been a little dreary.

John Leeson: When I first started doing the voice of K-9, they used to put it through a ring-modulator or some such device to put a very tinny edge on it, but the treatment's been getting less and less and I've been finding myself sort of growing into the voice of K-9. On the filming of *The Five Doctors*, the sound supervisor came up to me and said, 'Look, no, we don't want any treatment; just do it yourself.' So I did!

The fourth Doctor (Tom Baker) and Romana (Lalla Ward) are relaxing on a punt on the river Cam. As they steer the boat under a bridge, they too are snatched.

PM: That was the footage from *Shada* that John provided. I had nothing to do with the selection of material.

As each person is taken from their own time, the black-gloved figure places a large figurine of each on a big, circular games board, split into five zones, each radiating from a sinister castle-like structure in the centre. All except the fourth Doctor and Romana, for they have been caught up in a time eddy and are trapped in the temporal void.

JB: I always enjoyed designing consoles and setting up all the lights to flash underneath. On the consoles here, underneath the perspex were lots of square egg-box-shaped compartments with the lights in so that when they lit up in sequence, you got the little cubes of light appearing on the perspex panel.

The fifth Doctor, in a rapidly weakening state, operates the TARDIS controls and collapses.
  Sarah Jane Smith is snatched by the spinning obelisk as she waits for a bus.
  In the TARDIS, the fifth Doctor lies on the floor. As Tegan and Turlough watch, he starts to fade from sight.

PM: We wanted a high camera angle on that shot so that he could disappear without getting Janet's or Mark's feet in shot.

The TARDIS materialises on a bleak and windswept plain. In the distance can be seen the Tower, and on the games board the final three figures are placed.

The remaining members of the High Council of Time Lords on Gallifrey – President Borusa (Philip Latham), Chancellor Flavia (Dinah Sheridan) and the Castellan (Paul Jerricho) – are aware that there is evil afoot, for all four Doctors' time traces are found to converge in the newly-activated Death Zone on Gallifrey

PM: With regards to the casting of the Council, Paul Jerricho had been in *Doctor Who* previously as the Castellan. I cast Philip Latham as Borusa mainly because of the final scenes. I considered him to be a very thinking actor and wanted someone with a bit of authority. I had worked with Dinah Sheridan years ago at Yorkshire television and loved the experience. She's got an elegance too and I also thought she looked authentically aristocratic.

[The standard Time Lord costumes were eight years old as they had originally been made for *The Deadly Assassin*, and fibre glass has a limited life. After a while it tightens up and becomes very brittle. This made getting into the formal Time Lord collars very difficult as they needed to be flexed open to get them over the artistes' shoulders. They were also very heavy and tended to fall back which meant the actor had to keep his arms around the collar to stop it doing so. This made movement very restrictive and as most of the time the Time Lords were sitting down, the formal collar was used only at the end for Flavia.

Borusa's costume was a variation of the Time Lord costume, using different fabrics. The colour was pale to make it look bigger and the costume cut square off the body to maximise the shape.]

JB: We designed the little handsets that the Council members are using. They were supposed to be small machines that you rest your palm on and then use your fingers to tap out the digits. They're nice little props to design and make.

There is only one hope of escape for the Doctor and for this the

Council have summoned the Master (Anthony Ainley). In exchange for a free pardon and a new regeneration cycle, he must enter the Zone and rescue the Doctor.

[With the costume for the Master, there was again the problem of two costumes being needed for location, so a second black velvet outfit had to be made. The original one had Victorian embroidery on the neck which had to be copied as near as possible. This was not too easy as it had oxidised silver in a North African pattern. The embroidery was done by Locks, who embroider for the Queen and Queen Mother.]

In a metallic corridor the first Doctor meets up with Susan (Carole Ann Ford), his granddaughter. They narrowly escape from a rampaging Dalek (Operator: John Scott Martin; voice: Roy Skelton) by tricking it into exterminating itself. They then begin the long trek towards the Tower.

[In an early draft of Terrance Dicks' script there was a scene where Susan was picked up by the obelisk while she was walking through an outdoor market in London. This was cut at the scripting stage.

Colin Lavers had originally thought that Susan had been left on present-day Earth and so clothed her as a woman of today. As it turned out the costume could well be suited for the time she was left in.]

PM: Working with reflecting corridors can be tricky, but as long as you work it out beforehand and don't point your cameras directly into the mirrors then there are not too many problems. It was very difficult to light because of the enclosed space and it was tricky for the sound booms as well.

JB: The moving Dalek was taken from stock, but we replaced the top half with an exploding version for the shot when it blows up. Malcolm James was one of the assistants on this and I remember practising the explosion in the effects workshop. The top part of the Dalek had to be created with all the insides in place. The explosions were titanium magnesium flash charges. There would have been eight or nine charges in the Dalek's casing and they were contained in steel mortars which, when they went off, blew the various outer panels off revealing the pulsating creature inside. There were airlines in the Dalek creature that is revealed, to make its tentacles thrash and writhe using compressed air from a bottle. The wall behind the Dalek was pre-cut, hinged and held together with some fine line which was broken with a small charge at the appropriate point.

The other Doctors also begin making their way towards the tower, each hampered by different menaces: the second Doctor and the Brigadier are nearly caught by a lone Cyberman (Emyr Morris Jones), and the third Doctor meets Sarah when she tumbles down an incline at the side of a road.

PM: There should have been a greater drop there. I think the problem was in trying to find somewhere where the path was on the edge for the car. It would have been better if we had used a stunt girl and a proper cliff. As it is the Doctor could just have stepped down and helped her up.

[End of part one.]

JB: We used smoke guns to create some of the mists and smoke that drifts across to obscure the roadway. There are a couple of shots here when a smoke effect has been overlaid on the picture afterwards.

The first Doctor and Susan find the TARDIS. They go inside and, the first and fifth Doctors meet and discuss the situation.
    The first Doctor suggests that Tegan make some tea while they decide what to do.

PM: Janet nearly had a fit over this. 'Why pick on the woman to make the tea? Why pick on me? Why should I make the tea?' She only agreed to go with the scene when Turlough went with her to help.

[In the rehearsal script it was Susan who suggested she help Tegan to make the tea.]

The Council give the Master their seal and a recall device which will bring him back to the conference room when activated. He enters a transmat device and is transported into the Death Zone.

PM: In that scene it's nice that Diana Sheridan is in shot when the Master disappears. She had to stand very still while it was being done and it worked very well.

The second Doctor explains to the Brigadier that the Tower is Rassilon's tomb, placed in the centre of the Death Zone on Gallifrey which was used by the ancient Gallifreyans. They would kidnap different races and set them in the Zone. This barbaric practice was stopped by Rassilon when he became President. The Zone was closed off and the Tomb placed in its centre as a warning.

The Master comes across a desiccated corpse lying on the ground. He recognises it as one of the Council who had preceded him. A fire bolt shoots from the sky and the Master moves off.

[The shot of the corpse was edited out of the American version of the story as it was felt to be too strong.]

JB: I think the body might have been created by Stan Mitchell, another of the workshop assistants.

In the TARDIS, a meal has been laid out which the companions help themselves to as the Doctors argue.

PM: I don't know what the idea behind all that food was. I think that nobody ever knows what food they have on the TARDIS. It was sort of like manna from heaven, ambrosia, because the Doctor never eats.

The third Doctor and Sarah meet up with the Master but refuse to believe him when he says that he has been sent to help them. They drive off when more lightning bolts crash from the skies. The Master runs off, dodging the bolts. Shortly after, Bessie is hit by a bolt and is immobilised. The third Doctor and Sarah continue on foot.

JB: What we had there were nice balls of flame. We used small camping gas cylinders with a small charge in the dimple at the top. What we had found was that if you wanted a ball of flame, you'd fill up a polythene bag with gas and then ignite that. Under these conditions that would have been difficult and you also wouldn't have got the nice spout of gas that takes the flame up into the air.

The fifth Doctor, having gained strength from the presence of the first Doctor, sets off for the tower along with Susan and Tegan. Once they get there they will deactivate the force field that is holding the TARDIS in place so that the first Doctor and Turlough can join them there in the TARDIS.

  The third Doctor and Sarah are making their way up a mountain when they see a squad of Cybermen (Lee Woods, Richard Naylor, Myrddin Jones, Gilbert Gillan, Emyr Morris Jones) lower down the mountain.

PM: It's sometimes tricky to get the timing right when you are directing a group that is far away from the camera and they have to make timed separate entrances into shot.

[There is a big problem with claustrophobia in a Cyberman costume. It takes ten minutes to get into the suit, and two more to get the head on, fastened with two large screws. The actors are very aware that they cannot take off the heads themselves and so Colin Lavers warned the director that if he saw any sign of panic he'd walk into the shot and stop it. The main problem with this was that Colin was always looking at the actors, but was never quite sure what the signs of panic would be.]

The second Doctor and the Brigadier find a cave into the mountain. The Doctor remembers an old nursery rhyme about the Tower which mentions three entrances: above, between, below. They are going below, and beside the entrance there is a flaming brazier and some torches, one of which they take to light their way.

PM: The torches had firelighters in the top so that they would light easily and flame well.

JB: We had to make these up and used the lightning logo which Malcolm Thornton had worked out. They had to be safe to transport about as well and reasonably practical to make.

The fifth Doctor, Tegan and Susan make their way across the wasteland.

PM: Poor Janet. John insisted that she wore these ridiculous high-heeled shoes and you never see her feet. They sank into the mud because it was so wet and she walked out of her shoes several times. It was awful. She really was shaking with the cold. I felt so sorry for her.

The Master hails the fifth Doctor from a gully and he goes to speak with him. A Cyber scout (William Kenton) sees them and reports back to the Cyber Leader (David Banks) and the Cyber Lieutenant (Mark Hardy). The Cybermen go to detain them but the Time Lords run off. The Cybermen open fire and the Master gets caught in an explosion and is knocked out.

PM: These explosions were tricky to time. Especially the one where the Master was running away.

JB: The action here really gives the whole game away. We wanted it to be very visual and there is a point when both the Doctor and the Master are looking back at the Cybermen, away from the explosion, and that's when we fired it off. It's the essence of a good explosion. You warn and work with the artistes and tell them what will happen step by step.

The fifth Doctor is trapped as he bends to check the Master. Susan and Tegan run back to the TARDIS, but Susan trips and sprains her ankle. The fifth Doctor takes and activates the recall device that the Council gave the Master and he is transported to the conference room. Meanwhile the Master recovers and swears allegiance to the Cyber Leader.

The fifth Doctor shows the Council the recall device – it has a homing beacon in it which is how the Cybermen found them so quickly. One of the Council is a traitor! Borusa orders the Castellan's office and living quarters to be searched.

JB: The homing device had a small but bright LED in it, and it also had to contain a battery.

The Cybermen decide to use the Master. When he is of no further use he will be killed.

The first Doctor and Tegan have already left the TARDIS for the Tower when Susan and Turlough hear sounds from outside – they operate the scanner and see Cybermen.

[End of part two.]

In the cave, the second Doctor and the Brigadier are chased by a Yeti (Lee Woods).

PM: There was this incredible great deep lake in the caves which was difficult to light because it was so vast. You couldn't see very much of anything. On a location like this you work out very carefully in advance where you're going to film as it can be very dangerous and slippery in places.

The third Doctor and Sarah encounter a Raston Warrior Robot (Keith Hodiak) on the mountain slope. They freeze – it is programmed to react to movement.

PM: The robot was played by a dancer, Keith Hodiak, and at one point when he was inside the costume he had to go to the toilet. He ended up with this terrible stain on the costume which wouldn't dry and so someone had to hold a fan up against him to try and dry it off before the next take. We had hired a dancer for the leaps because he had to be able to jump high enough not to land.

JB: We designed this robot with a smooth, reflective head. It was made from a vacuum formed silver chrome material which, once you thinned it out, you could actually see through like a half-silvered mirror. Unfortunately it kept misting up on location.

The Castellan is accused of being the traitor after the Black Scrolls of Rassilon are found in his quarters. The scrolls spontaneously ignite in their box and the Castellan is led off by the guards (John Tallents, Norman Bradley, Lloyd Williams) to be subjected to the mind probe.

PM: The number of times I tried to get Paul to say, 'Not the *mind* probe.' Yet he insisted on, 'Not the mind *probe*.' It doesn't sound like English at all somehow. We did about four takes but he never got it right.

JB: The box was electronically controlled. We had holes drilled through the table underneath to take the control wires. We had to use some hot coils to make it smoke first of all and then the flames had to come later. It also had to be self-extinguishing. We rehearsed it under studio conditions, to make sure it worked, without the pressures of time.

The Castellan is conveniently killed by the Guard Commander (Stuart Blake) 'whilst trying to escape'. The fifth Doctor does not believe this and suspects that someone else is the traitor.

[Eight-year-old costumes were being used for the Chancellery Guards. The helmets tended to be too large but were not too much of a problem. However, the original fibre-glass knee and elbow patches were tightening up and had become very brittle, so much so that the elbow patches could not be used.]

JB: We designed the guns you see here. The guard has one and there is another lying beside the body.

The second Doctor and the Brigadier move further into the caves. The Doctor finds a narrow cave and they squeeze in. Luckily, it is too small for the Yeti to follow.

PM: There was a huge drop down from the walkway but you can't really see it. We found a whole area with all these locations in and it was too good an opportunity to miss, really.

[An original Yeti costume, made of goatskin, was found rolled up in a box in the stores and had to be laid out for two weeks to get it straightened out. Colin got into the costume to try it out and see what size of person was needed. There was only one foot so a new pair was made. No beak was used as the costume would only be used in a cave with lots of cables and fireworks and the field of vision would be restricted too much.]

JB: We used lumps of dry ice in the pool to make it smoke and bubble.

The Doctor pulls from his pockets a firework – a galactic glitter – and after lighting it from the flaming torch throws it at the Yeti. Rocks fall from above, effectively trapping them. The Doctor notices that there is an air-flow and they move off deeper into the cave.

PM: The section of cave that they were in tailed off to nothing. The next sequence was in a different part of the caves.

JB: We constructed the firework that the Doctor held. It would have been safe for the actor to hold. When the rocks fall here, you can just see that they are attached to a net. We had to close the way out when the rocks fell, and the only way to ensure that was to have a net which we threw down over the entrance. Unfortunately you can just see it as the net shudders at the end.

Nicholas Courtney: Pat Troughton took one look at the cave mouth and said, 'You're not getting me in there!' But we did. There was also lots of polystyrene rock as opposed to real rock in the little niche that we hid from the Yeti in and so we had to be very careful with the flaming torch not to set the rock alight. One had to be sure to hold the torch under real rock and not under polystyrene rock, otherwise the whole place would have gone up in smoke.

They find a doorway across the cave and enter the lower section of the Tower.

PM: That was built across an existing tunnel by Malcolm Thornton.

Susan and Turlough watch as the Cybermen outside the TARDIS prepare a coffin-like bomb.
    The third Doctor and Sarah are saved when the Cybermen that were following them appear. The Robot quickly and efficiently destroys all the Cybermen, cutting them to pieces with steel bolts and discs (stunt Cyberman: Stuart Fell; other Cybermen as previously on location). The third Doctor and Sarah take advantage of the diversion and carry on up to the mountain having taken some of the Robot's spare weapons.

Terrance Dicks: The Raston Robot sequence came about because we had reached a point in the story where the Pertwee Doctor and Sarah were going to go through into the tower. We needed one last major obstacle. We didn't want another old monster like a Yeti or a Cyberman as we'd already used them and so this was the place to come up with something new. The robot was planned to be simple and effective; sometimes you write something regardless and hope the production team do it as well as they can. But by this stage everyone was screaming about the cost, and also Peter Moffatt was getting worried about the amount of location filming he had to get through. So we planned something that was both practical and good. Something we knew they could do, that at the same time would be effective. It was a kind of martial-arts robot. We worked out this business of the smooth egg face and the silver figure and the gimmick that it can practically teleport: it moves at such a speed that it goes from here to there without being seen, and that was it really. An idea that didn't make it to the final version was that the robot was very tidy-minded and would stack all the bits of Cyberman up into a neat pile outside its cave. One bit that was added was the Cyberman being sick, and another was when the Dalek exploded. I didn't write all that about the dying creature inside, but I was very pleased when they added it.

JB: We had three or four different things that happened to Cybermen. This one loses an arm, this one's head blows up and so on. It was quite a challenge to put together a battle sequence in an afternoon when you have the pressure of the weather and all that. It is all so quickly cut together that you don't notice the individual shots and it just creates the impression of overall carnage.

[From a costume-design point of view, the script required the Raston Robot to move its hand over one shoulder, which meant it could not be an armoured type and had to be flexible and more plastic. The headpiece had a mirrored visor: when it was light outside the actor could see out, but in Wales this was not always the case and often he was almost blind. With so many loose rocks, that was quite dangerous and often he had to be led on and off the location.]

The fifth Doctor speaks with Chancellor Flavia. The Doctor does not believe that the Castellan was the traitor and he decides to speak to President Borusa.

The third Doctor and Sarah arrive on a precipice overlooking the Tower. The Doctor starts to unravel the rope obtained from the Raston Robot's cave.

The first Doctor and Tegan arrive at the main entrance to the Tower. The Doctor activates an electronic bell-shaped device and the door slides open.

The third Doctor lassos one of the Tower's cornices with some steel rope. He and Sarah slide down it, much to the dismay of the Master and the remaining Cybermen who are watching from further down the mountain.

TD: That was originally a hang-gliding sequence. I thought that we could have the third Doctor turn his cloak into a hang-glider and just fly to the Tower. But it wasn't possible to do it in the time, so we came up with them sliding down the wire instead. It's always *Star Wars* on a shoestring with *Doctor Who* and you are always fighting against what's possible and what isn't. I think it's amazing that they do so well. It's always a part of your brief that you must come up with something amazing, astonishing and cheap!

JB: This was originally going to be a bow-and-arrow idea to fire something across the gap. In the end we had a bit of a problem with that and it broke, and I think that Pertwee couldn't use it. In the end we came up with the idea of a lasso. I remember rigging something up in the studio so that we could get them swinging along the line to the top of the Tower.

PM: There was an enormous pause in filming during this sequence for over an hour because Jon Pertwee refused to do the scene. The Doctor was supposed to build a bow and arrow from the bits he had picked up, and I had kept asking and asking how he was supposed to do this, and how this thing should be made and everyone said it would be all right. When we got to the scene, Jon couldn't see how it could be done. In the end, while the Cybermen were nearly frozen to death in the valley down below, John Nathan-Turner, Pertwee and myself went to a car somewhere out of the cold and worked out a way to make the scene work.

That was a great mixture of different shots that we were unable to do at the same time. Jon threw the lasso on a cliff-top in a howling gale in Wales; it landed on a pinnacle on a set in the film studio at Ealing; they slid down the wire at Ealing; the Master looking up at it, surrounded by Cybermen, was in the bottom of a valley in Wales; and the high shot of the Tower was matted in afterwards. But when edited together, it all worked like a dream.

The Doctor helps Sarah onto the top of the Tower.

PM: Lis is quite high off the ground there. The parapet was about eight feet off the ground. The composite shot there is really nice. It's the film at Ealing plus the painted Tower plus the filmed background.

JB: I know we had to make a bigger version of the top of the Tower for that. Jean Peyre got involved with this scene as well to match all the elements together.

The first Doctor and Tegan have arrived in the entrance hall of the Tower only to be confronted by a deadly floor pattern of electrified squares. They hide as the Master, followed by the Cyber Leader, Cyber Lieutenant and a group of Cybermen (Graham Cole, Alan Riches, Ian Marshall-Fisher, Mark Bassenger) enter. The Master demonstrates that the pattern is safe to the Cybermen by crossing it. The Cybermen follow only to be destroyed by bolts of electricity from the ceiling. The Cyber Leader demands to know the safe route, but the Master turns a cyber weapon on the Cyber Leader as he is following him across.

JB: You can't see any wires trailing from the Cybermen to trigger the explosions because there weren't any. My assistant on the show, Malcolm James, suggested that to avoid the problem of trailing wires, we got the actors playing the Cybermen to trigger the explosions themselves using small battery packs. This was a great idea and really worked well in the studio.

There was almost a problem in the studio when the Cybermen were being sprayed to cover up the various explosive charges placed there by Visual Effects. The spray could all too easily drift into the costume and choke the actor.

The first Doctor deduces from the Master's comment that it is as easy as pie, that the squares have a safe path across derived from the calculation of pi. He and Tegan follow the Master across.

The fifth Doctor finds that Borusa, who was in the conference room and has not left, is no longer there. He begins to search the room.

The third Doctor and Sarah move down through the Tower. Sarah is feeling scared so the Doctor checks ahead. He meets phantoms of Mike Yates (Richard Franklin) and Liz Shaw (Caroline John) which vanish screaming when he realises they are not real.

[In the rehearsal script there were no scenes present with the phantom companions. Instead, Sarah Jane was physically attacked by a phantom of the third Doctor after the real Doctor has left her on her own.

Colin Lavers chose for Liz some present-day clothes, simply something that suited the actress and was comfortable to wear. Yates wore a costume from stock, but to emphasise that he was a phantom and the mind conjuring it was not perfect, there were no UNIT insignia.]

The first Doctor and Tegan pass by a flight of stairs on their way through the Tower. The Master comes down the steps behind them.

[End of part three.]

The second Doctor and the Brigadier encounter phantoms of Jamie (Frazer Hines) and Zoe (Wendy Padbury) on a flight of stairs leading up. The phantoms vanish screaming when the Doctor realises that the real Jamie and Zoe would not have known who they were.

[Colin Lavers again used the 1973 *Radio Times* special for costume reference for Jamie and Zoe. There were two different tartans shown in the magazine in colour, but one had been specially shot for the publication. The actual McCrimmon tartan was mainly blue, but when Frazer Hines saw it he commented that it was not the right one. Eventually a red and green eighteenth-century kilt was hired that had been used in the film *Bonnie Prince Charlie*.

For Zoe's costume Colin wanted to reflect the sixties plastic look, particularly as Zoe had tended to wear plastic-looking clothes, and so he used packaging material. If Zoe had had to move around it would have been far too noisy but it was quite suitable for the short scene.]

The fifth Doctor notices the Harp of Rassilon by a wall and realises that a musical key must open a hidden door. He begins to experiment on the Harp.

PM: Peter played the harp himself at this point as he's quite musical.

The first, second and third Doctors all meet up in the main hall of the tower. They translate the hieroglyphs on a small monolith: whoever takes the ring from Rassilon's finger will have eternal life. The Master steps forward from the entrance to the room – now he will claim eternal life. He threatens the Doctors with his tissue compression eliminator weapon. The Brigadier jumps him from behind and he is tied up.

The fifth Doctor plays the correct tune on the Harp, read from a painting on the wall, and a door slides open revealing the forbidden games control room.

PM: Peter didn't play that sequence. We had a lady harpist come in for the sound dub to record the music.

In the games control room, President Borusa is dressed in black and is presiding over the game board – he is quite mad. He is after immortality and has used the Doctors to breach the tomb's defences.

[Borusa's black costume was almost an opposite to his normal costume. It was cut to emphasise height and thinness with converging lines, using various black materials. If only one black material had been used then only a black blob would have appeared on the screen. Colin Lavers had designed a new collar made out of black wire to give the impression of cobwebs and possibly provide the director with interesting shots through it. Unfortunately, Philip Latham found it rather inhibiting and couldn't wear it.]

JB: Some of the consoles in the room were practical and some were dummies. The walls were made from those milk crate things. Malcolm was always up against the budgets and if he could re-use materials then he would. In this case, the walls look really good with the lighting behind them.

The Doctors find a communication and control system in the tomb and the third Doctor reverses the polarity of the neutron flow, thus allowing the TARDIS to come through the force field.

The Cybermen by the TARDIS detonate their bombs just as the

TARDIS dematerialises and heads for the Tower on pre-set co-ordinates.

JB: The explosion was done with a locked-off camera and a cut immediately before the explosion so that the TARDIS could be removed. There's also another of our small props there, which the Cyberman uses to detonate the bombs.

Borusa is wearing the Coronet of Rassilon, and with his mind enhanced by this he takes over the fifth Doctor's mind. He and the fifth Doctor then go to the transmat, where the second Doctor is trying to make contact.

PM: The sequences on the monitor with the second Doctor were fed through live from the other set, but the Peter Davison sequence was pre-recorded. You can see that the background is different.

The fifth Doctor and Borusa arrive in the tomb and Borusa freezes the companions in time. The other three Doctors link minds and free the fifth.

PM: To do that sequence of cutting between the Doctors we just used the normal number of cameras and changed position if we needed to between shots.

The voice of Rassilon booms out that this is the game of Rassilon.

TD: Having put Rassilon at the end to resolve it all, I envisaged him as a kind of Valentine Dyall type actor; tall and gaunt and impressive. I think in the end it worked quite well because Rassilon didn't look the way you expected him to. I think I had envisaged a more elaborate projection of the giant Rassilon, you would actually see a giant Rassilon towering above at the end of the story, but again it's a matter of time and budget.

Rassilon's face (Richard Mathews) materialises and asks if Borusa wishes to have immortality. Rassilon asks the Doctors if Borusa deserves immortality and they all say no, except for the first Doctor who has realised what is happening. He says that Borusa should get immortality.

Rassilon agrees and tells Borusa to take the ring from the hand of his effigy, which is lying on top of the tomb itself.

At this, Borusa is immobilised in stone and set in the base of the tomb with other megalomaniacs who wanted immortality (Johnnie Mack, Frederick Wolfe, Charles Milward). He, too, is now immortal.

PM: All those actors behind the masks were lying underneath the hollow tomb. We had two versions of the side of the tomb – one with transparent faces and one with opaque faces – and we mixed from one to the other.

JB: I remember doing something with the ring on this. We set up a little rig to fire the ring off his hand but they've done it with a video effect on the final story. Obviously it didn't work too well and it got dropped.

Rassilon returns the Master to his own time zone, and the first three Doctors and their companions depart in copies of the fifth Doctor's TARDIS.

The fourth Doctor is freed from the vortex.

The fifth Doctor is proclaimed as President by Chancellor Flavia when she arrives in the tomb. Taking the initiative, the Doctor orders Flavia back to the Council as acting President until he arrives to take over from her later. He then hurriedly leaves in the TARDIS with Tegan and Turlough – a renegade, just like in the beginning.

[End of The Five Doctors.*]*

Post-production

While the filming and recording of a *Doctor Who* adventure accounts for what is eventually seen on screen, the diary of a production does not end there.

Once the studio recordings were complete, the next stage was to copy all the recordings onto tape for viewing and later editing by Peter Moffatt. This tape-to-tape transfer took place on 18 April and took around four hours to complete. The footage filmed on location was transferred to video on 13, 19 and 25 May and took three hours to rehearse in order to match the studio conditions to the film conditions, followed by an hour's transferring of material.

The video effects, which included the spinning time-scoop obelisk, as well as the various ray-gun bursts from Dalek, Cybermen and other sources, were created on 16 and 18 May by video effects designer Dave Chapman using a Quantel 5000 imaging machine in the gallery of studio TC6.

The opening and closing titles were created on the 23 May for both the single-part story and the four-part version.

The story was finally edited together by Hugh Parson, who had been requested specifically for the job by John Nathan-Turner, on 23, 25, 28, 29 and 31 May and the 2 and 3 June in editing suite B. The final day had originally been booked as a 'safety day' but it was ultimately needed to complete the work.

Two VHS copies of the edited programme were supplied to John Nathan-Turner, one at the end of Sunday 29 May showing the work so far, and one at the end of Tuesday 31 May. These were viewed by Nathan-Turner on Wednesday 1 June for his comments before the final edit on Thursday 2 June.

The dubbing of sound recorded on location to the transferred video footage took place on 30 May and lasted from 11.15 in the morning until 11.00 at night.

With the final edited version of the story complete, two VHS copies were supplied to the BBC's Radiophonic Workshop for work to start on the music and sound effects for the show. The tapes were delivered over the weekend of 4–5 June and were viewed on the following Monday by the studio sound technician Martin Ridout and by Dick Mills, who would be creating the special sound effects for the story.

The composer allocated to work on *The Five Doctors* was Peter Howell. 'I was actually very pleased to do *The Five Doctors* as it was rather an exciting idea,' he said when interviewed in 1984.

The Workshop staff don't start putting music and effects onto a

Doctor Who until they receive a finished tape from the production office, thus making their task a lot easier as they are able to time exactly how long scenes are and to compose and place the music in precisely the right places.

Peter Howell liked to approach the programme by getting a lot of inspiration from various pieces of equipment. 'I always like to take a couple of days just setting up the studio using slightly different pieces of equipment in the sort of style that I think is right for the story. In this particular instance I felt that the story really did divide itself into three sections; the first section was the gathering together of the Doctors with quite a lot of electronic hardware involved with the games board and all that, and having got that part over with you are then into the adventure story with the Cybermen and so on; the third part of it was the coming together of the characters with the Rassilon sequence which was to me much more of an epic legend. I found that in my mind I had divided it into three so consequently, when I started off, I was basically interested in setting the place up to do quite a lot of sequenced electronics and things like that, which I felt was right for the electronic hardware in the picture, and then further on I was using the Fairlight computer more. Much of the music in the later scenes was done using the "Rassilon horn", which by the way is the hooter from the *Queen Mary* which had been slid up and down and re-sampled into the computer so you that you can play it. It took about a day and a half to make just that one sound but I felt it was very important. I wanted to link it with the constant view of the Tower and in fact it was quite useful in the culmination of the story as I used it almost as if someone were playing bagpipes until you couldn't stand it any longer. There came a point when Borusa put his hands over his ears just as he was about to disappear into the stone; in fact he was putting his hands up purely as an artistic device but it occurred to me that he was putting his hands over his ears as the horn beat him senseless, so to speak.

'I did suggest to the producer early on that bearing in mind that there were five Doctors in this programme that I would like to use the *Doctor Who* signature tune in the incidental music, as that would be quite a nice way of linking it all together, as if ever there was an excuse to use the signature tune in the incidental music then this was it. I had done it before (in *Meglos*) and I enjoyed it, and it is actually a very adaptable piece of music. As a matter of interest, I sampled the original sounds from the original signature tune onto the Fairlight and during the opening scenes when the Hartnell character is taken, I was actually using the original sounds, only digitally.

'I also considered using some of Malcolm Clarke's excellent music from the previous Cyberman story *Earthshock*. I borrowed it, but it is incredibly difficult to get pre-written music to sync in with the actual timed sequences that exist. It was very difficult to get it in but I did try.'

One very notable aspect of the production was that the closing credits rolled over a version of the theme music which combined the original sixties and seventies theme with the then current eighties theme, which Peter Howell had himself arranged. 'I suggested it to the producer but added that I had no idea whether it would work or not,' said Peter. 'Once I had done it, he came along and listened to it and decided to use it. I personally was very pleased with it.

'I felt that because the end of the story was not a cliffhanger, it was not necessary to have the very strong start to the end music. I do have a version of the music that goes from a sort of 20-year-old mono with hardly any frequency response to a classy stereo version, and that really blows your mind. I'll tell you a trade secret here: the old signature tune is in E-minor and the new version is in F-sharp minor so the two didn't mix very well as they stood; also the new one is slightly faster, so I had to pass the old one through a harmoniser to jack the pitch up to that of the new and then I had to do a slight speed change on it so that it would match and it really was a major task. I did it quite a long time before I saw any of the programme because I had a couple of days at my disposal and I thought I'd try it to see if it worked or not. Most people thought that it was a nice touch. It's probably the right time to do things like that when you are doing a special, as you can get away with it.'

The other aspect of the production handled by the Radiophonic Workshop were the special sounds, created for the special by Dick

Mills. Mills had been with the Workshop since the early sixties and had been handling the special sound requirements for *Doctor Who* since the mid-seventies.

'As with all programmes,' explained Mills at the time, 'we tend to look at each *Doctor Who* story with a view to its complete form and so our first concern was to make it "moody" and "mysterious" – the actual sound-making part is easy once you've decided where all the sounds are to go.

'We first discussed with the director where sounds would appear and what they would be like. An early decision was to try and make each sector of the Death Zone have its own wind background so as to give a different location to each Doctor's adventures there. I'm not sure whether this subtlety came off or not in the final version. Another idea was to back Rassilon's presence with sound. Fortunately, with the amount of film material used, there was not a great deal of special sound required except perhaps to add to the Raston Robot scenes.'

One nod to continuity brought in by Mills was the use of established *Doctor Who* sound effects. 'There were the Cybermen and Dalek guns, and the Gallifreyan stasers, in addition to the Yeti roar (from *The Web of Fear*) and the standard TARDIS sounds.

'There is total liaison with the musician on the show now that both sounds and music are created under one roof at the Workshop. Discussions usually occur over dramatic matters and/or frequency ranges to be used to avoid clashing with one another. Often just one contribution from either music or sound is eventually preferred at one point in an episode. I usually insist that all dramatic effects in space are covered musically except for the final obligatory bang!

'We generally have a ten-day space between episode review and the dubbing session, and we always need all ten days. This is particularly true in my case where I have to visit studios, do reviews or dubs for other episodes as well, once the season has started. The ten days allows for composition, creation, playback to the director and any remaking to occur before the final dub; plus of course all the necessary paperwork (shot lists, dubbing instructions etc.)'

It was during post-production that it was noticed that Richard Hurndall had made a mistake in reeling off the numbers that comprised the value of pi during the studio scenes in the anteroom set. Therefore Hurndall was recalled to perform a short sound recording to be used to overdub the dialogue in error. This recording took place on 20 July.

The final sypher dub – the combining of all the aural elements of the programme with the visual elements – for the single episode edition of the programme took place over 14 and 15 September in the BBC's Sypher II suite. The same suite was used for the final dub of the four-part version which took place on 22 September and 6 October 1983. This involved the inclusion of several new musical 'stings' created by Peter Howell for the new episode endings.

The final dub marked the completion of production work on *The Five Doctors,* and all that remained was for it to be scheduled for transmission.

With all the work complete, Terrance Dicks was pleased with the final result. 'I was very pleased with it, considering all the obstacles and hassles that had to be overcome. It's difficult to say that without sounding self-praising, but there was nothing that disappointed me. I was very pleased with it; it all worked.

'Having said that, one of the problems with the story was that it wasn't written as four episodes. Normally you only have to hold the viewer's attention for 25 minutes at a time but when everything is all together, it is very long, so it's much harder to keep it driving along. You have got to have a series of climaxes or at least something happening all the time to keep the viewers interested.'

Peter Moffatt also felt the story worked. 'I think it is a great credit to everybody concerned in the production that it succeeded so well. To John Nathan-Turner for all his encouragement and his ever-guiding hand, to Terrance Dicks for his intriguing script, aided and abetted by Eric Saward, to the designers and technicians at the BBC for their wonderful enthusiasm and hard slog of work, to the actors who gave it such life. Everyone gave of his or her best, which is the way that good television is made.'

Transmission

John Nathan-Turner had initially been hopeful that the show would be broadcast in England on the anniversary itself, but this was not to be.

In response to a letter from David J. Howe as to why the programme would not be transmitted on the anniversary date, David Reid, the Head of Series/Serials Drama, Television wrote on 1 November 1983:

> Thank you for your letter concerning *Doctor Who*. You should know that the original schedule for *The Five Doctors* was indeed Wednesday 23rd November. However, other problems on BBC1 forced the Controller to move it by two days by which time we had given permission for other countries to transmit on the 23rd. It was not really possible for us to go back on our word particularly as other countries had already gone to considerable expense to line up simultaneous networking.
>
> Naturally I would prefer the programme to transmit on the 23rd but I do assure you that it is not possible and that hopefully the Friday slot is likely to attract a far larger audience.

The Five Doctors was eventually transmitted in the UK on Friday 25 November at 7.20pm as a part of the annual Children In Need appeal fronted by popular television and radio presenter Terry Wogan. Because the appeal was geared towards raising money via telephone pledges, in some regions of the UK captions were run across the bottom of the screen during the transmission giving the status of the amounts raised so far by the regions.

After the story had completed, Terry Wogan was joined by Peter Davison in a pre-recorded sequence as the actor was at the time travelling to America along with all the other major cast members, attending an anniversary convention in Chicago. Davison donated his Doctor's coat for telephone auction to raise funds for the appeal but it is unknown how much was offered or who finally obtained the coat. This sequence was only shown in the London region.

The Five Doctors was actually premiered in Chicago on the anniversary itself, 23 November.

The press coverage was very strong. The BBC placed the story on the front of their press information pack for the Friday and for the first time since the start of the eleventh season back in December 1973, the BBC's listings magazine, the *Radio Times*, afforded *Doctor Who* a front cover. This was a painting by Andrew Skilleter depicting the five Doctors and the Master around an image of the Dark Tower. Inside the magazine was an article about all the companions who have travelled with the Doctor.

Despite the twin attractions of the 20th-anniversary and the Children in Need appeal, the UK transmission only managed 7.7 million viewers, which placed it 51st in the week's top-rated television shows. This figure, however, matched the highest rated episodes of the 21st season.

When the programme was repeated as a four-part story in 1984, it only managed a maximum rating of 4.7 million, with the chart position dropping to 88 for the first episode and then falling as low as 107 for the third episode. This was notably lower than the stories in the surrounding seasons.

The press were less than kind about the special. The *Philadelphia Inquirer* said, after explaining why two of the Doctors were not 'the originals', that: 'What's left is a silly, occasionally entertaining story in which four Doctor Whos finally converge to solve a mystery and save their individual lives. Like all TV reunion shows, it falls short of the original – but in this case the original is still running.'

Closer to home, the *Sunday Times* said: 'Just why, in these days of sophisticated, multi-million pound films such as *Star Wars*, *Doctor Who* still attracts a regular audience of some 8 million remains a mystery even to the BBC. Part of the reason is that the viewing habit passes easily from one generation to the next, though that doesn't explain why, in America, *Doctor Who* has become a late-night cult show for adults.'

The Yorkshire Post, however, was slightly more critical. 'Last night's celebratory adventure on BBC1, *The Five Doctors*, was a partial misnomer, as the longest serving, Tom Baker, made no more than a token appearance. Richard Hurndall gave a convincing impersonation of the original Doctor, the late William Hartnell.

'But it did give the opportunity to contrast the styles of the three remaining, and it confirmed my view that Patrick Troughton had the character assessed perfectly.

'Splendid actor that he is, he was able to bring conviction to his highly eccentric and whimsical professor.

'Jon Pertwee took the eccentricity too far, while the latest Doctor, Peter Davison, was too easily recognisable as himself, and he was also too young, barely older than the obligatory mini-skirted female assistants, included to persuade fathers to join their children watching.

'The programme in which the Doctors were stranded in a death zone which looked like a cross between a fairground hall of mirrors and a slate quarry, also enabled the suavely villainous Anthony Ainley to live up to his description last night as "my best enemy", playing the Master. The deficiencies of some of the Doctor's past adversaries were mercilessly exposed.

'The Daleks, those rubbish bins on wheels which have inspired thousands of children's games, proved inefficient fighting machines as they blew off their own heads, and the Cybermen, predecessors of the *Star Wars* storm troopers, were massacred by a remarkable Jumping Jack Flash character who fired deadly bolts from his fingertips.'

The fans were, on the whole, positive about the show in the *Doctor Who* Appreciation Society's quarterly magazine *TARDIS*. 'A good traditional *Doctor Who* story, with an excellent dream-like quality. I would label it a classic but I think sentimentality made that near-inevitable' (Saul Nasse); 'The show relied too heavily on old material and ideas' (Christopher Denyer); 'What we got, as nonsensical as it all was, was entertaining stuff.' (Saul Gething); 'I think it deserves a 9.5 out of 10' (Ian Massey).

The novelisation of *The Five Doctors* was published by W. H. Allen in their Target range before the show had even been screened, the first time that this had happened. 'They were very keen to get the novelisation out as close to the show as possible,' explained Terrance Dicks, who adapted his own script for book form. 'I finished writing it before I saw the final playback of the programme, which does explain some of the minor differences between the show and the book. For instance, Patrick's furry Yeti coat, which I didn't know he was wearing until I saw the show. It's that kind of thing. When they get to the caves, they had put a little ceremonial entrance outside, with a torch. That wasn't in the script but it does give them a torch to carry and explains how they could see where they were going in the caves. It's the Brigadier's cigarette lighter that they use in the book. Other things, like Patrick's talking about Zodin the Terrible, came from a Programme as Broadcast script which I got in the last stages of editing the book so I knew pretty well every line and interjection – but nobody ever mentioned the fur coat! I wish I'd known: I'd have written it into the book!'

Credits

Director	Peter Moffatt
(Shada)	Pennant Roberts
(Inserts)	John Nathan-Turner
Producer	John Nathan-Turner
Production Manager	Jeremy Silberston
Production Assistant	Jean Davis
Assistant Floor Manager	Pauline Seager
Floor Assistant	Chris Stanton
Script Editor	Eric Saward
Production Associate	June Collins
Production Secretary	Jane Judge
Designer	Malcolm Thornton
Assistant	Steve Fawcett
Costume Designer	Colin Lavers
Assistant	Peter Halston
Dressers	Carl Levy
	Philip Winter
	Camilla Gavin
Make-Up Artist	Jill Hagger
Assistants	Naomi Donne
	Fay Hammond

Visual Effects	John Brace
	Mike Kelt
Assistants	Malcolm James
	Dave Rogers
Film Editor	M. A. C. Adams
Film Cameraman	John Baker
Assistant	Nick Squires
Sound Recordist	John Gatland
Assistant	Brian Biffin
Video Effects	Dave Chapman
Camera Supervisor	Alec Wheal
Crew	11
Technical Manager	Derek Thompson
Design Effects	Jean Peyre
Graphic Design	Ian Hewett
Videotape Editor	Hugh Parson
Studio Lighting	Don Babbage
Studio Sound	Martin Ridout
Grams Operator	John Downes
Vision Mixer	Shirley Coward
Lighting	Archie Dawson
Grips	Tex Childs
Film Ops	John Rice
	Les Thomas
	Brian Walters
	Eric Levey
Armourer	Tony Chilton
Prop Buyer	Robert Fleming
Film Operations Manager	Graham Richmond
Title Music	Ron Grainer and the
	BBC Radiophonic Workshop
Incidental Music	Peter Howell
Special Sound	Dick Mills
Writer	Terrance Dicks

8: Selling the Doctor

Media

During the first six years that Tom Baker had played the Doctor, *Doctor Who* had consistently maintained a very high level of popularity. The ratings had averaged around nine to 11 million per episode for most of the period and had even risen to an all-time high of 16 million at one point during 1979 – although this record figure had been attributable in part to a protracted strike that had hit the ITV companies and blacked out the third channel for several weeks across the country. In 1980, however, the programme schedulers at ITV came up with a secret weapon: a glitzy new American science-fiction series entitled *Buck Rogers in the 25th Century*. With its slick special effects, cute robots and lycra-clad ladies, this show was a big hit with UK viewers and had the effect of splitting the audience. *Doctor Who* was left with only around five million viewers per episode for most of its eighteenth season, and although there was a slight increase to around six million by the end of the story in which Baker left, this was still less than half the number who had been watching the year before.

There was, nevertheless, a large amount of press coverage generated by the announcement on 24 October 1980 that Baker was shortly to leave the role that had made him famous. Even the national news media covered the story, and speculation was rife that the new Doctor could be played by a woman (although this was in fact a publicity stunt dreamed up by Baker and producer John

Nathan-Turner).

In the event, it is doubtful that anyone could have predicted just who would be chosen as the next Doctor. One factor that Nathan-Turner certainly had in mind, however, was the need to cast an extremely popular actor whose presence would help to reverse the series' disastrous ratings decline suffered during Season 18.

Peter Davison's accession to the role was announced to the press on 4 November 1980 and, given that the actor was best known for playing vet Tristan Farnon in the popular series *All Creatures Great and Small*, the subsequent headlines were fairly predictable: 'Dr. Moo! TV Vet is New Space Doctor', 'Meet Dr. Tristan' and 'TV Vet's the New Dr. Who' were typical examples.

Davison could already be seen appearing on ITV as a regular in the comedy series *Holding the Fort* and in the children's story series *Once Upon A Time*, and he was also recording a new sitcom for the BBC called *Sink or Swim*.

By the time he made his debut as the Doctor, some pundits were suggesting that it was becoming almost impossible to turn on a television set without seeing him. The actor was even promoting Websters beer in a series of television commercials. After being announced as the Doctor, however, and only one year into his three year contract with the firm, he was replaced. The advertising agency were quoted as saying: 'As star of a children's programme, there's no way he should be advertising beer.'

A number of early publicity appearances followed for Davison (see Chapter 2), culminating in the unveiling of the fifth Doctor's costume at a press call on 15 April 1981 where the actor was photographed wielding a cricket bat in front of a set of stumps painted on the side of the TARDIS prop.

The BBC's announcement on 19 August 1981 of its schedules for the forthcoming Autumn season again saw *Doctor Who* featuring prominently, Davison being photographed in costume along with Pamela Stephenson and other stars of the shows included in the promotion. This was all the more remarkable given that *Doctor Who* was not actually a part of the Autumn line-up: its new season would not begin until 4 January 1982.

One major change when the series did return was the move from its traditional Saturday teatime placing to its new twice-weekly evening slot, where it was in competition with a wide range of ITV fare including initially the soap opera *Emmerdale Farm* and the holiday programme *Wish You Were Here*. It is unknown what prompted this change of scheduling, which appears to have been decided upon by BBC1 Controller Alan Hart, but it may well have had something to do with the poor ratings gained by the previous season.

Whereas Tom Baker had actively courted the press, Davison was an altogether more private person. Although during his time in the series he attended many conventions and made many personal appearances – which he was quoted as saying that he did because they came with the job of being the Doctor – the total amount of press coverage that he generated was not great. When interviews did appear, the actor's primary concern seemed to be the fact that he was recognised wherever he went and was becoming tired of signing autographs and being nice to people. The extent to which this public attention arose solely from his role as the Doctor is, however, debatable; Davison was such a prominent figure on television in the early eighties that he would no doubt have been recognised anyway.

Amongst the shows on which Davison guested during his time in *Doctor Who* were: *Multi-Coloured Swap Shop* (9 January 1982, publicising *Castrovalva*); *So You Think You Know What's Good for You* (11 January 1982, with his wife, actress Sandra Dickinson); *Pebble Mill at One* (March 1982, plugging a newly published anthology of science-fiction short stories to which he had lent his name for promotional purposes); *This Is Your Life* (recorded 18 March 1982 and transmitted 25 March 1982 with him as its subject); a BAFTA awards show outside broadcast (20 March 1983, presenting awards for children's programmes); *Saturday Superstore* (26 March 1983, with companions Janet Fielding and Mark Strickson); *The Late, Late Breakfast Show* (10 December 1983, receiving a Golden Egg award for a humorous out-take from *The Awakening*); and *Harty* (20 March 1984, with his successor, Colin Baker). He also took part in a number of radio shows, including one on BBC radio in May 1981 when he spoke about his interest in cricket.

As he himself had predicted, Davison ultimately decided to leave *Doctor Who* after only three seasons in the lead role.

'There was a danger of becoming stereotyped,' he told the press after the announcement was made on 28 July 1983, 'and I've always done three years of everything else. It's a nice round figure.' Some quarters of the press tried to suggest that his decision to leave was prompted by some 'backstage bust-up' but, as this had not in fact been the case, they were unable to get very far with this line of reporting.

Nathan-Turner again generated a certain amount of controversy by dropping false hints that the next Doctor might be played by a woman – 'I'm not ruling out the choice of having a lady Doctor,' he was quoted as saying – but the press seemed equally keen to report the recent decline in the series' viewing figures. While Season 19 had averaged over nine million viewers per episode, Seasons 20 and 21 had managed only just over seven million apiece. This was still a respectable rating, but Nathan-Turner no doubt had in mind the possibility of giving the series a further boost in popularity when he came to regenerate the Doctor once again. On the subject of Davison's successor, he was quoted as saying: 'The next Doctor will be older and a little more eccentric. We want to change the style of the Doctor completely. The new character will be vastly different from Peter.'

Just as press coverage of the series' lead actor seemed to diminish slightly after Davison took over from Baker, so the interest in the actors and actresses who played the Doctor's companions seemed to drop a little.

Matthew Waterhouse (Adric), Sarah Sutton (Nyssa) and Janet Fielding (Tegan) had all made their debuts at the tail end of the fourth Doctor's era, so their novelty value had been all but exhausted by the time that Davison took over.

Waterhouse's departure did gain a little coverage, having been publicised by way of a BBC press release issued on 3 December 1981, but the production team were probably less than pleased to see that this focused mainly on the actor's displeasure at their decision to kill off his character. The tabloid press had always shown rather less interest in the Doctor's male companions than in the glamorous '*Doctor Who* girls', however, and for much of the fifth Doctor's era it was actually Fielding who attracted the most attention.

Nathan-Turner, well aware of the perceived image of the female companions, contrived to dress Nyssa and Tegan in figure-hugging and impractical costumes throughout their time in the series. Perhaps the most well-publicised event of all, apart from the series' 20th anniversary (of which more below), occurred when the crew visited Amsterdam to do location filming for Season 20's opening story, *Arc of Infinity*, and Tegan was finally given a change of regular costume. No doubt to the delight of the assembled photographers, the new outfit was even more revealing than the old – a pair of culottes and a boob tube.

The recording of *Mawdryn Undead* again saw a number of newspapers running photographs of Fielding and Sutton, although these were rather less glamorous than was usually the case as the pair were showing off the old-age make-up that they were required to wear at one point during the action. The accompanying reports concentrated mainly on that fact that Fielding was getting married that week.

There was little noise made in the press when Sutton and Fielding later made their respective exits from the series. Similarly, the arrival and subsequent departure of Mark Strickson (Turlough) went largely unremarked, in line with the usual treatment of the male companions.

The arrival of Nicola Bryant (Peri) brought something of a resurgence of popular interest in the *Doctor Who* companion. The tabloids went wild, printing numerous photographs and articles about the newcomer, and Bryant made her television debut with an appearance on the BBC's *Breakfast Time* on 6 July 1983. By this time, however, the era of the fifth Doctor was almost at an end. The next story after Bryant joined the series, Davison bowed out to be replaced by the sixth Doctor, Colin Baker.

The 20th Anniversary

An anniversary is always a good opportunity to make an impression, and with *Doctor Who*'s 20th falling in November 1983, everyone involved was determined to make the most of the occasion – especially as the series had by that point really taken off in America.

A special programme, *The Five Doctors*, was planned to celebrate the anniversary on BBC1 (see Chapter 7). The other major event of the year was a convention organised by BBC Enterprises and held at Longleat House in Warminster, Wiltshire. Longleat had been the home of one of two permanent *Doctor Who* exhibitions in the UK since 1974 and Lord Bath, its owner, was keen to see its profile raised in this manner. The event would be open to the general public and would feature guest appearances by all four surviving Doctors – Patrick Troughton, Jon Pertwee, Tom Baker and Peter Davison – and numerous companions, as well as screenings of rare episodes and displays and talks by some of the BBC departments involved in making *Doctor Who*. Advertising trailers were placed after a number of Season 19 episodes, and other advance publicity for the event included mentions on Ceefax and fliers sent out with specialist publications.

The *Doctor Who Celebration: Twenty Years of a Time Lord* took place over the Easter bank holiday weekend, Sunday 3 April and Monday 4 April 1983, from 10.00 a.m. until 6.00 p.m. each day. Admission was £3.50 per day for an adult and £1.50 per day for a child. The main convention area was behind the House, where a number of marquees had been set up. These housed displays by the BBC's Costume, Make-up, Design and Visual Effects Departments and Radiophonic Workshop; a forum in which panel discussions and guest interviews were presented; a cinema in which the complete stories *The Dalek Invasion of Earth* (Hartnell), *The Dominators* (Troughton), *Terror of the Autons* (Pertwee), *Terror of the Zygons* (Baker) and *The Visitation* (Davison) were shown; and a sales area where large quantities of spin-off merchandise were on offer and an auction of *Doctor Who* props and costumes took place – the first time such items had ever been made available to the public to buy. A large conservatory adjoining the house was meanwhile converted into an autograph room.

Everything might have gone smoothly had it not been for the inclement April weather and the fact that far more people than anticipated turned up. The walkways and grass were churned into slippery mud-caked areas, and queues stretched into the distance as every tent was filled to capacity. The organisers had apparently expected around 50,000 people spread over the two days, but over 35,000 came on the Sunday alone, leading to many disappointed families being turned away at the gate.

The event attracted quite a bit of press interest, and a report by Colin Randall of the *Daily Telegraph* was typical: 'Long queues formed outside most of the main attractions and senior BBC officials apologised for the delays, saying that the event had proved "too successful". Families had to wait up to two hours for autographs from the members of cast, past and present. One visitor, Mr David Southwell, said he had spent more than £20 on the day's outing from Bristol with his wife and two children. "We have been here over two hours and all we have seen is a couple of sets," he said. "It is a complete rip-off and everybody is entitled to their money back." Others made similar points, though with more restraint.'

Bryon Parkin, Managing Director of BBC Enterprises, was reported as saying: 'We have been the victims of our own success. No one could have conceived that so many people would have come so early. There were queues at 8 a.m. and we have just done our best to cope with it.'

Parkin went on to promise that any ticket holders who were unable to get in would have their money refunded, and the BBC also made a statement that only ticket holders would be permitted entry on the Monday.

Interviewed from Longleat by BBC Radio 2 disc jockey Ed Stewart, Peter Davison put a brave face on the organisational shambles. Behind the scenes, however, many of the guests were extremely concerned at the poor treatment the public were receiving, and at the damage this could do to *Doctor Who*'s reputation. Particularly vociferous and forthright in his condemnation of the event's organisers was Mark Strickson, and he later admitted in interviews that this had almost cost him his job on the series.

In addition to several new ranges of merchandise launched to coincide with the anniversary (which are covered in a later section of this chapter), some special celebratory items were also produced.

W. H. Allen, the publishers of the successful range of *Doctor Who* novelisations, had put out the soft-covered *The Doctor Who Monster Book* and its sequel back in the seventies but had not so far ventured to produce a large-format illustrated hardback about the series. It was therefore something of a bold step when they decided to commission a celebratory volume of this type, *Doctor Who – A Celebration*, from writer Peter Haining. Haining was an obvious choice for the task as he was experienced at putting together overview-type publications. He had already completed books on Sherlock Holmes and Charlie Chaplin, and was also a good friend of W. H. Allen's managing director Bob Tanner, who would later become his agent. To ensure a degree of authority, the publishers put Haining in touch with Jeremy Bentham, a well-known fan historian of *Doctor Who*, who worked on a chapter chronicling all the Doctor's adventures to date. The remainder of the book looked at each Doctor in turn; gave brief descriptions of K-9, the TARDIS, Gallifrey and the Master; and presented interviews with Barry Letts, Terrance Dicks and John Nathan-Turner.

The other 20th-anniversary publication of particular note was a lavish special published by the BBC's listings magazine *Radio Times*. The precedent of the similar title produced to celebrate the tenth anniversary in 1973 had led to a widespread expectation amongst the series' fans that such a special would be issued, but it was only after pressure from Nathan-Turner that the powers-that-be capitulated and set one in motion. Brian Gearing, the editor of *Radio Times*, took responsibility for the project and commissioned one of his regular researchers, Gay Search, to provide the bulk of the text.

The format of the special stuck very closely to that established by its 1973 forerunner. Opening with a spread of photographs depicting the evolution of the series' title sequence, it continued with illustrated text features on: the Doctors; the companions; the Master; the fans; the aliens; some of the creative behind-the-scenes team; and the merchandise. A specially commissioned short story by the series' script editor, Eric Saward, told of the Doctor's original departure from his home planet Gallifrey, and also featured the Master and the Cybermen for good measure.

Rounding off the whole magazine was a piece by 'devoted fan' Ian Levine (who had been recommended for the job by Nathan-Turner) looking at all the Doctor's adventures to date.

All things considered, the special constituted a very effective skim through the series' 20-year history, and was nicely illustrated and put together. Even the recently announced sixth Doctor, Colin Baker, was included in its coverage, making it as up-to-date as it possibly could be.

Other activities connected with the anniversary included: a visit by Troughton and Davison, along with K-9 and a Dalek, to the 1 March 1983 edition of the BBC's *Breakfast Time*; a major photocall for *The Five Doctors* on 16 March featuring all the Doctors (Baker being represented by his dummy from Madame Tussaud's) and many of the companions; an appearance by Troughton, Pertwee, Davison and former producer Verity Lambert on the 17 March edition of the BBC's evening news digest *Nationwide*; and a further photocall, on 24 March, at which Davison appeared with many of the actresses who had played the Doctor's female companions over the years.

Merchandise

The boom in *Doctor Who* merchandise that had occurred in the late seventies continued into the Davison era.

The range of novelisations published by W. H. Allen under their Target imprint progressed unabated, with around eight new titles added to it each year. Other publications from the same company included Jean-Marc Lofficier's *The Doctor Who Programme Guide*, which came initially in two hardback volumes in 1981. This book, although containing numerous mistakes in its earliest editions, was to become one of the most influential and popular works ever written about the series; since its original publication, it has been revised and reprinted several times in rather more accurate versions. Peter Haining meanwhile followed up his *Doctor Who – A Celebration* with *Doctor Who – The Key to Time*, a 1984 book which presented a chronological history of *Doctor Who* but which unfortunately contained numerous incorrect dates and other factual errors.

World Distributors continued to produce their regular *Doctor Who* Annual during the fifth Doctor's era, and other publishers also began to exploit the potential of the *Doctor Who* market. Alan Road's *The Making of a Television Series* (Andre Deutsch, 1982) provided a case study of the making of *The Visitation* – the first instance of a single story being subjected to extensive analysis in a professional publication. More in-depth still was *Doctor Who – The Unfolding Text* (Macmillan, 1983) by John Tulloch and Manuel Alvarado. This was a university-level media-studies textbook which many non-academic readers and fans found not surprisingly rather heavy going. It looked at *Doctor Who* from a variety of viewpoints and featured much material about the making of *Kinda*, a story with a suitably deep religious subtext.

As previously noted, a large number of new products were launched to coincide with the series' 20th anniversary in 1983. These included: badges and a paper Cyberman mask from Image Screencraft (a commercial offshoot of Imagineering, the effects house that had created the Terileptils for *The Visitation* and the Cybermen for *Earthshock* amongst many other monsters and special props for the Davison era); sundry mugs, erasers, pencils, bags and balloons produced specifically for the Longleat event; a series of large artwork prints, generically called Profile Prints, showcasing the work of artist Andrew Skilleter (who had provided the covers for many of the W. H. Allen novelisations) and issued by his embryonic Who Dares publishing firm; and the first in what would become a massive range of *Doctor Who* video releases.

BBC Video had, in fact, carried out some market research amongst attendees at the Longleat event to discover which titles they would like to see made available in this new medium. The

Season 5 story *The Tomb of the Cybermen* had come out top of the poll, no doubt mentioned by many fans as a joke in view of the fact that all four episodes were at that time missing from the archives, but BBC Video reasoned that any other Cyberman adventure would do just as well and so chose the Season 12 story *Revenge of the Cybermen* to spearhead their range.

Other product lines to start up during the Davison era included a large range of pewter *Doctor Who* figures from Fine Art Castings, and Reeltime Pictures' series of *Doctor Who* interview tapes. Also in the shops were: *Doctor Who* wallpaper, featuring images of Davison, Daleks and Cybermen; a TARDIS tent; *Doctor Who* gloves and T-shirts; and a Dalek hat. The *Doctor Who* theme record was reissued with a photograph of Davison on the sleeve, and the *K-9 and Company* theme was also released. In addition, the first ever LP of incidental music from the series was put out in the form of the highly acclaimed if unimaginatively titled *Doctor Who – The Music*.

Marvel Comics' *Doctor Who Monthly* was still going strong, with numerous special publications being produced in addition to the regular monthly magazine; BBC publicity photographs from the series went on sale to the public thanks to a firm called Whomobilia; and eager fans could even obtain a *Doctor Who* umbrella.

In fact, the merchandise produced during this period almost rivalled that of the sixties in terms of its range and diversity. There was, however, one significant difference: whereas in the sixties almost all the merchandise had been issued by large toy manufacturers, in the eighties most of the items on sale were produced by small firms acting as cottage industries, or even by fans-turned-professionals. These firms and individuals usually escaped the overheads of the larger companies, but also lacked their sales, marketing and distribution functions. Luckily, the enormous fan interest in the series both in the UK and in America had resulted in a great many conventions being held, newsletters being produced and dealers setting up in business, and this had led to the creation of a ready market on both sides of the Atlantic for all the various items produced.

North America

The Peter Davison era saw *Doctor Who* approaching the peak of its popularity in the United States of America, as episodes – albeit mainly those featuring Tom Baker as the Doctor – were shown on an almost daily basis on PBS stations covering over two-thirds of the entire country.

Barely a weekend went by without a large *Doctor Who* convention taking place somewhere in America, and the show's stars, both past and present, were in constant demand to attend these celebrations, with large fees and travel expenses being offered to entice them from UK shores. John Nathan-Turner even began to act as a semi-official guest liaison officer for the organisers of these events. The biggest US convention of all, attended by an estimated 12,000 people, was the Ultimate Celebration, which took place in Chicago over the series' 20th-anniversary weekend in 1983 and achieved the unique feat of bringing all four surviving Doctors on stage together, along with many of their companions from the series.

The North American *Doctor Who* Appreciation Society which, like its UK sponsor, had been run essentially on a non-profit-making basis, now gave way to professional organisations such as Spirit of Light – who staged the Ultimate Celebration and many other conventions – and the *Doctor Who* Fan Club of America. The latter body was set up by two commercially minded fans, Ron Katz and Chad Roark, after they met Nathan-Turner at BBC Enterprises' Longleat event. Its members, who would eventually come to number some 30,000, received a regular newspaper entitled *The Whovian Times*, which featured interviews and news items and also numerous adverts for the masses of BBC-licensed (and, in some cases, possibly unlicensed) merchandise items produced in the States at this time, including T-shirts, jackets, mugs, key-fobs, pens, model kits and towels.

Elsewhere on the North American continent, fan support for *Doctor Who* remained particularly strong in Canada, where an organisation called the *Doctor Who* Information Network launched a regular fanzine, *Enlightenment*, around the end of Davison's stint

in the series. Circulation of this well-produced publication quickly
rose to around 400.

Australia

Doctor Who also remained very popular 'down under' during this
period of its history. The Australasian *Doctor Who* Fan Club continued to publish issues of its high-quality fanzine *Zerinza*, as well
as a more basic newsletter, and attracted a large influx of new
members. A number of *Doctor Who* Parties and other events were
held, with guests including former companion actress Katy Manning, who was now living in Australia. Other groups, such as the
Doctor Who Club of Victoria, produced fanzines and carried out
activities on a more local basis.

The public profile of the series in Australia received a considerable boost during April 1983 when Peter Davison and his wife
Sandra Dickinson made a promotional tour of major cities to meet
the fans and do a number of book signings at stores in the Myer
chain who had sponsored the trip and arranged an extremely hec-
tic schedule for the two visitors.

One unfortunate aspect of the Australian transmissions of the
Davison stories was that – as had also been the case in earlier eras
– a number of the episodes were edited by the censors to remove
material that they considered unsuitable for a family audience.
The most badly affected of all was Davison's swansong, *The Caves
of Androzani* part four, which lost over two and a half minutes of
material.

New Zealand

New Zealand, too, continued to constitute a strong market for
Doctor Who. An initial block of Davison stories, comprising
Castrovalva to *Mawdryn Undead*, was purchased by TVNZ (the
country's premier TV station) in 1982, although the episodes were
not actually aired until 1983. A second batch, comprising *Terminus* to *The Caves of Androzani*, was purchased around 1988 (the
long delay resulting from the fact that TVNZ had in the meantime

concentrated on screening stories from earlier periods of the series' history). Apart from *The Five Doctors*, which was shown out of sequence in 1988 as part of a Silver Jubilee season put together by TVNZ, the episodes in this second batch were aired in 1989 – although in slightly edited form, as the commercial half-hour slot to which they had been allocated allowed for only 23 minutes of actual programme time. *The Caves of Androzani* was shown in the even more heavily edited Australian version. The first batch of episodes had meanwhile been repeated in 1988, also in edited form, but the second has yet to reappear.

As in the UK, Davison could be seen in New Zealand not only in *Doctor Who* but also in a number of other series. His appearances in *Love for Lydia*, *Sink or Swim*, *The Tomorrow People* and *All Creatures Great and Small* were all screened during the course of 1983, and some of the country's newspapers were even moved to comment on the apparent flood of Davison material on offer.

UK Fandom

The *Doctor Who* Appreciation Society continued to be at the forefront of UK fandom during this period, although its dominance was now starting to be challenged by other fan groups and, in the publication field, by independent fanzines.

After its original organisers had bowed out in mid-1980, the Society had effectively been saved from collapse by David Saunders (who became Co-ordinator), David J. Howe (who had for some time been running the reference department) and Chris Dunk (the editor of the Society's newsletter, *Celestial Toyroom*). Over the next couple of years, the Society's executive body took steps to put its organisation and finances on a sounder footing. Dunk was succeeded as *Celestial Toyroom* editor first by Gordon Blows and David Auger, then by Gary Russell and then, until the end of the Davison era, by Gordon Roxburgh. The Society published much material during this period including regular editions of the fanzine *TARDIS*, edited by Richard Walter, and the fan fiction periodical *Cosmic Masque*, edited initially by John Peel and then, from early 1981, by Ian K. McLachlan.

The Society's membership was boosted considerably by a strong presence at the BBC's Longleat convention in 1983, and managed to top the 3,000 mark for the first time. The Society meanwhile continued to stage its own conventions under the aegis of convention department organiser Paul Zeus. In addition to the major PanoptiCon event each year, a number of smaller and more informal Inter-Face and DWASocial gatherings were held. It was, however, a constant source of irritation to the Society that the PanoptiCons had to be scheduled so as not to clash with major American events – such as the one held in Chicago on the series' 20th anniversary – as with their relatively high fees and travel expenses the latter would always be more successful in attracting guests. The fact that so many of the series' stars were always overseas on important dates such as the anniversary also meant that numerous opportunities for UK press coverage were lost.

Viewer Reaction

As previously noted, the Davison era gained very respectable ratings, although they were somewhat higher for Season 19 than for Seasons 20 and 21. One factor that impacted on these figures was the boom in home video recording that occurred in the early 1980s; the ratings system took no account of people who videoed shows to watch later. Another factor was that the UK's fourth terrestrial channel, Channel 4, started transmitting in 1982 and offered people a greater degree of choice about what to watch at any given time.

Further information on viewers' contemporary reactions to *Doctor Who* during this period can be gained from the BBC's own internal audience-research reports.

The summary report for Season 19 began by discussing the size of the audience, based on results from the BARB Audience Measurement service:

Audiences for this series were estimated to range from 16.1% to 20.5% (8.3 to 10.5 million) of the United Kingdom population, giving an overall average of 18.2% (9.3 million). There was no appreciable difference between the Monday and Tuesday audience sizes.

There then followed a section on audience reaction, based on questionnaires completed by members of the BBC's regular Viewing Panel. This recorded that the overall reaction index for the season was 66%.

The report continued:

Viewing of this 26-part series tended to be rather sporadic although…the majority of those reporting managed to tune in to at least half… Fewer than one in ten (8%) reporting deliberately decided to stop watching; frequency of viewing, perhaps predictably, tended to be governed by the convenience of the transmission time to individual respondents… The timing was only totally suitable for a minority, although only about one in ten (12%) found it completely inconvenient… Predictably, those who found the transmission time less convenient tended to tune in to fewer programmes. Just under half (47%) of the total sample watched with children under the age of 15, and these viewers tended to find the timing rather more suitable. There were several requests for a return to the old Saturday evening transmission time, albeit from a small minority.

Next came a number of sections relating comments on the actual content of the episodes:

Although only about one in seven of those reporting found the latest series of *Doctor Who* immensely appealing, the large majority reacted favourably and still enjoy the programme. The episodes in this series were considered well written and not too predictable, and most viewers felt that the storylines had been quite exciting… Reactions to the standard of acting were rather mixed, although still generally favourable… Peter Davison appears to have been accepted as the new Doctor. Although there were a number of unfavourable comparisons with certain predecessors (notably Jon Pertwee) and a couple of suggestions that he should stick to being a vet, the majority of those reporting clearly feel that he has got to grips with the part and now fits in rather well. There were few comments regarding the performances of the rest of the cast, although these were considered good.

All aspects of the production were thought to have been of a high standard. A number of respondents did feel that the special effects had been unbelievable and obviously false, but their opinions were heavily outweighed.

As mentioned previously, just under half the sample audience viewed in the company of children aged 15 or under. Boys were slightly predominant (55% : 45%). The children's ages were fairly   well spread; all ages between two and 15 were represented, but there was a marked concentration of children (particularly boys) aged between 6 and 10. In general, their comments were succinct ('great', 'brilliant' etc.) and very favourable. Boys tended to be rather more enthusiastic than girls (although both sexes liked the series) but there was a tendency among very small girls (under-sevens) to be frightened. Several children were rather disturbed by the death of Adric, although these were in the minority.

Interspersed with these comments were a number of tables giving detailed breakdowns of the figures in their respective sections. The report then concluded with a final table that the production team must have found particularly encouraging:

Finally, the sample audience was asked whether they would welcome a further series of *Doctor Who*. They responded as follows:

Yes, very much	36
Yes, quite	42
Not particularly	19
Definitely not	3

The audience research report for Season 20, which was accompanied by a three page computer tabulation of statistics, recorded an average audience of 7.0 million and an average appreciation index of 62. Its text read as follows:

This series of *Doctor Who* received a somewhat mixed but essentially favourable response from the members of the sample audience. Approximately half of those reporting regarded it as an entertaining and enjoyable programme which provided excellent viewing for the whole family. A number of this group thought it especially good for children, whilst others indicated that they had been fans of the Doctor since his portrayal by the late William Hartnell. These reporting viewers (who were most likely to be under 54 years of age) considered the storylines interesting, amusing and gripping, liked Peter Davison's portrayal of the Doctor and praised the other members of the cast.

Another group of respondents (between one quarter and one third of the total sample) liked the series, but were slightly disappointed in it. They tended to criticise the plots ('enjoyable, but stronger storylines needed'), the special effects or the transmission time. Indeed, the time at which the programme was broadcast was noticeably less popular amongst the 35–54 age group.

One in five of those reporting had not enjoyed the series. For 15% this dislike had led them to make a positive decision to stop watching. They were mainly over the age of 55 and criticised the series for being, in their opinion, boring and predictable. They also felt it had weak storylines, poor acting and disappointing special effects. A few ceased watching because their young children had been frightened by the programme.

57% of the sample audience indicated that they wished to see a new series of *Doctor Who*. A further one in three had no strong opinion on the subject. The desire for a new series of *Doctor Who* was strongest in those under 34 and weakest in the 55+ age group.

The average viewer and reaction index figures for Season 21, at

7.2 million and 65 respectively, were both slightly up on those for Season 20, but – although no audience research report is available for this season at the time of writing – it is known that there was a considerable drop in satisfaction levels after Colin Baker took over as the Doctor for the final story. Only 66% of those in the reporting sample thought that the sixth Doctor was a likeable character in this story, and only 54% thought that he was well portrayed by Baker. These figures compared with 73% and 71% respectively for the fifth Doctor and for Davison's portrayal during Season 20. While it was hardly unexpected for a new Doctor to encounter some initial audience resistance, Nathan-Turner must have known that a considerable improvement would be required the following year.

Peter Davison Stories in Order of Average Viewing Figures (Figures in millions of viewers)

Black Orchid	10.00
The Visitation	9.60
Castrovalva	9.57
Earthshock	9.33
Four to Doomsday	8.88
Time-Flight	8.88
Kinda	8.80
The Five Doctors	7.70
Resurrection of the Daleks	7.65
Mawdryn Undead	7.28
The Caves of Androzani	7.28
Warriors of the Deep	7.25
The Awakening	7.25
Arc of Infinity	7.15
Snakedance	7.10
Terminus	7.10
Planet of Fire	6.98
Enlightenment	6.83
Frontios	6.80
The King's Demons	6.50

Afterword

Following his appointment as *Doctor Who*'s producer at the beginning of November 1979, John Nathan-Turner set about transforming the series – his intention being, as he put it, 'To bring it into the 1980s.'

The new producer's influence was first apparent during Tom Baker's final season as the Doctor. A glossy new star-field title sequence and neon-style logo were commissioned; a more trendy theme tune arrangement was introduced; Dudley Simpson's relatively conventional incidental music, for so long a staple ingredient of the series, was dispensed with in favour of fully electronic scores provided by the BBC Radiophonic Workshop; the two established companions – Romana and K-9 – were written out, while three new ones – Adric, Nyssa and Tegan – were brought in to take their places; all the regulars, including the Doctor, were given heavily- designed, uniform-like costumes which went unchanged from one story to the next; and finally, of course, the Doctor himself was regenerated.

All these new approaches were carried forward to Peter Davison's tenure in the lead role. With a new Doctor in place, Nathan-Turner was able fully to realise his ambitions for *Doctor Who*, and the production became increasingly slick and sophisticated.

'I think you really have to look at the expectations of an audience,' noted the producer in a 1989 interview. 'The late seventies and early eighties saw a level of sophistication in television and the movies that no-one could have foreseen.

'Children particularly now, possibly due to the advent of computer games and so on, have very high expectations of television programmes in our genre. My idea was simply not to compete with the likes of *Star Wars*, but to use the resources that were available to us to the best possible effect. In that way, we would appear to be moving with the times.

'I hesitate to say this, but what happened in some – and I would emphasise not all – of the older episodes was very minimal. There were a lot of very long scenes, a lot of exposition, and not a lot of action or plot development. I like episodes sharply cut, with a strong narrative drive. The optimum length for a *Doctor Who* episode is now 24 minutes 15 seconds and, once you take away the titles, you have about 22 minutes to play with. So you really want to get on with a whole lot of story development – not just to hold the attention of the audience, but to make what you are handing them more substantial.'

Critics, however, expressed concern that Nathan-Turner's attentions were focused principally on cosmetic, essentially superficial aspects of the production, rather than on the dramatic content of the stories. Certainly this latter aspect was determined more by the respective interests and preferences of the series' successive script editors, namely Christopher H. Bidmead, Antony Root and Eric Saward. An interesting mix and variety of different story types was achieved – even down to the inclusion, in the form of *Black Orchid*, of the first *bona fide* historical adventure since 1966 – and frequently the scripts matched the production in achieving a level of sophistication and slickness previously unseen in the series. One common feature identified by many fan commentators, however, was an increased emphasis on concepts and imagery at the expense of *Doctor Who*'s more traditional strengths of good, straightforward plotting and solid characterisation. In other words, many felt that style was being given precedence over content.

Notwithstanding these common concerns about its artistic direction, the series gained very respectable ratings during the fifth Doctor's era – particularly so during the first of the three seasons, when it achieved a significant improvement on the previous year's unusually poor performance. One important factor underlying this upturn in popularity was the rescheduling of the series away from its traditional Saturday teatime slot, where it had recently been suffering in competition with ITV's imported American science-fiction series *Buck Rogers in the 25th Century*.

In its new weekday-evening slot, with its episodes going out at the rate of two a week in the manner of a soap opera, it reached a whole new group of viewers, many of whom would no doubt not have counted themselves amongst *Doctor Who*'s traditional audience.

Another factor contributing to the series' improved ratings was the high public profile that it continued to maintain. One thing of which *Doctor Who* certainly did not go short during this period was promotion. Nathan-Turner was very publicity conscious, and – working in conjunction with senior BBC press officer Kevin O'Shea – highly skilled at dealing with the media. This contributed greatly to the series generating extensive newspaper coverage, many television guest spots for its stars, copious quantities of spin-off merchandise and numerous promotional events – undoubtedly the biggest of which was the chaotic 20th-anniversary convention staged by BBC Enterprises at Longleat House.

The Davison era maintained *Doctor Who*'s position as an important and highly regarded element of the BBC's steadily diminishing output of family programming. It did, however, provide some portents of the coming fall from grace that would see the series just managing to escape cancellation in 1985 and ultimately failing to do so in 1989.

The changes in style and dramatic content that had so concerned many fan commentators would be taken still further during the sixth Doctor's tenure, when the overall look of the series would grow increasingly gaudy and stylised and the stories would become steadily more concerned with continuity and less with straightforward, comprehensible plotting.

The move to a two-episodes-per-week transmission schedule meant that the series was now on the air for only three months each year, rather than for six as it had been in the recent past, providing less of an opportunity for it to become imprinted on the minds of the nation's viewers as a permanent feature of the television landscape. This problem would also be carried forward to later years when, although there would be a return to the more traditional one-episode-per-week format, the number of episodes per season would be effectively halved (with double-length episodes for the sixth Doctor's establishing season and standard-length episodes thereafter).

In many ways, the fifth Doctor's era marked the end of *Doctor Who* as a series with a wide popular appeal amongst the general viewing public. In its declining years, despite presenting many good stories and ultimately undergoing something of a creative renaissance, it would find itself playing principally to an ever-dwindling audience of cult science-fiction fans.

				Script Editor - Eric Saward			
6E	Arc of Infinity	Johnny Byrne	Ron Jones	Dee Robson	Fran Needham	Chris Lawson	Roger Limb	Marjorie Pratt
6D	Snakedance	Christopher Bailey	Fiona Cumming	Ken Trew	Marion Richards	Andy Lazell	Peter Howell	Jan Spoczynski
6F	Mawdryn Undead	Peter Grimwade	Peter Moffatt	Amy Roberts Richard Croft	Sheelagh Wells Carolyn Perry	Stuart Brisdon	Paddy Kingsland	Stephen Scott
6G	Terminus	Stephen Gallagher	Mary Ridge	Dee Robson	Joan Stribling	Peter Pegrum	Roger Limb	Dick Coles
6H	Enlightenment	Barbara Clegg	Fiona Cumming	Dinah Collin	Carolyn Perry Jean Steward	Mike Kelt	Malcolm Clarke	Colin Green
6J	The King's Demons	Terence Dudley	Tony Virgo	Colin Lavers	Elizabeth Rowell Frances Hannon	Anthony Harding	Jonathan Gibbs Peter Howell	Ken Ledsham

TWENTIETH-ANNIVERSARY SPECIAL

6K	The Five Doctors	Terrance Dicks	Peter Moffatt	Colin Lavers	Jill Hagar	John Brace	Peter Howell	Malcolm Thornton

SEASON TWENTY-ONE

6L	Warriors of the Deep	Johnny Byrne	Pennant Roberts	Judy Pepperdine	Jennifer Hughes	Mat Irvine	Jonathan Gibbs	Tony Burrough
6M	The Awakening	Eric Pringle	Michael Owen Morris	Jackie Southern	Ann Ailes	Tony Harding	Peter Howell	Barry Newbery
6N	Frontios	Christopher H. Bidmead	Ron Jones	Anushia Nieradzik	Jill Hagger	Dave Havard	Paddy Kingsland	David Buckingham
6P	Resurrection of the Daleks	Eric Saward	Matthew Robinson	Janet Tharby	Eileen Mair	Peter Wragg	Malcolm Clarke	John Anderson
6Q	Planet of Fire	Peter Grimwade	Fiona Cumming	John Peacock	Elizabeth Rowell	Chris Lawson	Peter Howell	Malcolm Thornton
6R	The Caves of Androzani	Robert Holmes	Graeme Harper	Andrew Rose	Jan Nethercot Shirley Stallard	Jim Francis Stuart Brisdon	Roger Limb	John Hurst

NOTES: It must be presumed throughout that the respective story editors had input into all the scripts to a greater or lesser degree.

Production Credits

	TITLE	AUTHOR	DIRECTOR	COSTUME	MAKE-UP	VISUAL EFFECTS	MUSIC	DESIGNER
			SEASON NINETEEN					
		Producer - John Nathan-Turner; Script Editor - Christopher H. Bidmead						
5Z	Castrovalva	Christopher H. Bidmead	Fiona Cumming	Odile Dicks-Mireaux	Marion Richards	Simon MacDonald	Paddy Kingsland	Janet Budden
				Script Editor - Antony Root				
5W	Four to Doomsday	Terence Dudley	John Black	Colin Lavers	Dorka Nieradzik	Mickey Edwards	Roger Limb	Tony Burrough
				Script Editor - Eric Saward				
5Y	Kinda	Christopher Bailey	Peter Grimwade	Barbara Kidd	Suzan Broad	Peter Logan	Peter Howell	Malcolm Thornton
				Script Editor - Antony Root				
5X	The Visitation	Eric Saward	Peter Moffatt	Odile Dicks-Mireaux	Carolyn Perry	Peter Wragg	Paddy Kingsland	Ken Starkey
				Script Editor - Eric Saward				
6A	Black Orchid	Terence Dudley	Ron Jones	Rosalind Ebbutt	Lisa Westcott	Tony Auger	Roger Limb	Tony Burrough
				Script Editor - Antony Root				
6B	Earthshock	Eric Saward	Peter Grimwade	Dinah Collin	Joan Stribling	Steve Bowman	Malcolm Clarke	Bernard Lloyd-Jones
				Script Editor - Eric Saward				
6C	Time-Flight	Peter Grimwade	Ron Jones	Amy Roberts	Dorka Nieradzik	Peter Logan	Roger Limb	Richard McManan-Smith